DIGITAL UNSETTLING

CRITICAL CULTURAL COMMUNICATION

General Editors: Jonathan Gray, Aswin Punathambekar, Adrienne Shaw
Founding Editors: Sarah Banet-Weiser and Kent A. Ono

Digital Unsettling

Decoloniality and Dispossession
in the Age of Social Media

Sahana Udupa *and* Ethiraj Gabriel Dattatreyan

NEW YORK UNIVERSITY PRESS

New York

NEW YORK UNIVERSITY PRESS
New York
www.nyupress.org

References to Internet websites (URLs) were accurate at the time of writing. Neither the author nor New York University Press is responsible for URLs that may have expired or changed since the manuscript was prepared.

Please contact the Library of Congress for Cataloging-in-Publication data.
ISBN: 9781479819140 (hardback)
ISBN: 9781479819157 (paperback)
ISBN: 9781479819164 (library ebook)
ISBN: 9781479819195 (consumer ebook)

New York University Press books are printed on acid-free paper, and their binding materials are chosen for strength and durability. We strive to use environmentally responsible suppliers and materials to the greatest extent possible in publishing our books.

Manufactured in the United States of America

10 9 8 7 6 5 4 3 2 1

Also available as an ebook

CONTENTS

LIST OF FIGURES

Introduction

Unsettling

In 2020, amid the growing collective realization that we were living through a pandemic that would have monumental short- and long-term consequences, the mediatization of George Floyd's murder in the United States engendered a reckoning with enduring colonial structures of being and order across national contexts. A statue of slaver Edward Colston was thrown into the Bristol Harbor in the wake of this tide, even as the reality of Brexit had, after four long years, prevailed and ushered in a twenty-first century British sovereignty and with it an explosion of nativist "blood and soil" discourse. Calls to defund the police—an idea that had been developing in various social-historical contexts as a key strategy of contemporary abolitionist thought and that now was linked to global Black Lives Matter movements—emerged in various national and regional locations, from Nigeria and the United States to South Africa and France.

Simultaneously, white supremacists in the Global North and xenophobic populists in the Global South stoked the emotions of victimhood, powering their racialized politics with "fact-filled" theories and boisterous mobilizations around them. In India, right-wing nationalism tied to Hindu majoritarian ideologies reached new heights with the introduction of the Citizens (Amendment) Act in 2019, which targeted Muslim minorities through discriminatory actions, signaling an "attenuation of religious-neutral laws of citizenship" that had long defined the contours of secular India.[1] In the US, former president Donald Trump's support of right-wing groups and white supremacist agendas in the thick of Black Lives Matter uprisings in the summer of 2020 provoked violent racialized confrontation.

Across these multiple convulsions, the digital, as a means of communication, source of data generation, and networked potentiality, has been a consistent feature—a condition of possibility for the turbulences of the contemporary moment and what they might portend for the future. Why and in what ways should the digital be seen as a force and context for the turbulences that have shaken the first decades of the twenty-first century? What does such an exploration hold for the expanding scholarship on digitalization and digital media?

Situated in the historical juncture of computational capitalism, populist upheavals, and passionate calls for decolonization, this book offers a critical and reflexive exploration of the digital and its entanglements with ongoing churnings by centering processes and structures of coloniality and thereby pushing against presentist, liberal, and technocentric readings of the digital. Focusing primarily on the role of social media—arguably the most visible manifestation of digital technologies—and staging a number of examples of platform entangled politics and networked circulation, *Digital Unsettling* offers a critical ground to place the digital in the historical *longue durée* of coloniality.

The digital is a discursive channel and material extension of historical processes that began in the modern-colonial period. Over the course of six chapters, we explore structures and processes that have reinforced neocolonial relations within contemporary digital environments, paying particular attention to forms, infrastructures, and trajectories of online speech and audio-visuality and the capture and commodification of these forms as data. While assessing the digital in relation to the violence of coloniality, we also interrogate how the internet is entwined with persistent calls for decolonization that are fluorescing globally. As they emerge in online spaces, these calls for decolonization evoke the unfinished struggles for emancipation from Euro-Western domination that persist in settler colonial worlds and so-called postcolonial worlds, despite transfers of power in the mid-twentieth century that suggest otherwise. These evocations for decolonization, as they emerge out of different sociohistorical contexts and meet in the online spaces of social media, put into complicated and uneven conversation struggles for sovereignty, calls for epistemic freedom, and demands for institutional accountability.

Toward this dual analysis, we utilize *digital unsettling* as a heuristic to examine aspects and modes of digital communication that enable new participatory cultures and potentials for disruption, while reproducing colonial-modernity's foundational structures of extraction and dispossession in novel, twenty-first-century arrangements. Throughout the book, we refer to the digital as a composite expression to highlight the pervasive, almost ubiquitous presence of digital media and communications technologies as they mobilize and rework existing networks to shape a diverse range of activities. These mediated networks do not represent a single technological process or artifact, nor are they mere technological extensions. They are embodied and affective constellations within specific political economies that we reflexively navigate through a range of examples in this book.² We approach the digital as affective and material constellations by specifically examining internet-enabled social media as a central space where tensions between neocolonial structures and decolonizing rhetoric and related political actions become visibly manifest and materially consequential.

In exploring such constellations, we recognize the importance of the digital as a "bundle of historically new possibilities of constitution and connection," an arena of "multiple interfaces."³ The internet's profound mediations "lie in bringing distinct actors, levels of authority, institutions, ideologies, and motivations in close confrontation, [and] in creating new mediated spaces of contiguities and confrontations."⁴ These "contiguities and confrontations," inextricably shaped by history, are manifest in a variety of discursive forms that circulate online. These interfaces also inform the logic and material logistics of extractive data practices and tend to consolidate and naturalize Eurocentric and universalizing forms of knowledge.⁵

We take up the term *unsettling*, theorized in recent discussions of sovereignty, to mark the ways colonial formations persist despite the putative success of nationalist/anti-colonial movements in the previous century. The term also acknowledges a recognition that these formations cannot be undone so easily. Rather, coloniality and its histories of expansion, extraction, and dispossession and the ways they live on in the present must be "fundamentally brought into question," whether through grassroots movements or through scholarly enterprise, toward imagining other possibilities for vital life while critiquing existing arrangements.⁶

We also deploy *unsettling* to bring attention to how coloniality has retrenched itself in online spaces in the form of extreme speech, disinformation, and propaganda, animating violently exclusionary nationalisms that rely on racist, casteist, misogynistic, and homophobic discourses that disrupt the smooth surfaces of the (neo)liberal world order. In either case, the various affects—anger, resentment, fear, hope—that digital interfaces channel, intensify, and circulate are crucial.[7] In the age of platform mediation and interface, unsettling affects are braided with the algorithmically mediated iterative content they enable. We are interested in these iterative affective loops, the interfaces that make them possible, the extractive data relations they rely on, and the unsettling they enable to highlight how they make palpable an enduring coloniality across geographies.

We track multiple unfoldings of digital unsettling by navigating distinct yet connected moments. In the chapters, we take up examples from India, the US, the UK, and Germany that draw from our embodied and situated knowledges emerging from our experiences as subjects in-between each of these national contexts and as researchers invested in studying historical and contemporary processes of connection between them. We also touch on other instances of unsettling as they manifest in different locations globally, as they become digitally linked to places we are in relationship with, navigating these multiple homes and fields as critical sites that illuminate the workings of the digital and our embeddedness in them. Our progression through the chapters is not linear but rather telescopic, moving from local settings to global implications and consequences, between the modalities of retrenchment and generative disruption and between capture and contestation that the digital has variously aroused and augmented. We critically engage with the digital in this book as the two of us—each from our distinct positions—have seen, heard, and felt the deep push for change and reckoning with the past that has created our present and our visions for the future, alongside the effects of political, economic, social, and epistemological formations that continue to immiserate the racialized poor and expropriate resources for the few.

The critical reflexive journey we have undertaken provokes ways to unsettle some key frames used in the current scholarship for assessing what is enabled and damaged by the digital. In particular, we complicate ahistorical and mediacentric approaches to the digital as "universal proliferation of horizontal rivalry" and the corollary argument that social media networks as "machines for producing desire" have simply multiplied animosities "by converting all users into each other's potential models, doubles, and rivals, locked in a perpetual game of competition for the intangible objects of desire of the attention economy."[8] This kind of analysis, we contend, is weighed down by methodological individualism that imagines social media as "render[ing] all individuals instantly comparable in simple, quantitative terms . . . by embedding users in a standardized format [of competition and mimesis]."[9]

By highlighting broader structural forces, colonial histories, and the affects and affinities the digital brings together, we move away not only from methodological individualism that has typified studies of digital media proliferation but also from the more optimistic assessment that the simple universal binary code has technologically induced an infinite proliferation of (emancipatory) participations.[10] As such, *Digital Unsettling* leaves behind liberal tendencies that inform a significant part of voluminous scholarship on digital movements and practices. Such approaches, we contend, tend to result in the theorization of discursive contestation as a two-sided debate among equal parties. Rather, we draw on recent critical scholarship that reveals how the digital extends previous eras of technologies of racialized surveillance and expropriation, discourses of gendered racism, and politics of extreme exclusion, while reflecting how, in our own work and in the work of others, the digital also offers opportunities to reimagine and reconstitute subjectivities and collectivities in ways that were impossible in previous eras, in ways that entangle and blur multiple projects of recognition and liberation.[11]

Theorizing Digital Unsettling

Recent years have seen a quantum jump in the scholarship on digitalization, and digital communication technologies in particular, and how they have reinforced and disrupted twentieth-century political, social, and economic arrangements around borders, belonging, knowledge, and collective action. Digitalization has been theorized as a wide-ranging process of informationalization affecting the domains of politics, market, and culture.[12] More specifically, it has been parsed as *technopolitics*—the flow of political and market power through technology and the materialities of the internet in shaping political action—and as *cultural formations*—which enable new conditions for communication and sociality, often in close conjunction with the infrastructural possibilities and imaginaries surrounding the digital.[13] While digitalization is a far-reaching process of transformation, studies have especially focused on the importance of internet-enabled social networking sites that compose a variety of mediations, primarily hinging on user-generated content.[14] Internet-enabled social media is nested within a broader process of digitalization but is also digitalization's most visible and tangible manifestation. It is therefore not surprising that social media has remained a key area of focus for digital studies as a culture-theoretical program, in contrast to conceptualizing digitalization as a techno-deterministic economic discourse.[15]

Across a range of disciplines and interdisciplinary investigations that have placed varying degrees of emphasis on the technopolitical and cultural dimensions of the internet, the political consequences of digital social media—for democratic order, in particular—have been an area of major interest. In this regard, the shift in scholarly assessments of digital media's impact on political life is palpable. Studies that emerged in the second decade of the new millennium have recalibrated the initial optimism around the emancipatory potential of social media as facilitators of horizontal, peer-to-peer networking that can allow ordinary publics to talk back to established power and upturn prevailing hierarchies. Rejecting the views of techno-optimism and technology solutionism, these studies have identified the encumbering effects of social divisions, as well as how digitalization's opaque operations, propensity for vitriolic exchange on social media, and centrally controlled surveillance mechanisms could provide a fertile ground for authoritarian, anti-democratic, and populist regimes to take root by utilizing the logics and affordances of data capitalism.[16]

In recent theorizations of the digital condition, the contradictory impulses of the digital have been defined as the logics of "post-democracy" and "digital commons."[17] Post-democracy refers to a condition where the digital "expands possibilities, and even requirements, of (personal) participation, while ever larger aspects of (collective) decision making are moved to arenas that are structurally disconnected from those of participation and in the hands of a small elite (the commercial social media such as Facebook and Google)."[18] In direct contrast to this centralizing tendency, it is argued, are the logics of the digital commons incarnated by Wikipedia and free software communities, which are "absolutely crucial for the infrastructural dimension of digital networks."[19]

While recognizing the contradictory tendencies of post-democracy and commons logics of the digital, a large number of these studies focus chiefly on the dangers that unbridled digital communication networks are believed to have posed to the virtues and consensus of the liberal order and to the institutions representing and upholding them. Studies on media manipulation and propaganda, to offer one example, have highlighted the risks of digital communication to electoral integrity in liberal societies, mapping these threats in terms of geopolitics (for example, Russia's disinformation campaigns against the US), political partisanship within the nation-states, and bad actors such as authoritarian populists and complicit social media companies.[20]

The stream of scholarship on digital activism, on the other hand, has examined newer developments, including long-standing civil society and advocacy organizations adopting social media for mobilization and coordination and the emergence of radically new "connective action frames" with "highly personalized, socially mediated communication processes" that rely on "large scale personal access to multi-layered social technologies."[21] For instance, concepts like "protest collectivity" argue that digital social media have led to open structures for organizing protests.[22] Similarly, the new communicative paradigm of "the shitstorm" is seen as native to the infrastructural conditions of digital communication that is built for instantaneous expression and reaction, rendering the public as a swarm that is trained on the hyper-present, propelled by affect, and unconcerned with the articulation of collective futures.[23] These studies have been alert to the specific mediatic conditions of digital communication, but they have tended to elide longer historical forms of social divisions and structural conditions of participation, framing the tensions instead as contestations between equal parties—albeit with digital access as a key differentiator—or crises engendered by manipulative actions of resource rich actors.

Recent scholarship, emerging primarily from Black feminist and critical science and technology scholars in North America and ethnographic studies of digital politics in South Asia, Latin America, and other regions have offered a push back against mediacentric assumptions around digital empowerment and the liberal framing of the threat of the digital. For instance, grounded attention to historical structures of sociality and political action that are revived and disrupted by internet-enabled media in India shows how such developments challenge prevalent assumptions about digital media as spatially unbounded political articulations that give rise to affinities prior to identities and solidarities based solely on digital enactments.[24]

Beyond the social conditions of digital communication, critical scholarship has also revealed that discriminatory structures are deeply embedded in the technological architectures and affordances, puncturing assumptions of (digital) technologies as value neutral or enablers of equality. Sharpening the focus on technology design, Ruha Benjamin, in a fine-grained analysis of racial bias in emergent technological systems, offers conceptual tools to "decode the promises of tech with historically and sociologically informed scepticism."[25] Tech fixes, she argues,

> often hide, speed up, and even deepen discrimination, while appearing to be neutral or benevolent when compared to the racism of the previous era. . . . [It] encompasses a range of discriminatory designs—some that explicitly work to amplify hierarchies, many that ignore and thus replicate social divisions, and a number that aim to fix racial bias but end up doing the opposite.[26]

Importantly, Brendesha M. Tynes, Joshua Schuschke, and Safiya Umoja Noble draw on critical race theory to explore digitalization through an intersectional lens, scrutinizing how "gender, race, class, and sexuality are 'interlocking' . . . [and] oppressions, including those based on the categories of race, gender, and class (among others), are inextricably connected."[27] Focusing on the #BLM movement, they argue that an "intersectional lens permeates all aspects of the movement . . . the movement originated and is sustained through the intersectional critical praxis of Black women."[28] They emphasize the significance of intersectionality as "an analytical strategy (the ways in which intersectional frameworks provide new angles of vision on social institutions, practices, social problems, and other social phenomena associated with social inequality) and critical praxis (the ways in which social actors use intersectionality for social justice projects)."[29] We step into this discussion and build on the critical framing marked by an "intersectional internet" theory, but we chart our analytical paths differently.

Of foremost interest to our exploration are the repertoires and critical praxis surrounding decoloniality. Decoloniality is a capacious concept that, as Aneeth Kaur Hundle argues, "is part of a larger archive of anticolonial thought: the study of settler and/or nonsettler colonial projects and the colony itself, studies of colonial mind-sets and attitudes fostered in native people, and studies of the failures and limitations of anticolonial nationalist projects."[30] Our interest in the concept and our engagement with it in this text is prompted by three concerns. First, we are interested in the animated discussions and mobilizations that the term has provoked in recent years in digital arenas, particularly concerning the nature and politics of knowledge and the material conditions of the university. Second, we are interested in the ways decoloniality can be deployed as an analytic for examining the colonial continuities that the digital manifests and channels as it reinforces enduring unequal political, economic, and social relations. Third, we are interested in the ways that decoloniality can enable a praxis of connection and ethics of responsibility for researchers—what we are calling a decolonial sensibility—a way to engage in research that utilizes technologies of connection to build relationships beyond the academy toward fostering new collectivities capable of addressing various manifestations of coloniality.

With regard to our first concern, we propose that investigating a few examples of twenty-first-century projects across geographies that mobilize decolonization as a concept or that in practice manifest its historical program provide a critical lens to understand digitalization, since these movements do not merely channelize digital avenues but reshape these digital structures as they expand and evolve.[31] Decolonization's articulation on social media platforms as it is linked to various discursive/epistemic/material struggles, as Bill Ray Betancourt suggests in his reflections on the potentials of decolonization in relation to settler worlds, offers the hopeful potential of a "teleology of the elsewhere, gestating an attachment to an otherwise that might hold out for more radical genres of living, ones that do not resort to violence to survive the present."[32] We discuss these contestations and worlds imagined otherwise and the kinds of affective flows that these projects enunciate throughout the book, most pointedly in the "Campus," "Knowledge/Citation," and "Home/Field" chapters.

We recognize, however, that decolonization has become an increasingly contentious and debated concept. As Bhakti Shringarpure notes, "With hundreds of thousands of 'decolonize' hashtags, several articles, op-eds, and surveys on the subject—and plenty of Twitter fighting over the term—one thing is clear: decolonization is all kinds of trendy these days."[33] The debate around decolonization and the skepticism it generates in its evocation is linked to the ways in which the concept has been used to garner individual acclaim inside and outside academic worlds or is mobilized by institutions toward deflecting or diffusing critiques and claims, rather than put in the service of collective liberation.[34] We touch on the latter in the "Campus" chapter by discussing how various institutions digitally mobilize decoloniality, sometimes directly and more often indirectly, to perform contrition while leaving structures of domination intact.

The trendy evocation of decolonization is also met with necessary critique when Indigenous land-back struggles are either elided altogether or not given their due place as foundational to theorizing what is at stake in projects that seek to push against coloniality in the present.[35] With this in mind, it is critical to recognize that decolonization is not a historical event or legacy but rather marks the ongoing struggle for Indigenous sovereignty. The digital plays a crucial role in the disruption and retrenchment of colonial conditions of possibility in these struggles. In the chapters ahead, we touch on how Indigenous projects for survivance mobilize the digital in "Campus" and "Knowledge/Citation." In "Campus," we also engage with the ways in which digitally enabled anti-racist struggles in universities have the tendency to elide concurrent and digitally visible struggles for land, water, and sovereignty—and the historical backdrop and consequences for these elisions.

Finally, and nefariously, decolonization has been deployed in online spaces as a means to masquerade majoritarian and hegemonic political projects in postcolonial nation-state contexts as liberatory. In India, as Priyamvada Gopal points out and as we discuss with examples in the chapters ahead, decolonization has been picked up by the Hindu right wing as a way to justify a Hindu supremacist, upper-caste nationalist project.[36] Decolonization has functioned in this hyper-nationalist project to promote revisionist histories and to elevate Hindu knowledge systems above Western epistemological traditions. Undoubtedly, social media has become the means to enunciate and materialize these claims, which we discuss in "Knowledge/Citation."

Thus, far from generating a consensus around what the goals of decolonization in the twenty-first century might be or even what decolonization means and who its central actors are, such struggles, as they are articulated in and through digital networks, might be best understood as arenas where colonial orders are critiqued and challenged by activists, students, and scholars, producing a form of rupture that is incomplete, inchoate, threatened by the logics of market capitalism, aspirations for individual uplift, Indigenous erasure, and the potential for right-wing cooptation yet holding the capacity to imagine and incite change. Our exploration of decolonization as it circulates in networked, recursive communicative technologies related to specific struggles, therefore, pays attention to how related but distinct projects around the globe converge through a shared language of dissent while in some instances become divergent, coopted, and antithetical to an articulation and materialization of a liberatory politics.

Our interest in decolonization also lies in its potential as a critical analytical strategy that can place digitalization in relation to coloniality as an enduring structure of power. In this sense, we take up decolonization not as an object or process to scrutinize but as an analytical point of departure that places particular relational and structural conditions of coloniality at the forefront of analysis. Our analytical approach develops from an understanding that coloniality has been and continues to be a *global* process that reproduces and sustains, as Sahana has argued elsewhere, three interlinked sets of *relations*: nation-state relations established by colonial power that frame the boundaries of minority/majority and inside/outside, market relations institutionalized by colonial power now manifest as uneven data relations, and racial relations naturalized by colonial power that mark certain populations as disposable or less worthy.[37] The coloniality of power as a global process of colonial modern relations unfolds within and as external forces in different societal contexts.[38]

Without doubt, as Sharika Thirangama, Tobias Kelly, and Carlos Forment argue, "there are multiple genealogies of distinction and prestige that underpin regional hierarchical structures, and which often come to mingle with colonial projects but are not invented by them."[39] Yet conceptualizing coloniality as a set of relations allows attention to the overarching frameworks and historical continuities that undergird contemporary forms of digital action and turbulences as they intersect with regionally distinct hierarchies and exclusions. We discuss throughout this book, but more directly in the "Capture," "Extreme," and "Home/Field" chapters, how enduring forms of coloniality are now entrenched in the techno-networked infrastructures of the digital in the form of uneven data relations, the global hierarchy of digital labor, and digital surveillance of the state-market nexus. We develop this critique by building on the insightful scholarship on digital capitalism and data surveillance in critical race studies but expand our discussion beyond North America and in conversation with emerging scholarship on decoloniality and internet studies.[40]

We also show how the coloniality of mediated interactions on social networking sites is manifest starkly in the cantankerous cultures of exclusionary extreme speech and racial aggression against minorities, migrant Others within the nation-states, and global trends of right-wing trolling against progressive voices, including academics ("Extreme" and "Home/Field" chapters). These spaces of aggression and the political economy of data extraction they are embedded within reveal how colonial formations persist, mutate, and proliferate in and through the digital. As such, while we recognize that the digital sparks new hopes around decolonial struggles, its logics and infrastructures have also been critical in perpetuating a "colonial-modern matrix of power."[41]

The digital, therefore, falls right in the midst of the mutation and reproduction of colonial relations and strident calls for decolonization. While igniting efforts to reimagine power relations and potential futures, the digital, as a global capitalist project, embodies the most oppressive structures of dispossession, extraction, and exclusion that have colonial bearings. It is this dual process that *digital unsettling*, as heuristic and conceptual framing, signals and scrutinizes. Digital enunciations of the decolonial as a rallying cry, a praxis, an ambivalence, or a reactionary sentiment, we contend, offer opportunities to explore the potential to think and feel beyond liberal enclosures and their limits by engaging with these affective feedback loops as they emerge online, linking locations, histories, bodies, texts, and signs. However, these have occurred in the context of continuities in colonial structures of surveillance, propaganda, and extraction. By putting examples of the neocolonial inequalities that digitization has wrought into dialogue with the political potentials (and pitfalls of) digital communications technologies, we strive to productively analyze how affective participations and the crisscrossing links between locations that the digital has made possible lead to multiple and contradictory *digital unsettlings* in the contemporary moment.

Anthropology as Location and Lens

This book is neither a comprehensive decolonial deconstruction of digitalization nor a thoroughgoing representation of the vast political, epistemological, philosophical, and ontological dimensions of decoloniality. The scope of our offering is more humble. We see the expansion of digital communication processes as an important historical moment to engage with contemporary social movements that evoke decoloniality and the hegemonic politics that confronts, threatens, or suffuses them. Equally, we are interested in excavating the digital through an analytical lens that centers the enduring power of colonial relations. We undertake this dual task by reflexively engaging with the core assumptions and tropes of (media) anthropology as a disciplinary location we both, for better and worse, call home.

For each of us, the subdiscipline of media anthropology has provided a community of practice and methodological approach to critically engage with our ongoing, unfolding research projects. Anthropologists who study media worlds, infrastructures, and production cultures have recognized the possibility for cultural, economic, and social reproduction and rupture that the media in its various forms—the radio, the television, satellite TV, cassette tapes, and most recently, the internet— creates within specific sociohistoric contexts. Media anthropology, in each of our broader intellectual projects, has offered a genealogy of possibility to think through how present digital circulations on Twitter, Facebook, TikTok, Instagram, and other social media platforms create new opportunities for research of the particular as it travels across various sites, even as these novel communicative contexts challenge anthropological authority rooted in colonial knowledge formations and attendant area studies logics of partible socialities.

As importantly, we have learned from media anthropologists who have collaborated with and otherwise supported Indigenous media makers as they mobilize their "ontological resources" to "imagine otherwise."[42] These collaborations offer a way to think about digital scholarship as a means to work together with those most affected by digital technology's capacity to reify conditions of coloniality. Examining the digital through the (sub)disciplinary location of media anthropology has also produced different moments of unsettling when we have found ourselves critically examining the discipline and recognizing how contemporary data relations have a striking parallel to the historical trajectory of anthropology as a science of the colonizer (a point we discuss in the "Capture" chapter).[43]

We bring this disciplinarily shaped analytical attention, ethical learning, and reflexive navigation to bear on the ways in which the digital is entangled in neocolonial forms of extraction, surveillance, and control, while attending simultaneously to its mediating capacities for disruption, its important role in the creation and maintenance of counterpublics, and the potential it brings for imagining shared or collaborative research. Of particular significance in the analytical pathways we open up through our media anthropological location is the discussion around how digital world systems complicate long-held conceits in the discipline regarding the primacy of long-term fieldwork.

As we discuss in detail in the "Home/Field" chapter, it is evident that with the expansion of digital technologies, communities are able to converse beyond the mediation of academic voicing and are able to scrutinize academics who engage in their lifeworlds and point to aporias, falsifications, and narrow research agendas that obscure materialized inequalities.[44] The digital offers a particularly significant disruptive force for the discipline's anointed practices of fieldwork, home/field distinctions, and received wisdom regarding ethnographic encounter and its capacity to produce theory/knowledge. It enables a different relationship between here and there or between researcher and researched that recognizes the instability of either dyad. In so doing, the digital enables an analysis of comparative colonial relations that can throw light on the margins, the peripheries, and the Global South in a multipolar world system in which "the rhetoric of modernity is no longer unidirectional and unipolar."[45]

Indeed, our exploration of digitalization through a reflexive and critical engagement with anthropology has pushed us to experiment with a novel critical method of comparison. In (colonial) anthropology, comparison is used as a means to position the West in relation to the rest—sometimes explicitly, often implicitly—to develop culturalist insights about specific locations. This "West and the rest" paradigm has also informed comparative approaches in other disciplines, such as communication studies and development studies. Our reimagining of comparison as digital method primarily draws together mediatized examples from the US, the UK, Germany, and India—locations where the two of us have affective, social, economic, and political connection and places where we have ongoing fieldwork—and puts them in productive relation with each other. Our decision to think and theorize from these particular locations emerges out of a commitment, shaped by feminist thought, to center our partial and situated knowledges as they emerge in and between these locations.[46] We include other locations that become visible and linked to the US, the UK, Germany, and India on social media and in our collaborative research projects, but as researchers navigating multiple homes, we feel that these national contexts where we have had foundational experiences, done research, and find ourselves betwixt and between are the key locations where we feel ethically and epistemologically comfortable rooting and routing our inquiries about the globality (and coloniality) of digital mediation and our political engagement.

The digital invites and amplifies this sort of recalibration of comparison as a shifting, moving, and deeply affective strategy of knowing that is constrained and enabled by various power relations and affinities by placing, in the various networked platforms we traverse, the semiotics, repertoires, political economies, and histories of multiple locations into iterative dialogue and unstable encounter. Comparison in this sense is no longer the privilege of the researcher but is a ubiquitous feature of the digital condition that fosters a collective articulation and debate linked to multiple points of *felt* relation and connection. We might describe this ethnographic method shaped by the digital condition as montage that works by placing events and spaces—similar to a timeline on a social media site—into radical juxtaposition, in ways that hold the potential to reveal the enduring structures that connect contexts.

Montage emerged as a theory of the image in the Soviet era that recognized the capacities of the mechanical eye of the camera to produce, through juxtaposition and compression, new and wonderous ways of perceiving what is otherwise invisible, opaque, or just out of reach, with the potential to rupture the normalized and the normative conditions of modernity.[47] Montage and its corollary, surrealism, were taken up and repurposed by anti-colonial thinkers and artists in the twentieth century—notably Léopold Senghor and Aimé Césaire—as a means to crack open objectivist colonial renderings of worlds, and as a tool, as Césaire expresses, for "disalienation."[48] Our embrace of montage as a method to critically examine the digital is to recognize and be reflexively attentive to the juxtapositions of contexts and conditions that social media enables, the particular affective resonances they generate, and the situated knowledges they activate, and bring this sort of attention explicitly into our analytic practice.

A critical mobilization of montage as method requires an attention to the ways in which algorithms organize what becomes visible, audible, and sensible on social media, as algorithmic systems work to monetize attention and extract value from collectively generated data. A reflexive deployment of montage starts with a recognition that we, as researchers, are (also) consumers and producers in these contemporary circuits of neocolonial capital, functioning within its (colonial) matrix of power. As our opening paragraphs in this introductory chapter reveal, our attentions to political developments in the last two years are particular and linked to what gets amplified through the digital algorithms of sorting we are enmeshed in and attentions we have cultivated because of our own affective commitments to particular places and struggles. Montage as (digital) method, therefore, requires an attentiveness not only to what comes into adjacent visibility but to what is just outside of the frame, on the peripheries of our attention, and more importantly, to inquire into the historical processes that connect and shape their emergence. When utilized reflexively, critically, imaginatively, and inventively, a social media–inspired montage aesthetic of juxtaposition has the potential to unsettle normalized understandings of the contemporary world system as it is constituted in and through taken-for-granted forms of coloniality.

Montage as a critical digital method, for instance, offers one way to complicate culturalist assumptions that underlie comparative projects in approaching the Global South as either homogenous or radically different or inferior to the North, as well as romanticized notions of the South as holders of pristine ontologies that can salvage the world from environmental and moral decadence. In this sense our theorization and mobilization of montage is inspired by methodological critiques of colonial and imperial knowledge systems. As Katherine McKittrick notes, these systems, through the naturalization of disciplinary methods, "express and normalize discipline-based and place-based classifications."[49] By putting different places and contexts into critical conversation, montage holds the possibility to reveal shared material conditions and historical legacies that animate contemporary digital cultures.

In the chapters that follow, we place academic trolling among British ultranationalists in conversation with Hindu nationalist trolls in India and right-wing anti-immigrant groups in Germany, even as we turn critical attention to extreme speech moderation practices scattered across Berlin, Manila, and Gurgaon; the force of struggles that have shaken campuses in South Africa, the UK, and the US; and online citational practices that draw disparate geographies and their knowledges along uncharted nodes of connection and disjuncture. Our decision, shaped largely by our training as anthropologists to center particular locations from which to observe these phenomena—places where we have ties and commitments—afford us the opportunity to ground the analysis that montage as a digital ethnographic method makes possible. By locating ourselves in encounters we have had in different places and placing them in historical relief, we offer context to our networked research that extends across events and geographies.

Montage as method also holds the potential for establishing connections between marginalized groups fighting for justice within bordered nation-states across the planet. Through montage and its mobilization of reflexive juxtaposition, we strive to make visible a politics of connection and alliance building across borders as well as enunciate its potential for amplification. In so doing, we take up decoloniality not only as a subject of study or as an analytical departure point but as a political register of potentiality toward building meaningful opportunities to radically reimagine worlds. Throughout, we ask if the digital offers networked opportunities for cross-border organization toward forms of repair, reparation, and justice while recognizing the inherent contradiction that comes with relying on and utilizing corporate digital platforms toward the realization of liberatory political projects.

For scholars in the academy, this sort of query creates opportunities, even if on ambivalent grounds, to situate ourselves differently and in conversation with various struggles on the ground and to build research agendas toward goals for redress and change across borders. However, we are aware of and attentive to the pitfalls of what are presented as solidarities when they are expressed all too easily. Without doubt, as Eve Tuck and Wayne Yang pointedly caution, "Solidarity is an uneasy, reserved, and unsettled matter that neither reconciles present grievances nor forecloses future conflict."[50] Rather than taking up solidarity, which, whether intentionally or unconsciously, holds the potential to undercut substantive demands for land repatriation and reparations, we emphasize the need to work through the ruptures and tensions between multiple struggles for freedom, equity, and justice. We call this approach a "decolonial sensibility," based on, as Liu and Shange argue, "a radical belief in the inherent value of each other's lives despite never being able to fully understand or fully share in the experience of those lives."[51] By developing a decolonial sensibility, we grasp that a decolonial future cannot be an inverse mirroring of the liberal tendencies of drawing equivalence, something we vehemently argue against. Nor can it become a repertoire of well-intentioned reformist actions within institutional spaces that don't ultimately engage with the afterlives of slavery, Indigenous genocide, and settler occupations that have been foundational to the inception of colonial modernity. Rather, we see decolonial sensibility as an activist-conceptual space of dissent and rearticulation in the contemporary moment that could help us to imagine and realize connection in ways that each struggle, each story, and each act of oppression on the margins, borders, peripheries, and locations—and each body battered by hegemonic interests—is considered in its fullest weight. Connection thus becomes a way to deepen—and not dilute or distract—collective actions toward reimagining worlds and relations. We see the need for such connections as even more pertinent in the face of globally resonant, digitally empowered aggressions of right-wing movements that are not new but, as we will elaborate in the chapters to follow, are built on time tested colonial methods of control, capture, and disinformation as governance. Amid these grave realities, where oppressive regimes have repowered their attacks against anyone who speaks for social justice precisely through globally circulating tropes across morphing boundaries and the hectic pace of discursive engagements online, a decolonial sensibility might offer potentials for connection that can stand up to the confused conflations of right-wing politics within and across national borders. If the essence of decoloniality, as Priyamvada Gopal, drawing from Jamaica Kincaid, suggests, is "a demanding relationship with history," a language of connection across borders arises only when five hundred years of empire is recognized as a shared condition that particularizes struggle in local contexts, when it becomes a sensibility that is shared across locations.[52]

Alliance building entails mutuality and trust, but we do not anchor either to an abstract humanistic normativity that appeals to high moral values as a harm-reduction model employed by white people to shed their guilt.[53] Rather, we are interested in alliances built on a recognition of the actual structural conditions that implicates each of us in different positions of domination and subordination. We therefore suggest a decolonial sensibility, in this book project but more importantly in our current projects outside the academy that undergirds our thinking, as central to collaborative worldmaking. Adom Getachew suggests that this kind of endeavor "entails a critical diagnosis of the persistence of empire and a normative orientation that retains the anti-imperial aspiration for a domination-free international order."[54] In imagining this task of building a world after empire—a task that is collectively ours—we propose that a decolonial sensibility can work to unsettle colonial relations and build connections in ways that can account for the specificities of place and location, as an analytical approach that recognizes multiple genealogies of power and hierarchies entrenched by coloniality, and as an orientation that emphasizes the importance of centering experience as part of theory building.

It is thus not a surprise that this book has emerged from our experiences of navigating the Western academic institutions as immigrants from South Asia carrying the privilege of English education, upper-caste status, and middle-class comforts while facing the heat or bearing witness to the violence of anti-immigrant sentiments, right-wing populism, anti-Blackness, and anti-Indigenous sentiment in the various northern locations we have navigated, lived, and belonged. These challenges of being between national contexts and the privileges by which they are undergirded have produced complex and multiple interpellations and, thus, opportunities for each of us to develop a critical reflexivity.

Sahana's journey to the European academy after living and learning in India and the US has pushed her to reflect on the visa-stamped migration of educated people seen (and tolerated) as beneficial for the nation-state, while heightened right-wing sentiments marshal various means to dismiss, devalue, and even criminalize the "other kind of migration" as a crisis, and liberal "hospitality," on the other hand, tends to embrace all migrants as "guests" (by implicitly presupposing the ownership of the home guaranteed by the nation-state). In this moment in history, when guarded welcome to "qualified immigrants" is (once again) modulated by shared panics around "unwanted immigrants," academic and immigrant life has entailed confronting ossified forms of gendered and racialized inequities inside and outside the academy, while also benefiting from different kinds of scholarly opportunities. On the other side of the home/field, the foreign-researcher tag has afforded her privileges during fieldwork in India, and navigating right-wing actors has often triggered reflections on growing up in a southern Indian city, and on how Hindu-centered politics came as unmarked politics in her childhood years, seeking to draw into its fold all those active like her in any kind of civic struggles.

Gabriel's movements between India, the US, and the UK have also offered complex interactional frameworks by which to critically evaluate position and power. As an anthropologist-in-training in the US after years of doing grassroots education work in New York and San Francisco, he began to critically evaluate and explore the ways in which postcolonial belonging and diasporic affiliation were used to at once exclude and include him in Indian and US nation-state settler, racial, and caste politics while implicating him in both systems of historical oppression. Gabriel's time in an anthropology department in the UK has taught him something about being located in the center of the old empire and how being seen as a problem and a solution when it comes to long-standing issues of systemic racism in the UK in relation to the production of knowledge about the peripheries of the post-colony positions him in his encounters.[55]

Throughout the book, we each touch on how our racialized, caste, and class positions—as they overlap and are remixed through transnational movement and online encounter—shape our project to track the ways in which the digital unsettles. By writing collaboratively, we offer another layer of reflexive comparison that puts into conversation each of our experiences of encounter in offline and online worlds. As each of us has recounted moments that encapsulate the digital and physical worlds we traverse for this book, the text we have generated has offered us opportunities to discuss the power differentials in which they are entangled. Through these discussions we have engaged in the complicated and often difficult work of coming to understand ourselves anew toward participating in projects to construct worlds otherwise. As Lauren Berlant notes, collaboration and collaborative writing in particular "is like a super intensified version of teaching, where you and somebody else are working something out, and you are building on each other, but you're also missing each other."[56] We have navigated learning, building, and missing each other and have tried to make these processes—to some degree, at least—visible in the text that follows. One way we have signposted our distinct experiences and reflexive engagements in the field and at home, for instance, is by adding our first names in the parenthesis at the beginning of the relevant sections. By attaching first-name parentheses to particular sections, we have sought to give each other space to express our experiences in our own voice, rhythm, and affect.

The seeds for this project were first sown at the workshop "Decoloniality and the Digital Turn in Media Anthropology" in 2019 that Sahana organized with the Media Anthropology Network of the European Association of Social Anthropologists, inviting media anthropologists to consider how digital technologies have altered the temporal, spatial, and epistemological aspects of anthropological fieldwork, how decoloniality as a critical-historical perspective and an interventionist agenda allows for an interrogation of digitally mediated avenues for political activism, and how digital media is complicit with the colonial matrix of power. Following this approach, she presented a paper on decoloniality and extreme speech in the same year at the Media Anthropology Network's e-seminar, where Gabriel offered his comments as a discussant. This sparked conversations between us about the topic, and after the public exchange at the e-seminar, we planned a book project to expand the approach and explore our ideas and experiences around coloniality and the digital in some depth. Based on ongoing work, Sahana proposed the chapters on extreme speech, data capture, and the home/field conundrum, and Gabriel proposed the chapters on campus struggles and knowledge politics. We kept each of our distinct styles of writing and disciplinary/institutional training by dividing the chapters based on these interests ("Campus" and "Citation/Knowledge" chapters by Gabriel, and "Extreme," "Capture," and the first draft of "Home/Field" by Sahana). In the "Home/Field" chapter, we developed the discussion by adding sections to highlight our distinctive experiences across multiple homes and fields in our projects. We worked together to write the introduction and the coda.

Our experiences both within the academy and beyond have provided us with particular phenomenological and analytical perspectives to press the problem of the digital through the prism of decolonial thought. Reflecting on our methods, activist engagements, and complicities and entanglements with hegemonic institutions, we acknowledge that decolonization projects are always partial, unfinished, limited in scope, and fraught, yet necessary to build new worlds of connection by unsettling presumptions and preoccupations within and outside academic worlds.[57]

Montage—Moving through Concepts

Our chapters mobilize our methodology of digital montage and reflexive exploration through several conceptual frames—campus, extreme, capture, knowledge/citation, and home/field—to weave together a narrative of unsettling. Each of the conceptual frames that punctuate each chapter highlight distinct yet connected moments of disruption and entrenchment that have emerged in and through the digital. Through these chapters, we have engaged with the concept of decoloniality in three distinct ways: as a subject of study as it appears in online spaces linked to offline social movements, as an analytical strategy to push against ahistorical studies of digital media that obfuscate its undergirding colonial conditions, and as an ethical and political commitment to develop a decolonial sensibility.

Our analysis places the university campus at the center of struggles for the future and campus protests as incubators for imagining a way forward. It is precisely because of the symbolic and material coloniality of the university campus *and* its potential as a (mediated) space to imagine an otherwise that we begin this book here. The chapter highlights how campus protest, iconized through the phrase *must fall* as it emerged in South Africa, has become, as a result of digital communication, a permeable and expanded space of contestation that challenges norms regarding (economic) access, participation, curricular goals, and canonical knowledge formations across borders. First, we explore how campus-based protests have mushroomed across the globe in ways that create national counterpublics and transnational networks of connection and solidarity challenging the foundational presumptions of the university's function in a world system. These counterpublics and networks rooted in the university in the present moment, however, tend to elide concurrent Indigenous struggles to protect land and water. We argue for a digital decolonial politics on campus, particularly in North American universities, to include and amplify Indigenous struggles for survivance. We then discuss how these protests have pushed universities to adopt and appropriate decolonization as a means, method, and rhetoric that, whether purposefully or incidentally, dampen or quell protest through performances of contrition while simultaneously emboldening attacks on "left-wing" academics and student protestors from within and outside the university. Ultimately, we show how these developments unsettle the presumption of the university as a liberal settlement where speech is "free," ideas are neutral, and access is universal, and we push for a revised dialogue about the university that places its specific histories of erasure, elitism, and expropriation in settler colonial, imperial, and postcolonial contexts into relationship with one and other.

The second chapter, "Extreme," hones the focus further on attacks against progressive voices by moving outward from university campuses into broader political movements and showing how online speech is deeply implicated in the resurgence of xenophobic, reactionary politics often glossed as a "populist wave." The chapter explores the volatile and cantankerous social media engagements of the Hindu right-wing in India and white supremacists in Germany, the UK, and the US to argue that extreme forms of online speech commonly engaged by these groups reflect and reinforce longer historical processes of coloniality that continue to animate, inform, and shape racial relations, normative understandings of bordered geographies, and taken-for-granted market relations. By exploring how coloniality has retrenched itself in online spaces with extreme speech that flows through the affective infrastructures of digital capitalism, we also argue for a methodological impulse to question existing normative categories in liberal thought that tend to erase colonial continuities by framing the digital as a radically new constellation and the reason for an unexpected crisis.

Building on the critique of affective infrastructures of digital capitalism opened up in the previous chapter, our third chapter grounds the discussion in a critical political economy of contemporary data relations. Engaging recent scholarship on data colonialism and big data in the Global South, it shows how the most recent manifestations of data relations that aim to extract and monetize "behavioral surplus" share and normalize problematic anthropological tropes around "capturing the natives in their natural environments."[58] While critics of artificial intelligence and algorithm-driven surveillance capitalism are increasingly reclaiming humanism against the onslaught of the global data machine, we show that such criticisms do not recognize the historical trajectory of colonialism in which "capture" was the key modality for imperial capitalism and that the category of "human" as the European Enlightenment project sought to racially classify human, subhuman, and others.[59] Nor do these criticisms consider the vastly uneven ways in which algorithmic capture unfolds globally. By perusing emerging debates around algorithmic racism and scrutinizing extreme speech content moderation arrangements of the global tech industry as illustrative cases, this chapter anchors the political economy of contemporary capture in the historical *longue durée* that has problematic parallels to how anthropology emerged as the science of the colonizer.

If data relations enable exploitative forms of capture, within the academy and for knowledge politics broadly, the digital enables a different unfolding. Our chapter "Knowledge/Citation" argues for an attention to how the digital unsettles normative frameworks of knowledge/power linked to academia broadly and academic institutions more specifically. Focusing on several examples, including @citeblackwomen, a US-based campaign that advocates for the recognition of the scholarship of Black women across disciplines, Dalit Camera, a media activist group that uses YouTube to campaign for Dalit rights and the abolishment of caste, and IsumaTV, an Indigenous media project that spans continents, we look at the ways in which online worlds allow otherwise submerged knowledges to circulate in ways that create a cross-platform politics of citation that destabilizes formal institutional knowledge arrangements. We conclude the chapter by touching on the ways in which right-wing formations use the very same mechanisms to produce decolonial claims, to illustrate the potential dangers of over-valorizing the digital as a space for decolonizing knowledge relations and to highlight the ways in which decolonization—as a symbol and discursive strategy—can and has been coopted to fortify hegemonic power.

In "Home/Field, the final chapter, we dwell on our own predicaments as researchers in the midst of all these shifts, by opening a key methodological quandary that the digital has fomented within anthropology specifically and the social sciences more broadly, as well as in the development and humanitarian sectors. Digitalization has decoded some key methodological/conceptual tropes such as the distinction between "home" and "the field" and associated ideas of distance and nearness, now and after, us and them. With the always-on character of digital social networks now entrenching the fields of anthropology and other disciplines, the metaphorical distinction between home as a site of calm academic reflection as opposed to field as a site where "alterity is discovered" appears not only untenable but also unfamiliar.[60] This development that is linked to the growing digitalization of social and cultural lives has methodological implications. The field is no longer a set of "regionally circumscribed epistemic communities."[61] Under the digital condition, the decolonial decoding of problematic distinctions between home and field disrupts the methodological fixations that anthropologists and other social scientists working with the Malinowskian framework have stubbornly held fast to since the turn of the twentieth century. By inquiring about the partial dissolving of these distinctions, we ask what it means to do research when the comfort of home—a sign of the privileged location of the colonizer—is productively disrupted by the turbulences of digital communication, especially when the field follows and haunts the researcher in digitally networked ways.

Reflecting on these conundrums and how our scholarly, biographical, and political trajectories have inspired new collaborations beyond the home/field binary, we conclude the book with a coda that returns to the key arguments of *Digital Unsettling* and outlines the roadmap for a methodology that has made this project possible and that such a project envisions to advance. We present different methodological moves for a decolonial ethical praxis that can pry open the digital and its recursive communicative networks as a neocolonial technology while simultaneously exploring them as a tool for an alterpolitics of recognition and political change.

1

Campus

University as a Site of Struggle

The "educational danger" of student movements . . . lies in
their capacity to produce insurgencies, insurgencies that are
created by connecting social formations and processes that
are supposed to be understood as disparate.
—Roderick Ferguson

On March 9, 2015, students at the University of Cape Town (UCT) in
South Africa, fed up with the racism they encountered in their institution and the failed promises of the South African state to create
economic and social opportunities in the post-apartheid era, "occupied
the university's administration buildings, holding lectures on apartheid
history and beating drums."[1] Social media snapshots of the occupation
traveled, indexed by the hashtag #RhodesMustFall. Within a month, the
movement was picked up by students at Oxford University in the United
Kingdom.[2] The students at Oxford echoed the demands of the students
from UCT, pushing for the decolonization of curricula and pedagogy,
the hiring of Black professors, and the public recognition of the enduring legacy of colonial and imperial power. Statues of British colonialist
Cecil B. Rhodes—who, among other things, was one of the progenitors
of the South African apartheid state—became, in the words of organizers at UCT, "the natural starting point of this movement."[3] They argued
that toppling statues was just the beginning. As their manifesto claimed,
the statues' "removal will not mark the end but the beginning of the
long overdue process of decolonising this university. In our belief, the
experiences seeking to be addressed by this movement are not unique to
an elite institution such as UCT, but rather reflect broader dynamics of
a racist and patriarchal society that has remained unchanged since the
end of formal apartheid."[4]

In October 2015, the #FeesMustFall movement—drawing attention to the prohibitive increase in university fees in South Africa—shut down several universities across South Africa. As Kelly Gillespie and Leighann Naidoo explain, #RhodesMustFall morphed into a wider, more popular movement in South Africa precisely because rising fees represented a far more immediate, material challenge for young people who studied in non-elite higher education institutions in South Africa and felt the post-apartheid state in South Africa had not done enough to pave the way for a different future for their generation.[5]

The student-led movements against increasing fees in South Africa were echoed in Latin America, Europe, and Asia, in some cases overlapping, amplifying, and extending the demands #RhodesMustFall signaled to include critiques of the coloniality of the postcolonial state. In early 2016, the institutional murder of a key Dalit organizer in India, Rohit Vemula, led to the push for an international public reckoning of the university as a space that continues to be a site for collective aspiration and democratic struggle while it perpetuates casteist, religious, and gendered exclusion in the postcolonial nation-state.[6] Meanwhile, in the same period in Latin America, collective demands to open the doors of the exclusive university systems, modeled after their European counterparts, to Black and Indigenous students were linked to demands for the inclusion of non-European knowledges.[7] These on-campus protests overlapped with demands for a more just (and less corrupt) government.

These movements—whether explicitly calling out the coloniality of the university in terms of its teaching, its overwhelmingly white faculty, and its Eurocentric curricula or by drawing attention to issues of access and corruption—resonated with and amplified movements on university campuses in the United States.

In 2015, #BlackOnCampus emerged as a hashtag to index the variety of racialized experiences of Black college students across universities. Other hashtags soon emerged, #IAm, #RoyallMustFall, and so on, that linked material demands to racialized experience and US settler colonial history and revealed the stubborn recalcitrance of the US university system that, on the one hand, purports access and mobility, and on the other, polices its thresholds jealously.[8] In recent years, campus protests in the US have also taken on an economic undertone as student organizers and academics have pushed against rising student debt and the lasting penury it creates for working-class and middle-class students.[9] As Achille Mbembe rightly suggests, in the university, "to decolonize implies breaking *the cycle that tends to turn students into customers and consumers.*"[10]

Finally, and crucially, the university became a site of reckoning for the global #MeToo movement, which mobilized social media to call out sexual misconduct, abuse, and gendered predation in various professional spheres, including academia. Patriarchal systems of power, located in university patronage systems and academic hierarchies and in the embodied practices of deified "great men" professors, were called out as part and parcel of a larger move to dismantle various forms of hegemonic power steeped in colonial relational arrangements.[11] Here, Suren Pillay's words, as she spoke to students participating in #RhodesMustFall on the steps of UCT in April 2015, resonate:

> We, those outside your university, and at other universities, down the road and across the country, are watching with great enthusiasm and inspired by the courage and thoughtfulness with which you are conducting this moment of subversion. I have to say that I am in particular very encouraged by the connections you have made between subjections of different kinds, particularly two very neglected forms of subjection—in the sphere of knowledge production, and in the sphere of gender and sexuality. These are remarkable connections and the kind of leadership that is visible to those of us on the outside, shows a genuine effort to unsettle imperial hubris, but also patriarchal power relations.[12]

Precisely because they coincide and amplify one another on social media, student movements across the globe have opened the space to consider the university campus as a critical location where colonial structures of knowledge, unequal arrangements of academic labor, and gendered and racialized inequities in relation to access and belonging in the postcolonial nation-state coincide with material disfranchisement and widening economic inequality. The digitally mediated university campus has become a space/time that allows us to reckon with the generational shifts that produce a different response to coloniality from previous moments. As Black, Indigenous, working-class, and gender non-conforming students coming of age in the twenty-first century come into fresh contact with the inheritances of colonialism in our contemporary late-capitalist world system, they articulate new positions and demands based on a conjuncture of location, knowledge, power, and action.[13]

In turn, students are able to speak across institutional and national contexts about their particular and shared conditions through various social media platforms.[14] Digitally mediated conversations across locations become an opportunity to disagree about aims, theoretical orientations, and leadership structures in struggles to reimagine the university.[15] They also become an opportunity to share tactics, learn about other sites and stories of struggle, and expand the potential for a twenty-first-century decolonial praxis. These exchanges are steeped in various affective registers—anger, disappointment, worry, hope—that amplify the velocity of circulation, the intensity of exchange, and the potential for participation.

Discussions that begin in the radical organizing spaces of the university, as they channel affects related to questions of coloniality in the present through digital circuits, broaden, engage, and foster what we describe a bit later in the chapter as *affective counterpublics*, which work to collectively describe and interrogate the relationships between economic disenfranchisement, racism, and their colonial antecedents. The digitally mediated campus, then, becomes a site by which we can apprehend a transnational struggle to unsettle and, therefore, potentially radically reimagine the university—one built on emergent formulations of enduring principles that have been the hallmark of the struggle against coloniality—abolition, collective potentiality, and radical access.[16]

What we are interested in engaging with in this chapter are the ways in which hashtags, images, and particular repertoires of digital performance create the conditions for students across national contexts to link institutional racisms and structural epistemic colonialities endemic to universities, even if unevenly and in tension, with issues of enduring economic inequality. This development signals a rebirth of an internationalist political project that does not pit "identity" against a critique of capital but polyvocally narrates each as awkwardly intertwined between and within the campus networks that the digital facilitates. As such, it places the university campus at the center of struggles for the future and campus protests as incubators for imagining a way forward. It is precisely because of the symbolic and material coloniality of the university campus *and* its potential as a (mediated) space to imagine an otherwise that we begin this book and our theorization of *digital unsettling* here. For us the university, not least because it is where we work, is a key site of unsettling, a location from which to understand the affective and temporal politics of decolonization and its potential to rupture enduring colonial arrangements as it manifests in online spaces in ways that shape, connect, and amplify transnational protest.

This, of course, has not gone unnoticed by university leadership, right wing groups, and other arrayed interests that seek to maintain the status quo. Later in the chapter, we touch on how the digital has been mobilized to counter student protest. These digital moves enable university management and entrepreneurial academics to appropriate decolonization as a shorthand for fundable, sexy, and inevitably shallow engagements with the histories of anti-colonial struggle inside and outside the university that inevitably work to retrench enduring systems of privilege and power.

Other tactics taken up by universities have included doubling down on free speech and debate to justify platforming right-wing speakers and legitimizing racist, sexist speech and mounting impassioned defenses of the classics and the Western liberal tradition. As Priyamvada Gopal notes, these defensive postures—as they emerge inside and outside the university—rest on the idea that calls to decolonize are simply measures to exact revenge against those that have had "inherited advantages deriving from dispossession and genocide."[17]

In what follows, we focus on student activists' digital tactics and complex articulations of gender, race, and economic justice and university responses to them in the form of gestural and appropriative moves toward their demands for redress. We conclude by discussing some of the ways in which the imperative to decolonize has been appropriated by the university to shore up its position and monetize minority difference while managing its institutional effects. In so doing, we set aside the conversation about the kinds of digitally circulating disinformation and vitriol under the guise of free speech that is currently embattling university campuses, picking it up in the following chapter on extreme speech.

The university campus, of course, has long been the site where demands for minority redress and justice are voiced and where, as Roderick Ferguson argues, hegemonic power is cultivated.[18] In the US, for instance, upheavals and calls for a "third world revolution" on college campuses across the country in the late 1960s located the university as a space where racially excluded difference could have a voice and find ways to equalize material inequalities in the university and society. Efforts on university campuses, as they resonated and drew from various social movements across the country—the Red Power movement, El Movimiento, and the Black Power movement—paved the way for the creation of ethnic studies, Indigenous studies programs, and the like.

What marks this moment as unique is how the digital makes the university campus permeable, visible, and virtual—a key node in a "network of outrage and hope" that potentiates dialogue across specific sociohistorical contexts and comes to symbolize the entanglements between here and there, then and now.[19] While incipient online spaces have been central to social justice and civil rights organizing in the US since the 1960s, the university campus shows us the transnational and multipronged potentials of on-the-ground protest supported and amplified by twenty-first-century digital organizing.[20]

Decolonize This Campus!

(Gabriel) In 2019, another round of campus protests began across the world, including one at the institution where I teach in London—Goldsmiths, University of London. Students at Goldsmiths, like students in other movements from the last decade, wed on-the-ground activism with strategic digital engagement to firmly position the university campus as a location of decolonial rupture by fostering a critical and transnational conversation regarding the twentieth-century mythology of higher education mobility and by historicizing the university as an enduring location for the reproduction of colonial norms. Their efforts, echoing Eli Meyerhoff, sought once again to disrupt "the romance of education" linked to the university campus.[21] Goldsmiths Anti-Racist Action (GARA) offers a way to think through how the digital facilitates transnational organizing and creates the conditions for teaching and learning across time and space about coloniality in the present.

GARA-involved students spent 137 days occupying key administrative buildings on campus to protest institutional racism, generating a list of demands directed toward the institution that addressed deep epistemic and economic inequalities.[22] The breadth of their list of demands took management and faculty by surprise. On the one hand, they, like some of the UK campus-based movements that preceded them, pushed for a reckoning of curricula, hiring practices, and so on. However, they also added to their list of demands the need to address the unfair labor conditions of security guards and cleaners on campus, the majority of whom were Black or from other racialized minority groups, and the imperative to reinstate scholarships for Palestinian students, which were offered by the university for a number of years but had inexplicably been discontinued. In creating a broad platform of demands and representing their complex relationships to one another intertextually in online spaces, Goldsmiths students reflected what they had learned from movements that preceded them outside of the UK, particularly lessons from the recent South African Fallist movements: that the colonial legacies of racism are intertwined with economic disenfranchisement and that movements for justice must broaden its imagination beyond the institution or even the naturalized borders of the nation-state to include those who are under threat of dispossession.

Of course, these broad imaginaries for justice and solidarity within and beyond the institution or the borders of the nation-state don't always emerge in campus organized protests. Take, for instance, the campus-based protests in the US we mentioned earlier, signified by the hashtag #BlackonCampus. While this campaign unfolded, there was another social media campaign underway organized by youth from the Standing Rock Sioux tribe "to fight against the planned construction of the Dakota Access Pipeline through the sacred Indian Reservation lands."[23] Over the course of a year and a half, this campaign, marked by #ReZpectOurWater and #NoDAPL, brought international attention and tremendous material and bodily support through various crowdfunding efforts to those on the frontlines of the Standing Rock reservation as they physically resisted the construction of the pipeline. That the hashtag campaigns pushing for racial justice on campuses in 2015 and 2016 in the US did not braid with and amplify coeval struggles for Indigenous sovereignty speaks to how, as Tiffany Lebotho King reminds us,

"U.S. racial discourse tends to be organized by a white-Black paradigmatic frame that often erases Indigenous peoples."[24] It also reminds us, as Vine Deloria argued during the US civil rights struggles of the 1960s, that struggles for inclusion in the settler state are not commensurate with Indigenous struggles for sovereignty.[25]

GARA offers some insights on how movements that work, even if imperfectly, to decolonize can broaden their agendas, make visible multiple concurrent struggles without collapsing them as equivalent, and develop novel digital strategies to amplify and materialize them. I spent several days with students leading the GARA, attending teach-ins, eating meals, participating in planning sessions, and actively engaging in negotiations with the university. As I spent time with student organizers, I began to grow more interested in how the digital figured in their strategies, particularly how they used Facebook, Instagram, and Twitter. As we sat in regular meetings, one of the key conversations centered around how students in the occupation might use social media to raise awareness and incite discussion, first among students and faculty on campus, then, as time went on, across linked publics in London, the UK, and globally. I also became increasingly interested in how previous digitally mediated campus movements shaped their understandings of occupation, not just in instrumental terms but in ways space and time were felt, perceived, and inhabited.

It became clear early on that the space/time the students at Goldsmiths occupied during their active protests was not only delimited to South London and the university they attended as fee paying students. As they held teach-ins, potlucks, sleepovers, and planning meetings in the administrative building—once a townhall for Deptford, a neighborhood in South London whose historic wealth was built by shipbuilders in the eighteenth and nineteenth century—they/we inhabited a colonial space. Portraits of the local area's favorite sons, all beneficiaries of colonial extraction, decorated the walls of the large chamber. The frescoes of the building, all in a nautical theme, spoke to England's implication in the transatlantic slave trade and other depravations of the colonial period. The physical space they inhabited, when seen through the filter of the student occupiers' demands, clearly collapsed the distinctions between a colonial and imperial past and the present moment.

In this physical space steeped in coloniality, hashtags that referred to previous actions and occupations elsewhere that foregrounded the removal of the edifices of colonial figures—#RhodesMustFall, most importantly—became significant. Hashtags that emerged out of the Goldsmiths occupation—#MyRacistCampus—began to comingle with #RhodesMustFall on Twitter, creating a sense of event whose space/time spanned years and crosscut geographies and that was linked to material concerns, naturalized edifices, and marginalized students' experiences of the colonial university. One could easily argue that the Goldsmiths occupation was an extension of the space/time that was initially created in Cape Town.[26] In other words, the disruption of the workings of a colonial university in one location, as it was mediatized through the hashtag, generated the possibility for its space/time to become public, shared, and retrievable in another moment and location. Among student organizers at Goldsmiths, this feeling of a digitally enabled sharing of anti-colonial space/time created a sense of continuity and shared struggle—a means to link one's own experience to that of others on another university campus to sustain occupation and movement.

Social media, of course, has been a key tool and virtual shared space/time for various movements in the last decade. From the Occupy movement and the Arab Spring to Ferguson, Missouri, smartphone technologies and social media have been mobilized to disrupt hegemonic power, in part by materializing collectivity. Whether through the use of particular ring tones as a means of covert communication or by using messaging apps to bring together flash mobs to swarm public spaces as a means to collectively amplify a message or to make visible otherwise obscured positions, places, or temporalities, the digital emerged as a repository of practices and capabilities that offered an opportunity to foment, rupture, and (re)claim. These online social media/new media practices mesh with visceral face-to-face techniques of struggle. As Jeffrey Juris, in his reflections on #Occupy everywhere argues, "It is clear that new media influence how movements organize and that places, bodies, face-to-face networks, social histories, and the messiness of offline politics continue to matter, as exemplified by the resonance of the physical occupations themselves."[27]

We have come to know about the Janus-faced nature of these technologies in recent years and how the data that social movements generate in social media spaces have been used against them. As Simone Brown points out, the state has long used technologies of surveillance to mobilize against perceived challenges to colonial power.[28] We discuss these technologies in our chapter on capture, paying close attention to how algorithmic racism and the political economy of data surveillance reify colonial categories of the human.

Yet despite this, given the events of the last decade, it is clear that digital communication technologies have continued to lend themselves in service of social movements and that actors on the ground have resorted to "agentic circumventive adaptions" and "creative vernacular strategies" to navigate the emergent challenges and threats in digital spaces.[29] For instance, platforms deemed under surveillance or that do not have sufficient end-to-end encryption are abandoned, while corporate platforms like Twitter, Facebook, and Instagram are used strategically to create visibility. With regard to campus actions and occupations like the one at Goldsmiths, student protestors employ a multiple platform approach, relying on common social media platforms—Facebook, Twitter, Instagram—to draw attention to the enduring coloniality of the university while creating loose networks of solidarity and connection across national contexts through other platforms, with the understanding that all these different interfaces generate individual and collective risk.

#HashtagCampusProtests

The first, and possibly most obvious, place to think about the mechanics of these connections and the multiple registers of solidarity that are evoked to sustain them is the hashtag. The hashtag is a ubiquitous symbol used on Twitter and other social media sites and, when thinking about social movements, does the work of linking offline protest with online discourse related to protest. The hashtag offers a means to index the localized distinctiveness of a protest or movement while functioning as the connective tissue that references other ongoing campus-based struggles in other parts of the world and at other moments in time. They also become a way to link, in clear, concise terms, various problems of the university.

As Rahul Rao argues:

Students' claims, often articulated on social media with the pithiness that hashtags require, have shed light on the content and pedagogical premises of syllabi (#whyismycurricullumwhite), the underrepresentation of students and staff of colour particularly in more prestigious institutions and in the upper echelons of the profession (#whyisntmyprofessorblack) and the hostile built environment of British universities that reflects their entanglement in the histories of slavery, colonialism and apartheid (#Rhodesmustfall).[30]

The hashtag, in this sense, creates a persistent index of coloniality in the present, what Yarimar Bonilla and Jonathan Rosa rightly describe as a filing system, by which to collate, iterate, and retrieve thoughts, feelings, ideas, and even news linked to (campus) protest to create a meaningful, homophilic archive of resistance.[31]

The hashtag, however, exceeds its use value as a way to link, file, and retrieve content within social medias' vast and iterative digital archive insofar as it functions, simultaneously, as a way for those involved in protest to actively mark as relevant an utterance, an image, or a multimodal semiotic formation. This active potentiality enables users to mobilize their experiences as they are rendered in textual or audiovisual content to, as Rao suggests, shed light on how individual encounters with marginalization are entangled with structural issues in and of the university. A portrait, a short utterance, the image of a building—this content textures and diversifies the hashtag's meaning and shapes its potential for uptake. Those who encounter mediatized struggles for access and justice in the university on social media and share these experiences, political affinities, and positionalities are able to engage in a kind of participatory witnessing of coloniality as it unfolds in contemporary institutional contexts. By evoking witnessing, we point to recent conversations in media studies around the ways in which media circulations facilitate multiple forms of witnessing. More specifically, we draw from Alissa Richardson, who, working with recent protests against anti-Black police violence in the United States, argues for a theorization of witnessing that recognizes and takes seriously the differential affective resonances that media forms generate as they circulate in online fora.[32] Hashtags, when approached as a technology to mark the potential for participatory witnessing that is shaped by the afterlife of slavery and the dispossession of land and resources across continents, plays a vital role in facilitating the linkages between racialized student protestors, the campuses they inhabit, and the common experiences between them by becoming a means to self-identify, participate, and become enmeshed in a shared struggle.

Bonilla and Rosa describe the process of hashtags bringing together experiences, attentions, and people at various scales as an intertextual chain. This chain links a "broad range of tweets on a given topic or multiple topics."[33] This chain can extend under the umbrella of a single hashtag or under a combination of hashtags, each of which creates another tendril of connection and holds the potential to amplify multiple related struggles when deployed simultaneously. Moreover, these various chains work to make visible mediatized places that crosscut space and time.[34] The campus as place becomes the central referent for intersecting ad hoc publics if a hashtag is picked up and becomes a trend through the proliferation of unique tweets and retweets.[35] Bonilla and Rosa argue that this sort of mediatized place offers an intriguing site for fieldwork, a way to unsettle the received wisdom of the field as a neutral geographic location on a colonial map. Rather, this place, as it is constituted through tweets, subtweets, and retweets that each seek to tell their addressees what the hashtag or hashtags are really about as they are linked to unfolding events in physical space, create a volatile and conflicted interdiscursive location. This "place" allows us to understand the contours of a struggle across territorialized locations, but as Bonilla and Rosa warn, it doesn't provide enough context to "assess the context" of each mediatized utterance.[36] For us, this insight is important because it reveals how the university as a digital place and context can connect variously divided geographies in ways that highlight shared colonial relations and their contestations. It also reminds us of the specificity of struggle and the continued need to think about connectivities as we are grounded in located struggles, in this case (for Gabriel) in New Cross, London.

Another way we think the placemaking potential of the hashtag matters—in relation to campus-based struggles—is that it is generative of a shared temporality. The shared temporality that the hashtag produces is generative of "public time," where people across time zones can feel a sense of togetherness and shared engagement.[37] One consequence of the creation of a shared public time linked to a movement or protest is that a multisited public conversation converges around the broader historical conditions that it signifies. In some cases, these conversations can span the contours of empire and illuminate its temporality in ways that engender conversation in unprecedented ways. As John Newsinger points out, "The Rhodes Must Fall campaign has provoked more public discussion and debate on the rights and wrongs of the British Empire than any number of academic books and articles."[38] Newsinger's comment suggests that events taking place in Cape Town during the period when the Rhodes Must Fall campaign was active could be simultaneously accessed in London, Delhi, or Lagos through #RhodesMustFall in ways that were generative of a shared time across locations. This suggests that the immediate transnational potential of a hashtag is that it creates a shared temporality of struggle in simultaneity that invites specific modes of witnessing and participation.

The potential for sharing in this temporality, as we intimated before, stretches beyond the duration of a protest event. Years after #Rhodes-MustFall in Cape Town was a physical occupation and synchronous event, it became an asynchronous and digitized chronotope for further anti-colonial protest.[39] As such, not only did #RhodesMustFall create participation in the form of debate and discussion across various locations as it unfolded, it also sowed the seed for future actions and protests. The hashtag #RhodesMustFall, in this sense, congealed counterpublics around its organizing symbols and demands in ways that fostered the possibility for its decolonial impulse to materialize elsewhere.

Counterpublics is a term that Nancy Fraser coined several decades ago as a critique of Jürgen Habermas's normative theorization of a singular public sphere.[40] Fraser's conceptualization of counterpublics took stock of power as it manifests in differentiated classed, racialized, and gendered positions, recognizing its hegemonic positions and its counters in media worlds as part and parcel of what Antonio Gramsci has described as a war of position—one that sought to resist domination with culture rather than through force.[41] As a concept, *counterpublics* has been refined over the decades to account for the role mobile devices and social media connectivity have played in the congealing of social relations, actions, and the circulation of knowledge while acknowledging that access to public spaces for meeting has greatly diminished as a result of the twin forces of neoliberal capital and the increasingly restrictive surveillance state.[42]

Social media offers those who are the subjects of surveillance and control to turn the surveillance apparatus toward the state and its institutions and create digital (counter)publics. For example, discussing organizing efforts in the wake of anti-Black state violence in the US, Mark Lamont Hill shows how smartphone cameras became a means to produce an alternate account of events, while Twitter became a channel to distribute them, thereby solidifying what he describes as a Black counterpublic as it takes shape on the sub-platform—Black Twitter.[43] While Lamont Hill focuses on Black Twitter's impact on organizing efforts in the US context, our attention to the campus allows us to see how the connective technologies of social media create transnational connections between Black diasporic, African, and Indian students who experience the university as hostile and inaccessible.

Hashtag circulations have the potential to inextricably link instances of anti-Blackness in the university to other forms of systemic exclusion and marginalization—Indigenous, gendered, and caste-based oppressions—and to raise the question of what higher education is good for in the wake of pandemics, climate change, and right-wing nationalism. Here, what Katherine McKittrick calls Blackness as livingness, a site of intervention on coloniality, becomes palpable.[44] The connective technologies of the digital enable Blackness to animate, connect, and collectively rupture normative ideas of the university across contexts and link multiple struggles for justice. In other words, the shared temporality generated on social media mediation offers the potential for a recognition of a shared struggle against coloniality across borders.

In the last decade, for instance, university students in India who are seemingly the beneficiaries of the reservation system established during independence that sought to create a more level playing field by creating access to education and government jobs for caste marginalized and tribal communities have begun to protest the unequal and hostile conditions of the universities they attend. Dalit, tribal, and other caste-excluded students have argued that the system reinforces an upper-caste discourse of merit that negatively affects their mental health while at university and their long-term prospects long after they leave its halls. Their positions in the prestigious universities in India are always marked by the stigma that they are present only because they have been given a place by the state, not because of their intrinsic capability or worth.[45]

The protests against casteist hostility in India's universities emerged digitally under the banner of #DalitLivesMatter, speaking to the conditions of impossibility for Dalit and other Bahujan students. The hashtag, which mirrors the semantic structure of #BlackLivesMatter, calls for an attention to commonalities *and* particularities of the Dalit struggle and is an invitation for a transnational conversation around sociohistoric maintenance, hierarchical difference, and subordination and the shared histories of colonial rule that have given birth to or amplified conditions of impossibility, disposability, and struggle. The counterpublics formed during the #DalitLivesMatter protests on university campuses in 2016—which affectively resonate and link with struggles for Black lives elsewhere—have spurred global action around caste-based subordination and the role of the university in the maintenance of the structures that reproduce it.[46] #DalitLivesMatter, in more recent years, has broadened its iterative intensity and now indexes violence of all sorts committed against Dalits in India.

Affective Flows

As from the example above, key to understanding and engaging with the ways in which social media engenders the livingness of Black solidarities across contexts is to think with the affects they channel, circulate, and intensify. Affect, as a conceptual category and heuristic, has made its rounds in the social sciences in the last decade. We are interested, in this chapter and in this book, in how affects—age, fear, guilt, excitement—are channeled and accumulate in and through social media in ways that create the conditions for material ruptures and shifts. As Zizi Papparachisi notes, feelings or sentiments as they animate particular narratives—in this case of Black livingness in the face of enduring coloniality—are generative of affective publics.[47] How might we extend this theorization to think through what constitutes an *affective counterpublic*, those who push against the grain of normalized conditions of exclusion and have the potential to connect experiences across borders?

Turning to Thulile Gamedze, who in her reflections on her experience with the Rhodes Must Fall campaign in Cape Town, points to how the university suppresses "Black expressions of pain or rage" which students then channeled into activism, we might begin to think about the ways in which images, texts, and the hashtags that bind them draw together and intensify affects that ultimately have the potential to create collective action.[48] One way this happens, of course, is that racialized students share the harsh or difficult experiences they have in the university. These experiences can accrue in relation to one locus of contact—a specific university campus—and/or be linked to hashtags like #Iam, which collates the experiences of Black students across campuses in the US, or through multiple hashtags, to create the potential for a transnational affective engagement with experiences of marginalization in the university.

Here, an individual's narrative—as it is briefly articulated online and tagged with one or more hashtags—becomes part of a digital archive of complaint. Complaint, as Sara Ahmed teaches, is a register through which one can express "grief, pain, or dissatisfaction, something that is a cause of protest or outcry . . . or a formal allegation."[49] When complaints are expressed online and are indexed through hashtags, they form an archive that serves as a particular kind of collective witnessing and shared affective experience of the colonial university. This digital archive, as it resides on Twitter, Instagram, and elsewhere, effectively becomes a site where one can listen and be listened to when it comes to the colonial harms inflicted inside the institution.[50] Listening, of course, specifies witnessing as an aural engagement, one that is intimate and intersubjective. In social media timelines, opportunities for listening to students' experiences of hostility *in* the university are juxtaposed against images of colonial statues and edifices *of* the university, as both modalities often share the same hashtags. This collocation creates a powerful montage—where what is sensorially alienating is put in tense relation with experiences that are relatable, even if difficult to bear witness to.

Another way affects are channeled and congeal counterpublics, particularly in the context of university social movements that seek a particular set of goals or aims, is to strategically use social media to *generate* feelings of outrage, shame, and so on. At Goldsmiths, for instance, student occupiers strategically circulated images on Twitter, Instagram, and Facebook of the correspondence they had on email with senior management. By making private correspondence public, they created the potential for a shared public outrage and, if management was listening, potentially shame as well. GARA's tactics to name and shame in social media spaces were effective in so far as they garnered listeners within and outside of the institution. GARA occupiers' tweeted content that highlighted Goldsmiths' institutional responses to the occupation were joined by other tweets that called out the complicity of the senior management team, sometimes by name, in reproducing the racialized climate of the institution.

#MyRacistCampus emerged as a way to link all of these tweets, an eloquent articulation of the double bind that GARA activists/students faced as they disavowed a place that for better or worse they also had a stake in. Inducing shame as digital tactic hinges on people's reticence and even fear to have their public persona tainted through circulations of their complicity or misdeeds. Naming and shaming as an affectively charged tactical maneuver, of course, has precedent as a digital phenomenon in recent times and in pre-digital social movements of the twentieth century.[51] Calling out specific people and specific occasions of discrimination in no uncertain terms, while locating responsibility, targets a politics of respectability that governs action and maintains the status quo by saying what, in normative terms, can and can't be said and/or by policing how things are said. For a recent and related example, we can look to the #MeToo movement as it spread onto university campuses.

Starting in 2017, as part of the #MeToo wave of action in various national contexts, a student named Raya Sarkar used Facebook to publish a list of upper-caste male professors across national contexts who were accused of sexual misconduct and harassment in their various university contexts.[52] The hashtag #MeToo connected this list to a growing number of accounts and accusations of sexual harassment and violence across professional domains and geographies. Naming, under the banner of #MeToo, was an invitation not only to call out or name but also an invitation for other women to share their experiences. The public spilling of emotion spread across national contexts and, very quickly, exceeded a particular domain and generated broad and specific conversations about gender, power, and intersectional oppressions. The conversations this tactic enabled, however, weren't always generative, particularly when they focused on the tactic of naming and shaming online rather than on the sexual harassment it revealed. There was, for instance, a very brief statement signed by prominent feminists in India decrying Raya Sarkar's use of the tactic. They stated that "this manner of naming can delegitimize the long struggle against sexual harassment and make our task as feminists more difficult."[53]

Similar to the key actors in the #MeToo movement who published online lists of offending male academics (as well as artists, media makers, and so on), arguing that they were forced to do so as a last resort because there was no accountability at the institutional level or within the communities of practice to which they belonged, GARA core members expressed that systems of accountability at Goldsmiths were woefully inadequate to deal with issues of racial inequality and exclusion and that involving various publics by directly naming the issues and the actors responsible was their last but necessary recourse. Naming and shaming, coupled with a willingness to make transparent processes of negotiation with management, forced Goldsmiths' management to sit down and negotiate with student organizers. Of course, naming and shaming, in this case, also created a similar backlash. Several teaching staff declared in offline and online spaces that students should use the appropriate channels to voice their grievances rather than publicly airing the issues—repeating almost verbatim what prominent feminists in India had voiced in response to Sarkar's publication of the #MeToo lists on Facebook.

What the tactics above demonstrate, as they mobilize and channel affects across space, is that Twitter and other social media platforms can effectively link experiences of marginalization and the energies they engender across contexts and channel them through specific repertoires of social media performance to create affectively charged counterpublics that have the potential to impact outcomes. Some of these tactics, however, can also mobilize unexpected resistances by those who might otherwise be considered allies or, at the very least, sympathetic listeners because the mode of address (naming and shaming) and the mediated mechanisms amplify and disturb the order of things.

Sharing intimate testimonials, naming and shaming, and making private correspondences public are three repertoires we have briefly analyzed, each of which mobilizes social media to make visible the experiences of the marginalized and put pressure on institutions to enact change. Through these repertoires, racialized, class, and gender marginalized students who are otherwise invisible in their respective national contexts are, through the distributive technologies of the digital, seen, heard, and felt and—temporally—become part of something larger than themselves. Campus movements are born and sustained through these moving affects as they are channeled through multiple social media platforms. Affects, enmeshed in hashtags, images, texts, and so on, become both a cause and an effect for protest; in so far as they express, they amplify, and they signal the deep pain and struggle caused by the colonial university while mobilizing others to challenge and unsettle their premises.

As affects are channeled through social media circulations, they engender active connections between student activists in different locations who are actively protesting conditions in their respective universities. These digitally facilitated connections, in the form of direct contact and shared strategic planning, push us to consider the ways in which affective connections that congeal counterpublics and that can be used as deliberate tactic to create a broader visibility around an issue can also be mobilized to create the conditions for direct contact, communication, and knowledge sharing between campus based activist groups across national contexts.

For instance, students at Goldsmiths reached out to their peers in Baltimore, who were also occupying their institution to protest against the racialized policing practices of their university. The two groups scheduled multiple Zoom conversations during their respective occupations not only to share strategies but also to educate each other on the histories of white supremacy, policing, carcerality, and gentrification linked to each of these institutions on either side of the Atlantic. Their conversations across campuses offer a way to understand how platforms like Twitter and Zoom, each of which monetize participation and generate their own forms of surveillance, continue to be used in ways that subvert their designed intent. The sort of multiplatform engagement that student protestors engage in blurs the distinction between (affective) counterpublics and networks, demonstrating how campus-based social movements are utilizing multiple tools to create visibility around their specific struggles while creating persistent links across and within them. If, as danah boyd has argued, networked publics are "publics that have been transformed by networked media, its properties, and its potential," then networked (affective) counterpublics signal a way to think about the transformative potentials when the intensities of resistance-in-place are connected across national contexts.[54]

The campus as such poses an important example of an affective counterpublic that is generative of networks that straddle offline and online

worlds and that offers the potential to deepen and solidify contestations and link struggles. Universities offer one of the few physical public
spaces for organizing and collective action in a moment where public
space across nation-states is increasingly surveilled. University campuses across the contexts we have described above—South Africa, the
United States, India, and the United Kingdom—are inhabited by digitally savvy students from historically marginalized backgrounds who
have gained access to the university space in their national contexts as
a result of struggles for access from previous eras. These students, dissatisfied with colonial conditions of the university, are able to mobilize
against it, creating spaces for face-to-face and social media disruption
and using platform technologies to share logistics and coordinate with
campus organizers elsewhere as well as share vital knowledge with each
other.

Of course, these affectively charged digital tactics, because of the
freely available data they accrue in online repositories, have potential
repercussions. As the GARA core members negotiated with senior managers on their demands, senior management surreptitiously collected
online protest data to use as evidence against GARA organizers in court
were they to fail to vacate the space they were occupying. Hundreds of
pages of Facebook posts, tweets, and Instagram videos were meticulously
compiled in a document. This, of course, suggests that the strategies to
prevent or mitigate surveillance and a punitive response we discussed
in the beginning of the chapter might fall short if an institution decides
to relentlessly pursue its agenda to individualize agitators and punish
them with the goal to nullify protest. This sort of direct confrontation,
of course, produces bad press. Several news publications picked up the
GARA occupation at Goldsmiths, no doubt pushing the university to
accede to student demands but also to accelerate existing strategies to
prevent these sorts of eruptions from happening in the future.

Indeed, the university, particularly elite institutions across the world,
have recognized the threat these movements signal and have sought
to mitigate their effects. They have done so by explicitly and publicly
embracing diversity projects. Here the logic seems straightforward. By
inviting more of the formerly colonized into the spaces of the university, one can short-circuit the potential for disruption but, more importantly, demonstrate the university as the vehicle for realizing a telos of

universality. It is the same logic that undergirds neoliberal policy and ideology—that participation creates stability and eventual upliftment for the deserving.[55] In the university, this strategy not only has the potential to quell or counter grassroots organizing but also, as Roderick Ferguson argues, makes diversity monetizable.

If we look at the US or the UK, its only in the last twenty years that the idea of prioritizing diversity—of opening up the university to non-white, non-male students—has taken hold as policy and practice as a means to assure the future profitability of university. We are interested, quite specifically, in the role that the digital plays in more recent efforts to promote the university as a space of neoliberal diversity and, more recently, as a location for institutional performances of decoloniality, where contrition regarding the role universities have played in support-ing and benefitting from Atlantic world slavery and other forms of co-lonial extraction is performed. How is the campus articulated and how does it proliferate in online worlds through these efforts? How do these efforts work to dampen or limit the effectiveness of university-based so-cial movements?

The #Diverse Campus and Projects of Colonial Contrition

Historically, the university has been a site of accumulation, disposses-sion, and production of colonial knowledge formations in service of empire. If we take the US as an example, slavery and Indigenous dis-placement made available the very land that many private and public universities were built on and the labor and capital it required for their construction.[56] In the UK, universities have just begun inquiries into the wealth they and those associated with their powerful institutional struc-tures accumulated as a result of the slave trade, in part, we contend, in response to student activist movements demands. As such, higher edu-cation institutions, particularly the elite ones, have also taken to online spaces to perform rituals of recognition of their past in order to block critique and guard the future value of their respective brands.[57]

University tactics to promote their reckoning with institutional co-loniality in online spaces coincide with the increasing focus on diver-sity initiatives within institutional space (diversity, equity, and inclusion policies and practices in the US, widening participation in the UK), ostensibly meant to create access and new pathways for mobility. These initiatives circulate images and narratives of students and faculty who exemplify diversity without changing the structural conditions in the university.[58] As with other attempts to publicly recognize coloniality, this sort of institutionally whitewashed politics of recognition under the banner of diversity and, more recently, their claim to the very concept of decolonization as a sanitized institutional framework for measured change, as Glen Clouthard demonstrates with regards to US governmental acts of contrition toward Native Americans, ultimately reproduces the conditions of coloniality they make visible.[59]

As scholars who have contributed to the formation of an interdisciplinary, critical university studies agenda have argued, "The 'corporatization' of academic institutions and universal ideologies of equality and meritocracy in the modern university in liberal and secular democratic societies" create conditions such that the salutary image of diversity is seen as sufficient to publicly demonstrate an institution's commitments.[60] The need for images of diversity in the university creates a cottage industry of workers who consult with institutions.[61] Diversity consultants utilize the digital to promote the university as either already always utopias or as utopias in the making. These narratives require the production of audio-visual material to viscerally buttress them.

As posters of Black and POC (people of color) students smiling on the campus green and images of staff diversity are circulated in online spaces, they create the image of the contemporary university that has reconciled its historical problems. These sorts of online visual strategies, of course, rely on a superficial image-based definition of diversity that obscures structural issues that continue to plague university hiring, student recruitment, retention, and the mental health of minority students in various contexts across the globe. These campaigns work to obscure and even erase histories of oppression, exclusion, and the need for systematic redress. Images of Black, Indigenous, and POC faces, as they circulate on Facebook and other social media platforms, become part of a larger strategy that many universities are using to mobilize social media as a marketing tool, retention strategy, and method for securing alumni funding.[62]

As Aneeth Kaur Hundle explains, universities in the US have come to rely on these sorts of diversity initiatives, which also include staff trainings, the production of various sorts of reports, and so on, after affirmative action programs that sought to dismantle structural inequalities that affect women and minority communities came under scrutiny and sustained attack.[63] As states across the country effectively banned affirmative action, in their place emerged neoliberal initiatives that were taken up differently across various campuses that celebrated exceptionality while recognizing that minoritized groups offered another student market to cultivate and financially benefit from. This economic logic, of course, extends beyond the US. As Gabriel and his colleague Akanksha Mehta have discussed elsewhere, universities in the UK recognized, based on long-term demographic projections, that they would need to recruit minority students when fees were introduced in the 2000s to maintain financial viability.[64] Diversity initiatives in this light, then, become strategies of capitalist accumulation that are mobilized in and through digital circuitry.

In the last few years, image-based diversity campaigns, in the face of campus protest and ongoing racialized state violence in various contexts, have been supplemented by other kinds of online circulations meant to remediate racial tensions. In the wake of George Floyd's murder at the hands of the police in Minneapolis, Minnesota, in 2020, campus officials across North America, Europe, Australia, and elsewhere have written long statements condemning racist violence.[65] These statements circulate on social media, offering what some have critiqued as a politics of white innocence on the part of their authors insofar as they perform surprise, shock, and a passionate rejection of racialized violence without recognizing its enduring nature or their own complicity in its unfolding.

Gloria Wekker describes white innocence as "the passion, forcefulness, and even aggression that race, in its intersections with gender, sexuality, and class, elicits among the white population, while at the same time the reactions of denial, disavowal, and elusiveness reign supreme."[66] The statements, often written at the department level but also by managers and institutional higher-ups, offer an alibi for the university. Moreover, these sorts of statements—as they are put into social media circulation—allow departmental faculty to feel that they have done something significant, while posing a very real danger that the hard work of changing the lived structures of the university will be deferred for another day.

It is also worth noting the campaigns that universities in the UK and the US have undertaken in recent years to publicly explore their role in the transatlantic slave trade. Indeed, the contemporary university—particularly the most elite of institutions in the US, the UK, South Africa, and elsewhere—has recognized that its history is no longer submerged or imagined in various publics as unblemished. Glasgow University in Scotland is the most notable of these. In a historic move, the university announced that it will pay £20 million as reparations for its part in the slave trade.[67] It set up a partnership with the University of West Indies and has pledged £20 million to create a research center with them as part of efforts to foster a restorative justice and reparations program to acknowledge the tremendous benefits the institution accrued through the transatlantic slave trade in previous centuries.

Compared to the UK and US, political calls for and semiotic formations around decolonization have traveled with far less momentum on the university campuses in Germany. These limited circulations have reinvigorated public discourse around Germany's colonial past and demands for repatriation of stolen remains and reparations over violence against the Herero and Nama people of Namibia. If, on the one hand, public discourses congealing around museum spaces and genocide in Namibia have expanded the debate of who Germany owes a reparative debt to beyond Germany's wartime reparations to Holocaust survivors, on the other hand, the language of decolonization is also actively sought out and imbricated within large funding initiatives that have a longer institutional history of facilitating research alliances between countries in the Global North and the Global South.[68]

We can read these developments as a necessary materialization of reparations and laud this sort of initiative, in particular, instances where these measures have led to active scholarly and outreach creations challenging hegemonic power. However, there is a more cynical reading of the moves colonial institutions take up to reconcile the past with the present. These sorts of materialized gestures—offering some form of reparation or repatriation as instantiated through research partnerships, alliances, and so on—have the potential to serve as a short-circuit to student and, more recently, precarious university worker demands and protests regarding their experiences of racism, critiques of unequal laboring conditions, and attention to enduring neocolonial relationships between nations.[69] Debates around the stakes of such endeavors, of course, take place in the digital sphere adjacent and always in tense relation with digitally circulating traces of concurrent student and worker protests. We might look to #SlaveryMadeGlasgow as an index of the kinds of debates that Glasgow University's reparation efforts have engendered around the relationship between performance contrition for the past and present day conditions of coloniality.

It seems clear, then, that in the Global North, university efforts to dismantle enduring colonial structures need to move beyond policy enactments that guarantee seats or performative gestures in online and offline spaces that represent diversity or that, more recently, have picked up and mobilized decolonization as a way to demonstrate their commitments to change. In the UK, for instance, a recent report from the Higher Education Policy Institute recommends a broad decolonization agenda to address what they describe as a "silent crisis" in UK universities.[70] During the last year, particularly after George Floyd's murder, this has been translated into action by some university officials who have replaced the language of diversity with the language of anti-racism and decolonization. At Goldsmiths (where Gabriel teaches), for instance, there has been a push to create several anti-racism and racial justice steering groups to materialize change and an effort to bring in student activists from the Goldsmiths occupation to the table. However, these efforts run the danger of being rhetorical rather than substantive, bureaucratic rather than foundational.

The shallowness of the university's commitments to decolonization come into sharp relief when academics who vocally push against racism and other forms of enduring coloniality on social media, in their teaching, and in their writing come under attack by right-wing trolls in online worlds, on campus, and eventually, in the offices of the decision-makers and trustees of the institution who either don't support their faculty or who outright condemn them. Across the globe, right-wing groups have emerged to lay claim to the university and shut down voices of dissent or critique. As Dalia Gebrial notes, this hegemonic force has "had a louder, wealthier voice; newspaper columns across the political spectrum— particularly in the US and the UK—bemoaned the death of free speech and academic enquiry on campuses at the hands of over-sensitive, easily triggered student activists. This phenomenon became a meme that garnered unprecedented traction throughout the commentariat."[71] In addition to using the mainstream media apparatus to decry student activism as "snowflake" politics, right-wing forces working in concert have platformed and promoted speakers who traffic in twenty-first-century versions of late nineteenth-century race science and eugenic thinking by demanding the right to be heard in the halls of the university, under the banner of liberal enlightenment values.[72]

As importantly, some academics have taken it on themselves to push against those who would limit their or other's academic freedoms by evoking the excesses of the "regressive left" in the university. In a popular podcast series hosted by Sam Harris and promoted across the host's website, iTunes, and Spotify, marketing professor Gad Saad appeared as a guest in an episode in 2016.[73] The episode was revealingly titled "The Frontiers of Political Correctness." Saad ran his own podcast, "The Saad Truth," but he also appeared in the podcast episodes hosted by other online celebrities, signaling the mutually magnifying intertextual culture of the internet—a form of citational politics we will delve deeper into in our chapter on knowledge/citation in digital worlds. In the episode, podcaster Sam Harris introduced his guest as a professor of marketing who "pioneered the use of evolutionary psychology in marketing and consuming behavior" by tracing the "biological and evolutionary roots of consumer." Saad was invited for the podcast particularly because of his public record as an academic scholar who, in the words of the host, had been "battling some of the battles against the regressive left." The introduction of the podcast went like this:

> HARRIS: You are a very committed enemy of political correctness and
>   moral relativism, postmodernism, identity politics, and all of these
>   intellectual and ethical frames that seem to be going in a wrong di-
>   rection. You are a professor in a university. Do you ever regret getting
>   into this swamp and dealing with this shit?
> SAAD: (laughs) You know, it's funny because you have probably heard
>   this term *having skin in the game*, right? So it is difficult to have more
>   skin in the game as someone who is in a cesspool of all of these ideas
>   that you mentioned a few minutes ago and try to critique them from
>   within. . . . I cannot sit idly while the humanities and some of the
>   social sciences are being infested with movements that are genuinely

grotesque to human reason, they are an affront to human decency I
dare say. And I speak against it . . .

PODCASTER: . . . among the many things that are on the menu that
people are [asking] not to talk about . . . which is the most radioactive . . . do you have a sense of what gets you into trouble the most at
this point?

SAAD: It depends if you mean in the general campus or science. Let's do
both. If we are talking about science, there was a paper I published
in 2005 either in *Nature* or *Science*; I think the title was "Forbidden
Knowledge." There are some research questions or research topics that you should stay away from. Probably the top two ones that
are, to use your term, the most radioactive, would be racial differences . . . any research on racial differences, and probably second
would be sex differences. Of course, that's definitely where I come in
because a lot of the research that I do from an evolutionary perspective recognizes that human beings are sexually dimorphic by definition, that is how we define the species, and so to have a debate as to
whether there are sex differences that are innate is preposterous . . .
but yet much of the social sciences have built theoretical and empiri-
cal edifices completely rejecting this possibility.

This sort of public discourse against the "radioactive" left is amplified by right-wing groups like Turning Point in the US who—using free
speech as a premise—have organized online sites that name and monitor
professors who promote "Marxist" or radical thinking on campus, have
supported student activism, or have specifically supported liberatory
movements in Palestine and the Boycott, Divestment, Sanctions (BDS)
campaign to sanction the state of Israel. In several well-publicized cases,
Twitter became the site through which right-wing groups policed and
attacked professors on the grounds of hate speech and racism, forcing
university administrators and their boards to publicly renounce these
professors and in a few notable cases, terminate employment.[74] In these
cases, the university campus represents what right-wing actors imagine
is its promise to uphold dominant, supremacist views cloaked under the
banner of the universality of a (neutral) science.

These strategies signal a longing for the Euro-Western university
prior to its changing commitments to a postcolonial world order. But

as we discuss in detail in the next chapter on extreme speech, these developments do not simply signal a backward-looking stance, a kind of hegemonic longing for an idealized university of the past. Rather, they demonstrate a campus future—and indeed a vision for the digital commons more broadly—where the internet and its multiple platforms allow right-wing actors to place pressure on institutions by subverting the ideals of free speech, scientific freedom, and, in the most twisted cases, utilize the language of racism and anti-Semitism to root out dissent and retrench the colonial university by attacking individual academics. These digitally mediated strategies, when seen in productive juxtaposition to our discussion of decolonial campus activism, offers those who are invested in an unsettling of the liberal status quo a clear sense of what they are up against as well an understanding of how easily (and readily) hegemonic colonial power instrumentalizes liberal thought, and importantly, how its racist and exclusionary discourses that belie liberal conceit perpetuate through extreme forms of speech. In the next chapter, we explore the various ways the digital cocreates the conditions for attacks on progressive voices beyond the campus, bolstering the boisterous politics of a resurgent, xenophobic far right.

2

Extreme

Right-Wing Politics and Contentious Speech

When you're used to supremacy, equality looks like
oppression.
—Maurice Mcleod

(Sahana) It was early 2020, a month before the COVID-19 pandemic
forced sweeping restrictions on physical gatherings, driving the world
to a colossal public health crisis. At an elite social club in Munich, I was
chatting with a journalist who was at that time writing a book on the
fashion industry in Germany. "Digital revolution is destroying French
revolution," the journalist exclaimed with urgency as she tightened the
fold of her arms in stiff disapproval. In stating the crisis so piquantly,
she was voicing an anxiety that had gripped liberally leaning elites in
the last two decades of digital decadence—of lies, vitriol, and invectives
that had capsized the early euphoria around the digital as the harbinger
of participatory equity and emancipatory globalism. In the view of the
journalist, values of liberty, freedom, and emancipation established after
much hardship and struggle during the European Enlightenment were
now being decimated by the hate and lies of digital media favoring the
far right.

Keeping my voice low and intending to not agitate the well-meaning
acquaintance before me, I murmured that the past that she nostalgically invoked as an embodiment of liberal freedom had flourished at
a time when the same ruling powers unleashed numbing violence in
the colonies by rationalizing the suspension of liberal values in places
beyond the metropole as a necessary phase in the civilizing mission of
modernity. I saw a mild frown and discomfort on her face when I stated
this. The reference to violent colonial histories that implicated the "liberal" regimes of the Global North appeared to unsettle her diagnosis

of the present as an abrupt aberration. I didn't press the matter further, but it was also not hard to recognize the kind of current developments around digital communication she was referencing when she weighed the turbulence of the digital revolution against the historical effects of the French revolution.

Voicing a similar moral panic, recent academic studies have described such developments as the worrying trends of fake news, filter bubbles, lies, vitriol, naked slurs, and the downright comical nuisance that have suffused social media conversations, from top leaders to ordinary users.[1] Such trends signal how the particular turmoil on university campuses that we discussed in the previous chapter reflects a broader online culture that pins the locus of trouble to the figure of a public critic who is a member of or advocates for racialized groups, immigrants, LGBTQIA+ communities, women, Indigenous communities, and ethnic and religious minorities. Directing vitriol at the "progressive figure," ranging from journalists and academics to community leaders and politicians, self-fashioned upholders of online freedom of expression regularly shower a slew of sobriquets, insults, and aphorisms, feeding an emergent online populist style that Rogers Brubaker defines as a "'low' rather than 'high' style that favours 'raw' and crude (but warm and unrestrained) over refined and cultivated (but cool and reserved) language and self-presentation."[2] Some of the choicest name-calling stunts flaunt a knack of combining and twisting words in awkward angles and rendering a panoply of derisive labels in English including *libtards* (liberal retards), *sickular* (as opposed to secular), *race baiters, regressive left, the politically correct, presstitute,* social *justice warriors,* to *Gutmensch* (overly politically correct person, named as the buzzword of the year in 2015 in Germany), *commiechootiya* (communist dumbass, with a vulgar connotation) in Hinglish (Hindi and English), and Islamophobic terms such as *halal hippies,* circulating in the Danish public sphere.[3] Coined and powered by individual actors or groups that pride themselves on knowledge of internet jargons, local cultural expressions, and seemingly ingenious witticisms, this vitriolic culture has recharged public concerns over hate speech, while paradoxically cementing "lulz-fed' colloquialism as a form native to internet 2.0 communication.

Although such developments appear to confirm the anxiety of the journalist at the social club in Munich—that the digital revolution is decimating the gains of the French revolution—we argue that this moral panic belies a deeper problem that is both epistemological and political. Clearly, as the journalist saw it, her world was falling apart. Digital communication posed grave dangers to the painfully cultivated values of truth-telling, objectivity, and cool and distanced language in the liberal profession of journalism she had come to practice, and the problem appeared more severe considering how modern journalism is also shaped in the German context (and continental Europe more broadly) by a strong public-service media culture.[4] However, whether as unacknowledged blind spots or willful erasures, such self-understandings are weighed down by several epistemological and political problems. By positioning online vitriol as an antithesis of liberal communication and as a contemporary crisis instigated by digital channels, they gloss over the grave histories of how modern journalism, like the university we discussed in the previous chapter, was a central edifice of the expanding colonial-modernity matrix in the twentieth century. The perception of danger in the digital age in such accounts, therefore, develops from and reinforces a liberal self-understanding of calm rationality. Our key focus in this chapter is to highlight the limits of this self-understanding and to complicate the framing of online vitriol as a contemporary crisis in the liberal social order and associated moral panics that recenter the "rational West" as the locus and subject of crisis. Building on this critique, we show how a decolonial reading of online vitriol opens up new critical pathways to inquire into the nature of online vitriol—who is targeted and how—as well as ways of knowing what is damaged through speech.

We begin this inquiry by problematizing the implicit epistemological edifice of the liberal rational center that both frames the critique of and is perceived to be endangered by contemporary forms of online vitriol. We follow this critique with a close reading of a troll attack against an academic in the UK on Twitter that bore out the key ideological elements of white supremacist hateful speech. We tease out the comparative value of this episode by reading it alongside insights gained from ethnographic interviews with far-right activists in Germany and right-wing Hindu nationalists in India. We will then situate this political formation in relation to specific features of digital mediation and the broader "participatory condition" of digital communication that have enabled reinvigorated forms of right-wing extreme speech. Finally, we weave these analytical points together to conceptualize coloniality as a *global unfolding of the interrelated relations of the nation-state, race, and market* and argue that coloniality continues to shape the macro-historical structures within which proximate, affect-intensive battles of words are fought online, often with grave political consequences. This decolonial reading leads us to propose that vitriolic exchange is not a level playing field of profanities distributed equally among different ideological groups but a volatile arena where deeper colonial histories press on the present, allowing contemporary digital communicative forms to affect vulnerable groups in particular ways. In other words, the sheer use of vitriol and profanities says less about the implications of speech acts, since the mere occurrence of certain kinds of speech does not lead to comprehending who is affected and in what ways.

We see the need for what we call "deep contextualization" of longer histories in conjunction with "close contextualization" of the proximate worlds of online practice as an analytical and methodological exercise necessary for a fuller understanding of online vitriol. Our journeys in the West as immigrants have also overlaid our analysis with reflections about our own positionalities as upper-caste, middle-class subjects falling within the privileged bracket of desirable migrants. Some of these feelings suffused encounters with elites in the West, like the journalist in the club in Munich. In these interactional frames, because of our location in the North and our privileged positions in the university, we are interpellated into liberal framings of crisis. We are included by the very speech act into a reproduction of a glorious European legacy or a geographical division of here and there, them and us. This requires grappling with the feelings these articulations produce and a recognition of how our possible complicities in their reproductions might enable us to respond with critique or develop methods that rupture the epistemology of calm distance. We will ruminate on this further in the "Home/Field" chapter, but as regards online vitriol, far from a calm distance, a sense of alarm ran through us each time we wore the researcher's hat— knowingly as well as out of compulsive habit—and scrolled the swelling number of racist and anti-immigrant comments online. We felt that we were on a precipice where the comfort vested by our privileged academic positions that afforded us various forms of access was toppled by the racism on the streets and the emotional charge of insinuation and insult unfolding on our screens. We examined with horror several incidents of physical violence—from mob lynching of minority Muslims in India to the burning of refugee homes in Germany—and how wounding words and dehumanizing language circulating online translated into violent events on the ground. In these moments, our "embodied experience intertwined with political feeling," forming a visceral ground for decolonial thinking.[5] It brings to relief that *decoloniality* for us is not a fashionable term to parade for career gains in the academy but an evocative political space where the analytical edge of research comes fused with the viscerality of our embodied experience, pushing us to think through online vitriol and aggression with a new set of epistemological, analytical, and political lenses that are sharply attentive to colonial histories, geographies, affects, and lived meanings. To word it along the key framing of this book, online vitriol has been unsettling for us as a phenomenological fact, and such toxic exposures to online hate have impelled us to unsettle existing normative approaches to a phenomenon that is seen—in liberal understandings—as an obvious demonstration of what is out of place in the current digital age. Here, we return to our theorization of digital unsettling as ways to draw attention to how coloniality has retrenched itself in online spaces through racist, casteist, misogynistic, and exclusionary discourse and as the methodological impulse to question existing normative categories in liberal thought that tend to erase colonial continuities by framing the digital as a radically new constellation and the reason for an unexpected crisis. In the next section, we briefly outline the framework of extreme speech as a theoretical gateway toward such an analysis.

Ambiguity and Continuities in Extreme Speech Practice

The concept of extreme speech recognizes that any effort at drawing an overarching explanatory framework for diverse forms of online vitriol and their target communities is not only theoretically ambitious; it also runs against the emphasis that ethnographic practice places on excavating specific cultural and social conditions that shape political cultures of speech within the lived worlds and situated contexts of shared meanings.[6] Overarching normative frameworks common within the legal-regulatory discourse of hate speech and recent iterations of online extremism come with the additional risk of pathologizing speech based on a set of predetermined criteria that are often tied to the implicit goal of maintaining the liberal order or are used as a weaponized regulatory tool to squash political dissent. Analytically, diverse phenomena such as online misogyny and trans-exclusionary gendered discourses, or hateful and prejudicial speech about various groups—whether the Romani people in Europe, the Kurds in Turkey, or the Rohingya Muslims in Myanmar—require a fine-grained analysis of local power struggles, histories of ethnic tensions and persecution, gendered power structures, and translocal forces that intersect to define who is able to hurl online vitriol, to what effect, and with what degree of impunity.[7]

Highlighting the risk of reducing diverse contexts of abuse and vitriol to a single, overarching theory, extreme speech pushes for ethnographic sensibility and contextual understanding of actors, affordances, and practices that compose vitriolic cultures. Above all, it departs from a blanket approach to vitriol as gross violation of dignity deserving no further academic scrutiny. In place of the normative and regulatory question of classifying and isolating hate speech and disinformation, extreme speech turns to an analytical exercise to understand how this phenomenon has come about.[8] As mentioned in the previous section, crucial to this understanding is the navigation between different orders of analysis ranging from proximate contexts of digital use and situated cultures of speech to broader historical and political economic structures within which they unfold and which they reshape in turn.

At proximate levels of digital media use and circulation, extreme speech enacts its force as a performance with a definitive audience effect.[9] This is evidenced by how abusive actors seek or gain celebrity status or at the very least some traction online through transgressive performances.[10] Hence, such vitriol is not merely about expressivity but concerns active, embodied performances with an audience effect that is intended, socio-technologically mediated, or both. For this reason, the extreme speech framework calls for an analysis that goes beyond purely linguistic analysis of textual features and extends into exploring the phenomenon as an aspect of social media practice shaped by the contextual specificity of speech cultures.[11] For the same reason, it is important to move beyond assumptions around politeness, civility, and abuse as universalist features with little cultural variation—a perspective common within a large crop of studies in political communication as well as concepts such as cyberbullying.[12] For instance, in India, online extreme speech unfolds as what might be defined as *gaali* cultures that constitute the interlocking practices of insult, comedy, shame, and abuse that expand in a blurred arena of online speech.[13] On this slippery ground of shifting practices, comedy stops and insult begins, or insult morphs into abuse in mutually generative ways. While it is not true that abuse is the only means to participate in online political debates, it nevertheless constitutes a key communicational context for online users who increasingly feel the need to develop the skills to hurl, dodge, or otherwise criticize abuse as prerequisites to remaining active within online discursive spaces.

This complexity in the interactional contexts emphasizes the need to understand extreme speech as performance—an embodied expressive practice seeking or effecting various kinds of valences online.[14] To approach extreme speech as performance suggests that we take an agnostic approach to the "internet's city of words," where the boundaries between the ludic, the intimidating, and the disruptively absurd intertwine in such a way that their political consequences cannot be foretold with certainty. Extreme speech can open up new lines of political participation—at least as a discursive engagement—for net savvy actors, although this occurs in a highly volatile conversational context. Naming and shaming as an affectively charged tactical maneuver in the student protests that we discussed in the previous chapter illustrates the disruptive potentials of extreme speech in unsettling liberal modulations of civility as an encoding of class and race privilege and a gloss for the status quo. In other words, as a concept, extreme speech gestures toward complicating the prognosis of online discourse in terms of the polar opposites of a normative order and toward those practices where the experience of participation through maverick tactics slides into abuse of a more intimidating nature as they interface with larger structures of hegemonic power.

Therefore, of crucial importance in determining the implications of online extreme speech is the need to place proximate contexts of online use and translocal mediations of internet media within broader historical forces that shape hegemonic power structures and the diverse spaces where these structures are consolidated, reproduced, upturned, and de-

flected. As a corrective to observations about contemporary technological developments and charismatic populist leaders as the primary drivers
for online extreme speech, a critical decolonial reading envisaged by the
concept of extreme speech draws attention to interconnections between
national and translocal contexts and continuities underwritten by longer historical processes. Such attention to longer histories begins by
critiquing the very epistemological grounds on which rationality and irrationality are assigned to diverse speech cultures and people inhabiting
them and how evaluations based on the rational/irrational divide—as
we discuss in the next section—can be analytically limiting and politically damaging toward comprehending and governing online speech.

The Rational We versus the Irrational Other

The journalist's comment about the French revolution and digital revolution referenced at the beginning of the chapter represents an evaluative
perspective that is deeply shaped by liberal self-understanding. While it
is true that liberal communicative order institutionalized the practices of
verification, balance, and objectivity (exemplified by a transatlantic style
of professional journalism) and went a long way toward stabilizing the
ideals of rational deliberation aspired to in the public sphere, this vision
had a normative edge that rendered other communicative cultures and
publics as irrational and that needed a lift in the eyes of the West. In her
incisive account of the role of the racial in Western modern thought,
Denis Ferreira da Silva has shown that the difference of non-European
regions of the world as a signifier of whiteness is the very condition of
possibility for the emergence and existence of such a thing like modernity.[15] Furthermore, she argues, the spatial modality of race that unfolds
as "globality" assigns geographical regions outside of Europe as "affect-
able" rather than transparent and self-determined—the hallmarks of the
European self-understanding of the modern, enlightened self.

Nowhere is the binary schema of the rational center and irrational
periphery as starkly evident as in the discipline of anthropology and
its stubborn remnants in the present. The origin of the discipline was
itself based on the idea of the exotic—"of what is absolutely foreign and
different about one place and another" and the charms, befuddlements,
and amusements around the "irrational" and "unusual" practices of

exotic peoples that needed systematic documentation and speedy as-similation with civilizing modernity.[16] The deep entanglements between anthropology's "discovery" of the exotic and colonial power are widely acknowledged in scholarship and public memory, but their far-reaching effects in other disciplines and contemporary media regulatory prac-tices are no less significant.[17] The schema of the liberal center of calm rationality (the self-imagination of the West) versus the irrational, im-passionate publics of the periphery (the rendering of the non-West) has long defined the contours of the hate-speech discourse.

Studies in the media development and media policy traditions that are engaged in tailoring solutions for hate speech implicitly assume that the emotionality of hateful speech in the Global North is an ab-erration that stands in contrast to calm rationality as a default value of the postwar Western world. By the same token, studies on Africa, South Asia, and Southeast Asia have approached conflict as a pro-pensity exacerbated by emotionally charged verbal cultures that are further amplified by long-standing ethnic, religious, and caste divi-sions.[18] This heuristic division between the North and the South, and the accompanying conceptual construction of the rational center and emotional periphery, originated in the colonial logics of power. As Dipesh Chakrabarty argues in relation to historical methods and mo-dernity's assumptions that underpin them, peripheralized pasts (and peoples) are those that "the 'rationality' of the historian's methods necessarily makes 'minor' or 'inferior' as something 'irrational' in the course of, and as a result of, its own operation."[19] Walter Mignolo suggests that the epistemology of the European Renaissance was as-sumed to be the "natural perspective," which was reinstated after the Enlightenment, when reason became associated with Northern Eu-rope and indirectly with whiteness.[20] In his critical inquiry into the coupling of evidently distinct doctrines of liberalism and secularism in modern thought, Talal Asad has shown that secular-liberal forma-tions in Western modernity led to a set of enforceable normative as-sumptions, provoking a panoply of affects and emotions directed at people marked as alien, irrational, or excitable religious subjects.[21] In India, laws related to hate speech (sections 153A and 295A of the Indian Penal Code) emerged from colonial administrators' assump-tion that Indians were "excitable subjects."[22] Media regulatory struc-

tures that resulted from this assumption aimed at "containing" and
"reining in" the media, which resulted in a law-and-order approach to
speech common in the hate speech discourse.

A decolonial approach to online extreme speech is geared precisely
toward disrupting the schema of the liberal center and emotional periphery that continues to mark groups and communities in racialized
terms and shape racialized media policy, and to argue for an analytical
compass that can recognize violence as it emerges in different forms and
across connected geographies. Moreover, following Mignolo's conceptualization of decolonization as "delinking," decolonial thinking exposes
the violent kernel of irrationality concealed in the "myth of modernity":

> It is a question of uncovering the origin of what I call 'the myth of moder-
> nity' itself. Modernity includes a rational 'concept' of emancipation that
> we affirm and subsume. But, at the same time, it develops an irrational
> myth, a justification for genocidal violence. The postmodernists criticize
> modern reason as a reason of terror; we criticize modern reason because
> of the irrational myth that it conceals.[23]

The digital has had a Janus-faced effect in this matter. While it has provided avenues and affordances to whip up and normalize emotionally
charged extreme speech that flies in the face of liberal calls for moderation, consensus, and reason, it has also exposed the conceits and
deceits of the liberal self-understanding, foremost by demonstrating
that publics in the West—as the racialized geography of whiteness and
rationality—are as emotionally prone and vituperative as they charge the
"irrational periphery" to be.[24]

The seemingly unexpected rise of right-wing populist regimes in
North America and Europe in the first decades of the millennium and
the accompanying affordances of digital communication have prompted
scholars to acknowledge how flawed the schema of the rational center
and emotional periphery had been throughout. These studies have
begun to highlight the role of "negative emotions" in powering right-
wing populism, generating a growing catalogue of emotions—anger,
envy, outrage, enjoyment, and so on—in pinning down the problem of
populism. The sudden enthusiasm to catalogue these emotions in relation to political cultures has ironically upturned the very schema of the

rational center and emotional periphery.[25] What has long been pointed out by postcolonial scholars is now acknowledged as a plain fact: there is no center and periphery when it comes to emotionality.

In his elegant formulation of the "participatory condition" of the social, anthropologist William Mazzarella fleshes out the theoretical stakes of this (re)recognition.[26] Delving into the duality between representation and participation, Mazzarella draws on Émile Durkheim to point out that "society can never be, as it were, self-sufficient . . . it can never be immediately present to itself." "Any kind of consciousness," he continues, "is only possible through the detour of a representation."[27] In Durkheim's formulation, it is some material object that provides the fixture around collective sentiment to become conscious of itself. "By the virtue of this fact it participates in the nature of this object, and reciprocally, the object participates in its nature."[28] Mazzarella picks up the constitutive salience of participation in Durkheim's argument and elaborates further. Not only is society as a form of collective consciousness possible only through representation, but "this representation works by *participating* in the substance of what it represents" (original emphasis).[29] Participation, in other words, is affective investment—libidinal energies that make the sign holding the collective come alive. Recognizing affective investment in the very constitution of the social flies in the face of modern social theory that disavows enchantment in the name of secularism: "Modern social theory, secular as it seems, is actually organized around an occult kernel."[30] Mazzarella describes this revelation as a scandal: "This is a scandal for thinking democracy because, after all, leaving magic behind is part of what is supposed to separate liberal democracy from divine kingship."

Important as it is, the observation about the participatory condition cannot stop with exposing the "scandal." It is helpful in so far as highlighting the limits of the current moral panics in the West around digital communication and populism, and anxious commentaries about how digital social media are throwing up sentiments in all the wrong places and in all the wrong ways, instead of enabling rational critical thought. Such moral panics do not recognize the scandal of the "occult kernel" in secular modern theory: that affects and emotions have always been critical to collective consciousness of any sort, whether in the West or the East. The structural constraint of collective formation—that the social is only possible via representation and participation—places libidinal attachment at the very center of the formation of the social.[31]

However, this recognition in itself does not say much about how affect travels, whom it courts, and whom it touches as its subject.[32] It is not sufficient to point out that in the absence of material objects like a totemic sign or material bodies like the king as the locus of "collective effervescence," what we see now is "loose affect"—"sensuous social substance . . . is now at issue everywhere."[33] We agree with Mazzarella about the loosening of sensuous social substance, but it is not *everywhere* in the sense that affect has no patterns of flow or precipitation. The argument around loose affect might lose the focus on the historical conditions that politicize affect in specific ways and the way in which history orchestrates feeling in and through specific semiotic formations. In other words, Mazzarella's reading of Durkheim fails to locate, in any precise way, the loci of collective effervescence and their historical antecedents. Rather than taking loose affect as the obvious condition in the absence of a fixed locus such as the body of the monarch or a totemic sign, it is thus important to analyze historical conditions and accompanying political economic transformations that give affect its specific tenor and target.

Political philosopher Wendy Brown's reading of Nietzsche in analyzing contemporary right-wing and white supremacist movements offers a segue.[34] Brown draws on Nietzsche's discussion of "ressentiment" to understand trolling "as grievous, resentful energies—just the opposite of self-overcoming, proud, world-making energies of the powerful."[35] Ressentiment, she says, is "a vital energy of right-wing populism: rancor, grudges, barely concealed victimization and other effects of reaction are the affective heartbeat of internet trolling, tweets and speeches at right-wing rallies."[36]

Brown characterizes the current explosion of "rancorous, disinhibited, anti-social and nihilistic aggression" as "aggrieved power."[37] She indicts neoliberal reason for making white working and middle class inhabitants angry, spurring them on to spew vitriol online. While Brown's observation is no doubt important, the argument about aggrieved power as the outcome of actual economic conditions of deprivation of neoliberalism does not explain why the very beneficiaries of neoliberal economy are avid patrons of online vitriol or active abusers themselves.

Take the case of Lissy (pseudonym) that anthropologist Peter Hervik portrays in his meticulous analysis of the resurgence of the right-wing in Denmark.[38] Lissy is a millionaire, a well-heeled socialite. Hervik describes her as an active member of a closed Facebook group of approximately a thousand members that advocates the idea that immigration is a threat to Denmark's cultural homogeneity and national security. Among several incendiary tropes that inform her anti-immigrant politics, the ideology of spatial segregation of people stands out. Pointing at refugees who entered Europe in recent years, she states emphatically, "They have to stay where they belong, where they are at home, and they shall not care to expand without permission. Nobody has ever allowed them to expand. I have nothing against Muslims. If I travel to their countries, they can do whatever they like." Hervik takes this spatial ideology as a trait of neo-racism that regards everyone (rhetorically) "as of equal morality and intelligence, but if you are in the wrong place, it is only 'natural' that xenophobic reactions will occur."[39] Dislocation is harmful not only to those who "receive" these refugees, Lissy and her compatriots avow, but to those who are migrating as well. Such arguments about the rights of people to remain in their homelands are admittedly more contrived than the obvious racist comments that far-right advocates express. Lissy gushes in impatience when Hervik asks her about the latest arrivals of refugees in Denmark. "We are a homogenous Norden in Europe," she asserts. "Basically, I think it is beautiful. We, in Scandinavia, we form a distinct race [folkefærd]. We are pale, light in our skin. We reason alike and we . . . we may ask when do people become genetically civilized. It is indeed a long process."[40]

Lissy's restless wait for people to "become genetically civilized" signals deep subjectivities that belie explanations of neoliberal reason for white supremacist aggression. It points to the endurance of racial ideologies formed in the nineteenth century and shaped by figures like Carl Linnaeus, which posited a linear continuum of civilizational development, with Nordic peoples placed at the pinnacle of civilization. To follow Denis Ferreira da Silva, physical proximity does not erase, but it deepens the spatial ideologies of race that "predicate the obliteration of those who do not share in the spatial 'origins' of the transparent "I" [the European modern subject]."[41] In Lissy's case, ressentiment as a mix of powerlessness, anger, and envy and an explanation for populist affect makes little sense. Nor can this be defined as resentment. If resentment is like "taking poison and waiting for the other person to die," patrons of vitriol in Hervik's study, with their sheer privilege, *can* make others drink poison or make them die. Although Brown acknowledges that "some educated whites, racial minorities, the ultra-rich, the ultra-Zionist, and the alt-right" supported US president Donald Trump, her elaboration of ressentiment is not meant to explain this odd, motley collection of supporters.[42] Above all, to see Trump's victory as the paradigmatic emblem of the crisis reveals the continued dominance of transatlantic concerns dictating the terms of argument for the rest of the world. This kind of analysis, critical as it is of liberal bigotry, glosses over the uneven ways in which the economic program of neoliberalism is rolled out around the world as well as the granularity of historical continuity that underpins what is anxiously termed as a strange "brew of bellicosity, disinhibition and rancor."[43] By considering neoliberalism as the pivot of problems, Brown is able to characterize white supremacists who indulge in online media vitriol as "malleable and manipulable, depleted of autonomy, moral self-restraint, and social comprehension."[44] From this characterization, it is a small step to explain away online aggression as misguided energies, cunningly shepherded by self-aggrandizing leaders under overbearing economic conditions wrought by neoliberalism. The assumption about manipulability of masses elides the grave history of systematic violence that installed unequal racialized relations through actions—past and present—that are orchestrated, directed, and economic, in as much as they are helpless reactions of backbiting revenge.

Consider the instance of a train journey recounted by the Black feminist Audre Lorde, an episode elegantly analyzed by Sara Ahmed.[45] Lorde recounts travelling with her mother as a young child when she encountered a white woman on a subway train to Harlem, New York. The white woman's action, to draw away from her and finally move out of the seat where she had clutched herself, provokes intense emotions in Lorde, pushing her to question if she had made any mistake that caused the white woman's eyes to enlarge, nostrils to flare—"the hate," Lorde describes her experience at the end of the passage. I will reproduce here a rather long excerpt from Ahmed's moving analysis of this encounter:

In the case of Audre's story, Audre's gestures mimic the white woman's. Her gaze is "pulled down," following the gaze of the white woman. This pulling down of the gaze and the transformation of the black body into an object of its own gaze seems critical. The hated body becomes hated, not just for the one who hates, but for the one who is hated. . . . When Audre's gaze is pulled down with the white woman's, she feels "afraid." She comes to recognize herself as the object of the woman's hate: she is "hailed," in Althusser's (1971) sense, as the hated. The "doing" of hate is not simply "done" in the moment of its articulation. A chain of effects (which are at once affects) are in circulation. The circulation of objects of hate is not free. In this instance, bodies that are attributed as being hateful—as the origin of feelings of hate—are (temporarily) sealed in their skins. Such bodies assume the character of the negative. That transformation of this body into the body of the hated, in other words, leads to the enclosure or sealing of the other's body within a figure of hate. The white woman who moves away from Audre moves on, of course. Some bodies move precisely by sealing others as objects of hate.[46]

The episode captures, in Ahmed's analysis, the unfolding of movement and closure: actions that create objects of hate as easily as they allow actors to exit the scene, leaving behind the person rendered as a hateful body to her own devices. In his incisive analysis of the anti-Black racist worldview, Frantz Fanon recounts a similar experience when a white child points to him on a train and declares, "Look a Negro."[47] In this instance, the very declaration constitutes racism; calling someone a Negro is not an aftereffect or an expressive supplement. Fanon is now aware of his body in a "triple person": "I existed triply," he recounts. "I was responsible at the same time for my body, for my race, for my ancestors . . . I discovered my blackness, my ethnic characteristics; and I was battered down by tom-toms, cannibalism, intellectual deficiency, fetishism, racial defects, slave-ships . . . My body was given back to me sprawled out, distorted, recolored, clad in mourning in that white winter day."[48] Recalling Jean-Paul Sartre, Fanon pries open the white gaze that affixes the identity of the other, fixing Blackness as a slur in the "racial epidermal schema."[49]

The rendering of bodies as hateful has continued into the practices of trolling and abuse in the disembodied worlds of online exchange through a similar process of movement and closure—of digital gazes that seek to affix alterity and let loose affective energies that can vilify after affixing. In the next section, we will offer an ethnographic glimpse of this process, unpacking the ways in which affective circulations animate and subjectify online actors through racialized histories and a phenomenology of hate where "aggressors can experience themselves as if they are victims."[50]

Right-Wing/Far-Right/Alt-Right Trolling

(Sahana) For as long as I could, I stayed away from Twitter because of its accelerated temporality, which I believed interrupted the temporality of slow academic reflection, self-critique, referencing, and correction that occurs in loops of forward movement and steps that tread back. A lingering anxiety added to the hesitation. As someone who carries out ethnographic fieldwork among right-wing online supporters and strives for outreach activities, I always anticipated the prospect of being trolled by rambunctious Twitter warriors online, since episodes of troll attacks on academics, public intellectuals, and journalists who openly advocate for inclusive societies had become a common story in the online world and beyond (we will return to this point in the "Home/Field" chapter). Yet I had to scroll Twitter for research data, and eventually also to publicize and announce research outcomes, outreach activities, prizes, accolades, and complaints and for a new logic of declaring solidarity through online mentions and replies to colleagues, collaborators, and funders in a digitally mediated citational field. During one of those "fieldwork days" on Twitter, I came across a slew of tweets embellished with GIFs, images, and wordplay, targeting a senior female academic of South Asian origin (identified here as @AB) employed at a prestigious university in the UK. The pinned tweet of the academic displayed a compilation of white supremacist rhetoric online and a clear stance of disapproval whetted by years of research on British colonialism. The flurry of activity on her Twitter timeline pointed in the direction of a recent tweet in which she had criticized a well-known bestselling author with conservative political views bestseller for his pro-Brexit views (identified here as @MG), criticizing him for personally attacking her on Twitter. The academic had called the ideologue—in no uncertain terms—a regressive retrograde who chastised academics like her as self-aggrandizing "race baiters" for drawing critical attention to the UK's imperial past and present turmoil. After @MG launched a frontal ad hominem attack on @AB with a caustic comment that degraded the merit of her person rather than the value of her charge, a slew of tweet attacks ensued. The episode had the features of a troll attack characterized by persistent provocation through linguistic aggression that had continued from the days of UseNet groups and mailing lists but had transmuted as a user category with ambiguous valences in the years of the expansion of quasi-public platforms like Twitter.[51] I decided to name the episode #Troll_event.

For a content-based analysis of the event, research assistants and I collected comments that were posted in response to three distinct tweets from the pro-Brexiter in August 2020 that were sampled to outline the contours of #Troll_event.[52] Following this theoretical sampling, a total of 702 comments comprising text, images, and GIFs were analyzed using a two-stage coding: primary coding (identifying concepts based on prior research work on right-wing online messaging and close reading of the current pool of tweets) and synthesis coding (connecting concepts across themes). Finally, a critical discourse analysis was conducted that involved parsing online texts in relation to their sociopolitical contexts and particular online cultures shaped by platform design and user practices.[53]

The largest volume of thematic categories in the tweet pool (46 percent) drew direct reference to the two key protagonists of the troll event, namely @AB and @MG, thereby framing this as a battle of two prominent public figures at loggerheads (see figure 1).[54] However, far from being a mere personal mudslinging game, the episode revealed how the figure of a left progressive academic stood as a metonym for the racial Other and all things seen as abnormal or a threat to white privilege secured by the nation-state. Thus, the pool of tweets (including retweets) oscillated between overtly racist comments or allegations of race baiting (13 percent of the total volume of tweets in terms of thematic content) and ad hominem attacks (16 percent of the total volume of tweets), both powering one another (see figure 2.1). Half of the total count of tones adopted in the tweets were direct allegations (tweets that made a statement that portrayed the target in a negative light without providing evidence or argument); 20 percent of them were sarcastic; 18 percent were praise and celebration (largely in favor of @MG); and 8.5 percent were confrontational (tweets that actively invoked the presence of the target, directly challenging and countering them based on alleged facts and "whataboutery"). In addition, there were thirteen instances of warning (asking the target to be aware of the dangers of retaliatory online action) and four references to graphic violence. The majority of commentators (92 percent) rallied behind @MG, while only 8 percent stood on the side of @AB.

"Nothing more amusing than affluent and upper caste Indians pretending to be oppressed," declared a tweet, setting up the first staging ground for delegitimizing @AB's attention to oppressive structures of racism and white supremacy in the UK.[55] Envy for the material affluence of successful people of color was pertinent, but it constituted a small portion compared to a large number of tweets that accused @AB for being a "race baiter" who made sure "every debate is about skin pigmentation." Accusations of reverse racism framed a significant 10 percent of the tweet themes, blaming people like @AB for "slamming white people for being white." It's "pathetic," "awful," "extreme woke," "a simple projection," cried commentators who rallied behind @MG. "Race baiting" implied an instrumental use of the "race card" and "minority super status" for self-aggrandizing career moves or for covering intellectual incapacity with the signboard of victimhood. Several tweets speculated that the motivation was simply to "push a book." "She'll get more woke sales if she attacks [him] that the wokelings . . . [hate]," announced a tweet. An intriguing thematic framing that emerged directly from such an assumption was the dismissal of @AB as a "huckster." One tweet conferred the title of a "race huckster," and another gave the label "race grifter." In these comments, envy for the material affluence of the target came fused with a resentment for publicity and media capital she garnered, and following which, the commentators declared every move of @AB as an empty tactic to hog the limelight. The default publicity frame implicit in these comments had the white figure at the center, and therefore a non-white figure in its place provoked a feeling of "dethronement," an aberration from the normal.[56] Additionally, within online interactional contexts, such ripostes provide the means to debunk the claims of the opponent. Some commentators called her an "actual troll" and a

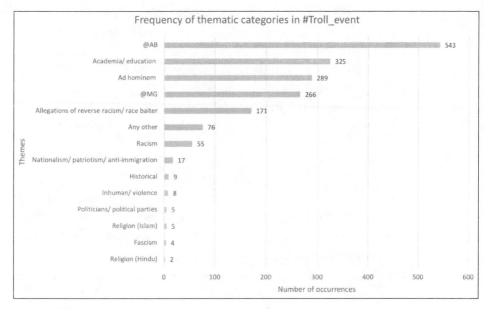

Figure 2.1. Thematic categories in #Troll_event

"bully." Following @MG's homosexual activism, some accused @AB of being homophobic and jumped in to articulate gay solidarities, evoking homosexual white supremacist voices spearheaded by figures like Milo Yiannopoulos.

The resentment extended beyond @AB, since for the most part, the outpouring of tweets represented a deep discomfort for what they believed she represented: a left progressive constellation comprised of universities, organized media, and political parties (anti-Brexit in this particular case). A significant 18 percent of tweet themes belonged to a category that we labeled "academia, education, press" (see figure 2.1). Commentators on @MG's side referred to the constellation by different names: "leftists," "globalists," "multiculturalists," "far left," and derided them as "utterly possessed by ideology," "spiteful," "libelous," "narcissistic," "hooligans who just want kiosk," people "with little self-awareness," and "Stalinist." "I am surprised the BBC haven't given her a job on . . . woke 'comedy' panel shows," remarked a tweeter sarcastically. In a similar sarcastic tone, one commentator defined @MG supporters as those who were blamed for going "against progress, immigrants, people of colour, Muslims," and adding, "I am beginning to see a pattern here, don't you?" One tweeter derided critical scholars as "typical woke activist[s], fueled by nothing more than unsophisticated hate and resentment," while another huffed that "the globalists won't stop until the whole earth has been brought to ruination." Tweets in this category dismissed universities as inconsequential in current times, while others worried about what would happen to their kids when they got into universities that had "such spiteful people."

Tweets that launched a string of violent obscenities indicted persons of color for desiring "colonial white man porn" and shot nasty comments on their physical appearance. Verbal abuses with animal names such as pig, pony, kitten, and bear that pro-Brexit tweeters hurled in the tweet pool were evocative of Edmund Leach's classic study on animal categories and verbal abuse in modern English culture, with some parallels with American and Kachin speech cultures.[57] Leach's theory considers animal categories as taboos that are "anomalous to clear-cut category oppositions" in a given lived language, and such taboos correspond to familiar animals on a scale of social distance (from edible to nonedible to edibility as outside the sphere of social recognition).[58] As he explains, "When an animal name is used . . . as an imprecation, it indicates that the name itself is credited with potency. It clearly signifies that the animal category is in some way taboo and sacred."[59] Without borrowing Leach's structuralist schema in its entirety, it might still be useful to stress the potency of animal categories—especially how the partly behavioral, partly linguistic features of animal categories imbue verbal slurs with a particular insinuating character that hinges on the social distance of edibility/acceptability.[60] Trolls calling on @MG to avoid a "pig fight" with @AB illustrated the potency of the animal category in the dual sense of taboo and sacred, but other animal categories, such as kitten to describe @AB and bear to depict @MG, also invoked masculinist imaginaries of overpowering and hunting down the feeble enemy. Ad hominem attacks were similarly nasty and ranged from ridiculing intellectual capacities and professional competence to the psychological state and social standing of the person targeted. One tweet drew the picture of innocent laymen unfairly attacked by a "race-baiter." "If you're not rabidly anti-fascist, you're wrong . . . most of [us] aren't rabid about anything. We just want to get along."

Territorial boundaries of the nation-state were a resource of immense empowerment for those who rallied behind @MG. A direct object of derision was @AB's resident status in the UK. "Why would an 'anticolonialist' choose to live in the home country of the colonizer," challenged a tweeter. Another stated, "Self-described as 'Anticolonial Resistance & British Dissent' . . . [they live] . . . in the UK. No way . . . [they] . . . will go and fight the real fight where needed: Africa or Asia (where you have all sort of authoritarian regimes, and imperialism under way through China). Useless people." These comments had the exact tone and content of Trump's infamous tweet that chided four minority Congresswomen to "go back" to countries they came from rather than "loudly and viciously telling the people of the United States" how to run the government.[61]

We found 405 tweets (74.6 percent) that fell into the category of extreme speech since they involved direct personal attacks, vilification, and unverified allegations. In terms of the type of extreme speech, an overwhelming majority (87 percent) were offensive to the individual, followed by 13 percent that were offensive to immigrants, two tweets called for exclusion from the nation (Britain), and one tweet called for violent action. @AB was the target of 81 percent of extreme speech instances, left liberals or academics were the target of 9 percent of extreme speech instances, and @MG had to contend with just 4.5 percent of extreme speech utterances. A small number of tweets that criticized @MG accused him of resorting to "petty insults," adding, "Remember in the morning she will be a fellow of X University . . . you will be in your underwear writing for the newspaper!" Some charged him for instrumentalizing homophobia to peddle racist, anti-immigrant ideologies, and others reminded the Twitterati about @MG's public statements that called for punishment of Muslims in Europe and labeled Black and Asian Britons as never belonging to Britain. There were at least two tweets that took a meta-view and dismissed the episode as a horrible spat, accusing both @AB and @MG for "trading affronts . . . like first year undergraduates who get drunk and snog each other at the summer ball."

Typical of Twitter troll attacks, comments that attacked @AB had a thick tone of sarcasm laced with in-jokes, boisterous shaming, name-calling, putdowns, aphorisms, and sobriquets that displayed familiarity with digitally native jargons that could trend and gain traction, at times expressed in a rhythmic flourish, such as rhyming race baiting with click baiting. A large number of visuals (a total of ninety-three posts including fifty-six GIFs, twenty-eight still images, and nine videos) that were shared by the tweeters embellished the nasty comments with extracts from pop music, YouTube uploads of everyday events, and memes. These ranged from YouTuber PewDiePie making a dropping gesture and exclaiming, "ABSOLUTE MAD LAD" and Prince Harry dropping the mic and saying "BOOM" to a sea mammal swimming by the camera to a word bubble "Halo," sci-fi creatures laughing loudly with an accompanying speech bubble, "LOL," and a group of Black teenagers drooling with bemusement, as though in a state of trance. One commentator provided a link to Ethel Merman's rendition of the Irving Berlin song "Anything You Can Do (I Can Do Better)" and twisted the lyrics in the tweet to chime, "Any racism you can do I can do better." One more drew a drab comparison with vegans: "Probably [she is] a vegan. They're always miserable." "Let's make SATI [medieval Indian custom of bride burning] great again," announced a tweeter. "I know Brits outlawed the custom, but for the sake of . . . [them] . . . I suggest it's brought back."[62] Restless to frame the ongoing deluge of tweets as "British humor," another tweet remarked snidely, "Too bad when her ancestors were colonized, they didn't get any British humor."

Throughout the episode, commentators who firmly stood by @MG and paraded their loyalty through a sling of insinuating tweets, patted each other's back—so to speak—on Twitter, exchanging the metaphorical high-fives and making merry of the little victories of words and online muscle power. "Enjoying your riposte @MG," applauded a tweeter, followed by emojis of faces with tears of joy and thumbs up. "I think your forensic takedown of . . . hucksterism . . . is hitting the target. Keep up the good work," cheered a commentator, and another praised him for "punching back hard." One other was deferential: "@MG sir this is reason #60XX why we respect you. Brilliant." "Fair minded and critical thinkers are with you," assured one more, and egged him on to take on "race baiters." "Think of it as a necessary public service," goaded yet another. "This is like a dystopian comedy sketch . . . race baiting evil #$& derides thoroughly nice bloke." A barrage of tweets, including "Almost a poetic put-down. Worthy of Wilde dear boy!," "its like watching kitten getting mauled by a bear lol," "Go #MG," "strangle the air of publicity," "get her @MG," and so on built up a momentum as though toward an exhilarating climax where the hunted would finally fall into the net.

We might develop a comparison here with right-wing Hindu nationalist trolling of critical journalists and left-liberal academics, including those employed in the Western academy. With minor tweaking, we were able to retain the same thematic grid we had used for analyzing Hindu nationalist messages in the case of the Twitter exchange between @AB and @MG (see figure 2.1). In the list of thematic categories that we discovered from the tweet pool around a set of right-wing Twitter hashtags and WhatsApp groups in India, we had to delete only the category "Muslim minorities" for the British episode, since we did not find direct expressions of Islamophobia in the #Troll_event. We had to add only two new categories, "accusations of race-baiting" and "academia/ education" to make sense of the UK #Troll_event. Moreover, the two new categories were similar to the category that we defined as "accusations against left-liberals who appeased Muslim minorities" in the case of India, in that the target group in both the cases was imagined to be unreasonable advocates for inclusion and stubborn critics of discrimination where none existed.

Shared Lexicon

Across the ethnographic vignettes registered in this chapter, there were shared tropes and rhetorical expressions among alt-right, far-right, and right-wing trolls. In the UK #Tweet_event, a commentator compared academics like @AB to "Uranium and Thorium which are radioactive without a reason." This was the same label that Sam Harris, in his podcast, invited his guest Gad Saad to comment on, as we discussed in chapter 1. Similarly, the alt-right derisive terms about "leftists" and "social justice warriors" resonate across Denmark and Germany.[63] A self-described "alt-right journalist and activist" told us in Berlin, "I like to troll yes, but I don't count it as a discussion. I write politically incorrect statements to provoke certain people, the *Gutmensch* [the good people], those social justice warriors." In a right-wing Hindu nationalist meme that condemned beef consumption (see figure 2.2), a gang of men wielding sticks is seen around a wounded man on the ground as one of

Figure 2.2. Meme representing the circulation of
"normie" in a Hindu nationalist message against beef
consumption in India.[65]

the attackers exclaims in Hinglish: "*Offend kyu ho rhe ho? Normie ho
kya?*" [Why are you getting offended? Are you a normie?] Peter Hervik
has documented how the far-right in Denmark uses the derisive label
of "normie" to dismiss left liberals as naïve, boring, and stubborn social
justice warriors who take offense at all manner of speech because they
"don't get the joke."[64] Documenting the alt-right in the US, Angela Nagle
gave her book the revealing title *Kill All Normies*. Evidently, "normie" is
a shared internet jargon that tries to avoid the indictment of prejudicial
and discriminatory language by resorting to the justificatory grounds of
juvenile joviality—a point we will elaborate in the next section.

Without doubt, right-wing troll communities have specific lexicons
powered by local cultural expressions, particular imaginations of the nation's enemies, and distinct linguistic registers, but the tropes and styles
of these online enthusiasts, including suspicion of liberal media and left-
progressive academics, gendered shaming, ad hominem attacks, caustic
wordplays, sarcasm, annotations with emojis, meme mashups, and so
on, have developed striking parallels across geographies. There is also a
distinctive pattern of diffusion that underlies this shared constellation of
words and speech acts.

The Long Tail of Underlings

A prominent feature of peer-driven extreme-speech practice common among online users (as opposed to organized top-down forms of targeted extreme speech) within constitutional liberal societies is what might be termed the "long tail" of underlings that attaches to a quasi-leader. In the British case of #Troll_event, @MG was evidently the quasi-leader. The leader appeals to reason, argumentation, and facts and figures without themselves getting directly abusive (in the sense of using direct dehumanizing language). However, this appeal to reason is precisely the condition for others to go down the line of vitriol and claim legitimacy for their comments. The leader, according to this thinking, has set the premises of reason, and anything in excess and unreasonable that follows is justifiable because of the "special circumstances" that the leader has already demonstrated with his "reasonable arguments." Typically, the quasi-leader has a public status, a record of publications or media appearances, and direct access to ruling power in various capacities. This kind of online abusive leadership is neither charismatic nor authoritarian. It is a parasitic form of leadership that relies on an explicitly abusive long tail of underlings that is volatile. For if the long tail is severed, the leader's existence will be jeopardized. Underlings are characterized by their flickering loyalties—they are ready to move to anyone who performs the task of legitimizing their abusive comments. Legitimization on grounds of reason is important because of the constitutional liberal conditions that frame political opinion in these societies. No formally educated, middle-class online abuser whom Sahana interviewed in India and Germany wished to be seen as a "plain abuser" devoid of reasonable grounds for justification or perceived by others as buffoons or pests or as being socially deranged. They all felt convinced they had a "strong point." The role of the "long-tail leader" is precisely to appeal and demonstrate that the trolls "had a point." For instance, British pro-Brexit ideologue Douglas Murray used this exact phrasing to describe the far-right English Defence League when he lamented that the authorities fail to see that "they had a point."[66] In India, troll attacks on online users who are critical of exclusionary extreme speech exhibit a similar pattern of the long tail marked also by bots and propagandistic activities sponsored by political parties.[67] In such cases, journalists and newly minted public commentators who are ideologically driven or opportunistic or both lead the frontline charge with an appeal to fact-based contestation, while underlings, paid trolls, and ruffian political leaders hurl swearwords and abuse in bot-amplified iterative cycles. Indeed, this reflects a distinctive pattern of content creation and distribution in online political messaging more broadly. For instance, a content analysis of four theoretically sampled hashtag datasets that emerged on Twitter during the student protests against nationalist politics at a major university in Delhi (a total of 70,662 tweets/retweets for #JNU collected between February 7, 2016, and May 11, 2016; 17,193 tweets/retweets for #CleanupJNU collected between February 16 , 2016, and May 5, 2016; 37,161 tweets/retweets for #ShutdownJNU collected between February 10, 2016, and May 6, 2016); and the Bharatiya Janata Party(BJP)-friendly hashtag #MainBhiChowkidar [I am also a watchman] that trended during the general elections (96,905 tweets/retweets collected between March 17, 2019, and April 19, 2019) revealed that a large volume of messages was sent out by the top two users who tweeted and retweeted most frequently, after which, the post-per-handle rate flattened (see figure 2.3). While hinting at the influence of automated amplification efforts in online discourse, this pattern of content flow also reflects a global trend in right-wing discourse online, as shown by the study that Bharat Ganesh has conducted on alt-right tweeters in Europe and North America, suggesting that a small number of key online users lead the content, and the long tail tags on by amplifying it through sharing and reposting.[68] In another study on Pegida and Alternativ für Deutschland (AfD), the anti-immigrant, far-right movements in Germany, Cornelius Puschmann, Julian Ausserhofer, and Josef Slerka (2018) have found that a large part of the commenting activity on the Facebook pages of these groups is carried out by a small number of highly active users.[69]

Moreover, when the long tail turns vitriolic and abusive, the leader sanctions the long tail by becoming a silent observer, drawing strength from what legal philosopher David Lewis calls "presupposition accommodation"—a "default adjustment that occurs, without fuss, when hearers take on board what speakers presuppose."[70] Once the abusive trail is fired with the leader's socially acceptable phrasing, the leader's silence becomes the key resource of ammunition for further vitriol by the long tail. In such instances, the "authority" of hate speech—that is, the

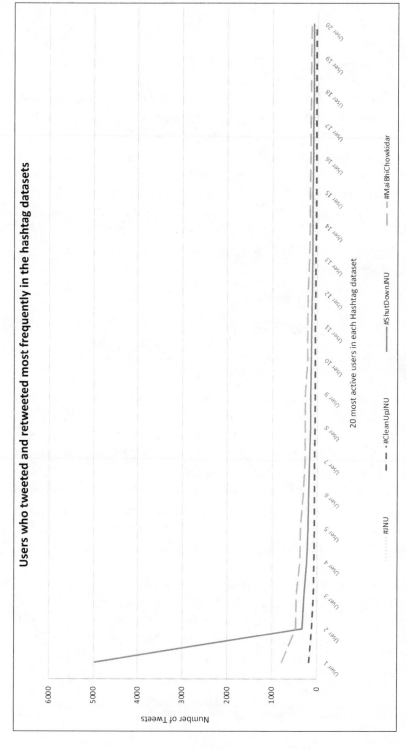

Figure 2.3. Twenty most active handles in four Twitter hashtag datasets during the 2019 Indian general elections.

ability to deliver hate as a knowable thing and an actionable directive—is outsourced to a larger group. Through speech acts that attach the leader with a long tail, "derogatory evaluation . . . becomes a done thing (shared social practice) and known thing (shared common knowledge)."[71]

Put differently, for the right-wing troll communities, the abusive long tail is as important as the presence of "decent" ringleaders who exuberate wit, success, and a certain grace in the public domain. In countries such as Germany, the appeal to reason and sophisticated theoretical formulations articulated by finely dressed ideologues is critical to the overall intellectual edifice of right-wing movements. A brief discussion of the ethnographic encounters with the intellectual sophistication of the contemporary German far-right might help illuminate the stakes of this performance.

Ethnopluralism and the Neu-Rechten Szene (The New Right Scene)

(Sahana) I arrived at the restaurant in a part-residential, part-commercial neighborhood close to the subway in Munich around the same time as Laura Csuka, the student researcher working on the project, reached the spot. It was November 2018. I stared into the sky and saw that there was no semblance of the sun. The air was cold and still. I clasped my hands in my overcoat pockets and clenched my teeth with a mild tremble as we stood in front of the main door of the restaurant, waiting for our interview partner to arrive. Laura and I did a quick rehearsal of the interview plan for about five minutes before we spotted a young man in a fine blue suit, matching trousers, neatly pressed white shirt, and shining leather shoes walking toward us.

We entered the restaurant and sat across a table. Laura, who grew up entirely in Munich before moving to the UK for doctoral research, started the conversation in German and introduced me as a "Ludwig-Maximilians-Universität München professor." I stretched my right arm spontaneously for a handshake and greeted him in English, "Hello, good to see you." His grip, I felt, was unusually loose for a handshake. In retrospect, I could see that the loose handshake hadn't emerged from pandemic-induced social distancing, since it was still the pre-pandemic time. As we settled down at the large rectangular table, I noticed lines of unease appearing on his face, prompting me to instantly speculate that this would not be one of the kind of chatty conversations I would typically have with right-wing interlocutors back in India. He appeared to be less uncomfortable with Laura. Perhaps the language, perhaps my age, perhaps my status as a professor, perhaps my skin color, perhaps all of them, perhaps none.

Felix (name changed) was twenty-one. His mother is Russian and his father German. Felix was a member of the conservative student associations called "fraternities" and Junge Alternative München, the youth wing of Alternative für Deutschland (AfD). As we were browsing the menu, I noticed a thick finger ring on him with an emblem. Laura noted that the engraved slogan contained the world *Recht* (right), pointing to the student association of Franco-Bavaria.

Felix started to take an active interest in politics at the age of fifteen. "It was during the Bundestag election in September 2013," Felix recounted. "I realized the conservative aspect was missing in all the major [political] parties. Then I saw that new party [AfD]. I helped them out, they accepted me in a friendly manner, and I feel quite comfortable there." What he liked the most about AfD was that it was "possible to be proud of Germany and German history, the German identity . . . that one can say these things without being attacked." The sense of freedom he experienced within the AfD contrasts with the heightened sensitivity around Germany's Nazi past in the national public culture, but Felix believed there was already a recalibration of this hesitation. This hesitation was "back then," when he was a teenager, he clarified: "Back then, it [talking about German pride and identity] was a contentious issue. We could not openly admit it. Now it's alright." Laura jumped on the point—sounding quite dismayed at the "it's alright now" expression—and asked him if he saw a shift already. He believed that there had been a change in the German public discourse, but that "it is more of a divide," he explained. "Both camps have become stronger." He described the camps as the "far left," represented by the Greens, and the "far right," represented by AfD.

Felix's attraction to AfD led him to volunteer for the party's social media promotions and street demonstrations. He coordinated with his AfD friends to post pictures on Junge Alternative München's Instagram account, which he said had 417 followers. The youth wing had started its accounts on Twitter, Facebook, and Instagram just three months earlier, although the youth wing in Munich was, in the words of Felix, "at least four or five years old." The wing organized hiking, regulars' table ("Stammtisch," a German way to hold informal group meetings on a regular basis), and street demonstrations and used their social media accounts to publicize these activities. One of the key reasons for posting on social media was to showcase that they were active on the streets.

Throughout our interaction, Felix looked evasive and hesitant. He was assertive and withdrawn at the same time. Curiously, he interspersed the entire conversation with the German expression *Ganz normal*, which translates literally as "quite normal" and means "nothing remarkable or unusual." When he switched to English, Felix used the expression *normal thing*. When I asked him about the kind of activities he carried out for the youth wing of AfD Munich, he said he would just post some things online, "Nothing, urg, directly nothing, but on some left-wing sites they post our pictures . . . so normal thing. So, but it doesn't matter for me. On the street, they say bad things to me and . . . [takes a deep breath] . . . normal thing, I think, its nothing special in my case." Laura expressed her surprise when we later did a post-facto analysis of the interview. "This guy seemed so genuinely insecure," Laura remarked, "I really felt it was necessary to walk on the eggshells in order to get some information from him rather than pushing him because he would have otherwise pulled up the defenses."

During the interview, both Laura and I were keen to get his views on trolling and other types of provocative speech online. Reluctantly relenting to our curiosity, he finally showed us a picture from the Instagram account of Junge Alternative München. As he held the mobile phone at an awkwardly wide distance, we strained our eyes to see what was in the picture, and with some effort, we noticed a banner that read "Asylmissbrauch: Konsequent abschieben" (Asylum abuse, forceful/consistent deportation).[72] This was a poster that the central AfD had distributed to all its regional wings to promote its anti-immigrant policies during the election campaign in 2017. Felix and his friends gave a particularly provocative twist to this centralized publicity plan. "We had to post this deportation poster. But we also had several more. Then we spotted a mosque. We asked ourselves what poster should we attach here? Why not the deportation poster? Why don't we attach that on the mosque!" he said, showing us the Instagram picture from his mobile phone screen. He was grinning for the first time. His voice was excited with a sense of pride and achievement. The picture of the poster on a mosque wall was the example he gave as a response to our question on provocative speech. "We are a youth organization," he added. "We're more provocative than others. We are the Unterpartei [below the main party]." *Unterpartei*—"under party" that figuratively stayed under rather than occupying the main stage of the party—signaled a sort of long tail where derogatory transgressions were allowed to froth as long as the ringleader (here, the main party) provided some semblance of acceptability in terms of prevailing norms of political discourse.

Aside from this brief moment when Felix looked more honest reveling in his bravado politics of anti-immigrant poster pasting, his responses were guarded. Yet toward the end of an hour-long interview, he went back to the point on German culture and identity. During his visits to Russia, his mother's homeland, he would hear a lot of praise for Germany. "I hear a lot from Russians that they envy us for our poets and thinkers."

Laura had a long comment in our post-interview discussion:

> When I listened to what he said about Russians praising Germany, I thought "Well, he's not wrong." Germany has a good health-care system, a social safety net, is providing its citizens with easily accessible education for free and is in general a functioning democracy. It's true that these things are all great and that many other countries are struggling with that. Especially Russia. But then [it] turns out he isn't thinking about these things at all. He literally thinks of the essence of a culture as made up of art and intellectual accomplishments from *the past* and that is what he relates to. Even though *now* is the time when wealth and well-being are as abundant as never before, he seems to be rather appreciating some intangible spirit of Germanness composed of the thoughts of dead people.

Interestingly, during the interview, Felix defined German culture not only in terms of artefacts, ideas, and art but also more importantly about the people who belonged to this culture and who had the right to claim it. "The question of *what* is German culture, *who* is part of it and *who* isn't," he declared rather emphatically, and when we pressed for more comments on the matter, he quickly retreated. "It's too political for me," he said, almost ready to end the conversation. Laura looked furious. "Too political!" she challenged him. "I thought I was here to talk about Instagram and the internet," he complained. "This goes a bit too much into [the] details." His gaze swept the room. He was pulling a face, and his words became steadily more inaudible and incomprehensible. It was our turn to retreat. When we turned the question back to "the internet," he sounded irritated and listed a couple of names indifferently. "WhatsApp, Amazon. . . . I don't think I am a great exception here." His favorite buffer expression spurted out once again: "Ganz normal," nothing remarkable. This time, however, it also signaled an intention for ending the interview.

Soon after the interview, Felix turned his Instagram account private. There was no evidence to suggest that our interview had prompted this decision, but we could speculate from his irritation and hesitation during the interview that he perhaps wanted a safe distance from prying academics. Fortunately, just before the interview, we had managed to check his Instagram profile. The first picture showed the Make America Great Again cap. The second picture showed him smoking a big cigar. In the third picture, Felix was hiking in the Alps in traditional Bavarian clothing, which struck Laura as something reminiscent of the painting *Der Wanderer über dem Nebelmeer* by Caspar David Friedrich, an iconic piece of art for the German Romantic movement from the eighteenth to the early nineteenth century. His profile picture showed him in the fraternity costume, hoisting a beer mug.

These images, registered in our notes, took us back to Felix's comments during the interview when he nostalgically extoled the richness of German culture, poetry, and philosophical thought, captured in the evocative phrase *German identity*. Although Felix was particularly evasive, other research interlocutors were more forthright about their views and attributed them directly to their grooming in German intellectual traditions. A self-identified alt-right journalist and activist in Berlin said to researcher Alexandra Deem, who was then assisting the project, that his involvement in right-wing politics was shaped by books. "It started quite early in my life with political philosophy," he said, stressing the bachelor's degree in philosophy he acquired from a top university in Berlin.

In December 2018, I met a senior far-right activist in Munich active on Facebook, who pontificated eloquently on the question of culture, shoring up the conversation with references to the Indian philosopher Jiddu Krishnamurthy and the theory of ethnopluralism. Ethnopluralism promotes the view that it is important to ensure the *rights* of people to live where they belong since dislocation of all sorts can be traumatizing (similar to the millionaire Lissy's comment referenced earlier). The modern Generation Identity movement in Germany, which grew from the founding ideas of Génération Identitaire (GI), the French youth section of the Bloc Identitaire that was aligned with the so-called Nouvelle Droite in the 1970s, has centered "ethnocultural aspect" as a key rationale for their political actions. Generation Identity movement started its chapter in Germany in 2012, declaring that their mission was to save the homeland from the perceived threats of "multiculturalism, mass migration and loss of identity." Indirectly targeting non-European immigrants and Muslims through the blanket term *migration*, GI has sought to draw strength from the concept of ethnopluralism. Extending the pride and anxieties about German culture and identity into a general anti-immigration theory, advocates of ethnopluralism aspire for a social order in which every ethnic group lives in its own culturally homogenous homeland. Proponents of ethnopluralism seek to draw legitimacy by defending the very discourse of difference and how people should strive to preserve and mutually respect distinct ethnocultural regions. Far from any direct references to denigration, hate, and exclusion, these theorists present themselves as defenders of difference, authenticity, and social-cultural security gained within homogeneous societies. The GI Germany website (*Identitäre Bewegung Deutschland*) states one of its missions as follows:

> Our goal is to create a patriotic civil society in which love of one's homeland and a fearless commitment to one's own identity are once again recognized as guiding values of social coexistence.[73]

Within German public culture, such articulations have served to draw a distinction from far-right groups that are condemned in organized legacy media as neo-Nazis and "Nazi hipsters."[74] By appropriating the seemingly progressive tropes of dislocation and pluralism, such reinvigorated intellectual articulations of right-wing nationalism and anti-immigrant sentiments reframe exclusion as a matter of rights of people who leave their homeland. In this clever twist of tropes, people who support mobility are portrayed as the real villains who foreclose the possibility of rooted coexistence by dogmatically insisting on globality. By essentializing cultural differences and promoting biological and ethnic origins as a necessary criterion for cultural belonging and membership to the German Volk, proponents of this *Heimatideologie* (homeland ideology) continue to peddle exclusionary ideologies but by rhetorically avoiding accusations of racism or discriminatory nationalism.[75] As anthropologist Sindre Bangstad has astutely observed in relation to Western Europe and Nordic regions, such articulations based on "theories" have extended the intellectual trajectory of far-right identitarianism that "serves the function of distancing from more overt and obvious forms of racism through rhetorical means."[76]

It might be recognized that a more fundamental historical process underlies theories such as ethnopluralism. These theories could not have emerged without the exclusionary ideology of nation-states as distinct territorial and cultural spaces etched out during the colonial encounter and European imperialism. Within the moral order of the nation-state, the distinctions drawn between insider and outsider, and minority and majority, instigate affective economies of immense intensity, fueling extreme speech in the form of both crude remarks and intellectually sophisticated arguments aimed particularly against racialized immigrants and minoritized publics.

In these instances, hate, to follow Sara Ahmed, does not "reside in a given subject or object. Hate is economic; it circulates between signifiers in relationships of difference and displacement."[77] As expressions such as "rape-refugees," "pseudoliberals," "presstitute," "commies," and an ever increasing list of derogatory expressions circulate on online media, "hate . . . [becomes] . . . distributed across various bodies" and "through the association between the figures . . . they acquire 'a life of their own' as if they contain an affective quality."[78]

Although Ahmed does not elaborate the point, mediation is involved in every step of the affective economy. Evident across @MG trolls, AfD Instagram posts, and Hindu nationalist aggressors online, digital mediation materializes the surfaces of hateful bodies through association, alignment, displacement, and 'stickiness'. If hate is part of the "production of the ordinary," digital exchange realizes it by bringing hateful expressions closer to one's everyday conversational realities—a certain mundaneness that muddles moral positions.[79] Tagging onto small-screen intimacy of digital exchange, hate evokes no moral judgement, because it passes onto the ordinary. This passing on to the ordinary occurs in continuous loops powered by systematic channeling of affect—of anger, glee, envy, and transgressive pleasures of online vitriolic exchange—within the participatory condition of digital capitalism.[80] We highlight this logic of (digital) market relations as the third aspect of coloniality, tied to but distinct from the nation-state and racial relations we have examined so far. We will now turn to the specificities of digital mediation as a critical element of the affective economies of extreme speech.

Participatory Condition of the Digital and "Radicalization by Design"

The racialization processes in the digital age are powered by the translocal mediations of the internet, while also offering avenues for their radical requestioning. Across ethnographic vignettes of right-wing aggression in the UK, India, Denmark, and Germany discussed above, internet media have allowed distinct affordances and possibilities of action that augment specific user cultures facilitating vitriol as an everyday infrastructure for exclusionary politics. Some fundamental features of digital capitalism might be identified as shaping these mediations that cut across political contexts and conflicts, while also highlighting, on a higher level of abstraction, that digital capitalism is itself a manifestation of coloniality's institutionalization of market relations.

Digital capitalism does not necessarily determine the content of participation to the last detail, although algorithmic tweaks are shown to have a real effect on content. More fundamentally, however, digital capitalism's force lies in the *rendition* of compulsive participation as a normative political behavior and socially desirable trait. Darin Barney et al. have defined this as the "participatory condition," "a situation in which participation—being involved in doing something and taking part in something with others—has become both environmental (a state of affairs) and normative (a binding principle of right action)."[81] This is shaped in part by online architectures that reward self-expressivity in a data driven marketplace that converts the self-activity of online users into a commodity for data analytics.[82] Sangeet Kumar notes that "the affordances and default settings on social media platforms . . . reward self-revelation and disclosure while penalizing reticence and non-participation."[83] The compulsion to participate connects with the related process of digital capitalism that merges leisure with labor.[84] Embedded within the gigantic algorithm-driven, data-hungry machine of what Shoshana Zuboff calls the "Big Other," patterns of content sharing are prodded by the rationale of *positive abundance via participation* as opposed to restraint and containment.[85] We will discuss the political economy of data regimes in greater detail in the next chapter, but we will highlight here how particular features of data capitalism have augmented the conditions for extreme speech.

The logic of positive abundance and continuous engagement has tilted everyday forms of online exchange toward confrontational styles often referred to as "counters" in internet folk jargon. Ethicist Tristan Harris, described as the "closest thing Silicon Valley has to a conscience," has criticized this state of affairs as "radicalization by design," characterized by algorithmic actions that keep the machines of online engagement active through communicative styles of provocation and polarized messaging.

At the level of online practice, these structures manifest as meso-level mediations of digital circulation that have a certain transcultural force and crosscutting effect. Online abusive cultures, for instance, are shaped by a dynamic set of translocal scenes characterized by, in the Goffmanian terminology, "a lack of insulation of observability for the group members."[86] For instance, online Hindu nationalist actors in India feel they are constantly watched by their peers when they tag, tweet, retweet, and troll. The pattern of exchange in the UK #Troll_event reveals that @MG supporters were taking cues from each other, deriving strength from each other's observable actions and simultaneously feeding this observability. The argument about observability runs against the common wisdom about digital anonymity as a key factor in facilitating disinhibition, deindividuation, and lowered evaluative cues in abusive exchange. Instead, it shows how at a phenomenological level and in terms of the online architectural design that is composed of hashtags, retweets, mentions, and profiles as elements of digital traces, internet interactional contexts set up a condition of observability. In other words, extreme-speech actors perform to their peers online, and this observability shapes their self-awareness as online subjects doing different things in the networked space/time of the internet media and face-to-face situations where they might hesitate to use the same brash language they hurl online. This observability paradoxically sits with an experiential sense of autonomy. A member of the AfD youth wing articulated this paradoxical mix of experiences when he said, "We feel protected by this alleged anonymity. Although everyone knows who he is, who I am, they feel protected and are considerably ruthless in their words."

Closely tied to experiential autonomy and observability is the cross-cutting mediation of online "fun" both as a format and as a practice. Fun as a meta-practice embeds distance and deniability in online extreme speech, in ways that allow right-wing actors to evade the moral and regulatory gaze by framing it as "merely funny" or by experiencing the fun of aggression by drawing strength from one another in the collective paticipatory culture of the digital.[87] The UK #Troll_event revealed how a panoply of word games and derogatory jokes facilitated the slide to hateful expressions. On quasi-public forums such as Twitter to image boards such as 4Chan, hate sticks to bodies through signs that are constantly innovated upon in "creative funny" ways, allowing the affective economy of hate to spread horizontally. In France, la Ligue du LOL (Laughing Out Loud League), an online group formed largely of male Parisian journalists, jolted liberal sensibilities with their sexist and racist imprecations at women, racialized groups, and LGBTQIA+, to men who did not subscribe to their "toxic masculinity."[88] "LOL culture is to present oneself with self-mockery," observed political communications professor Arnaud Mercier in a newspaper interview. "[It is] to be ready to die for a good word."[89]

In India, Hindu nationalists are not only adept at composing funny messages for online ideological battles, but they also derive fun from making their hashtags trend online or by winning arguments over opponents. In Germany, when we asked the self-identified alt-right journalist about how he meets his opponents, the *Gutmensch* (the good people, a derogatory term for progressive voices) online, he remarked, "It's something that just happens, usually in the evening when I am bored. It's not something I actively do. I don't have a plan; it's more fun." In these instances, fun greases the surface where hate could "slide between signs and objects."[90]

In addition, in countries such as Germany and Denmark, online "fun" has allowed far-right activists to escape the strict regulations around speech; simultaneously, these actors derive pleasure from escaping the legal nets through their clever twist of words, suggestive phrasing, and coded language. Our alt-right interlocutor in Berlin said:

> I'm good at writing what is possible within the frame of the German hate crime law. That's the fun part—if you write something in a way that everybody knows what I mean but I'm not writing it, and that makes them freak out because they don't want to have a discussion or come with an argument. They just want to put me in jail.

Responding to our question on right-wing trolling, a young member of the *Identitäre Bewegung* in Munich vividly connected this with the gamified contexts of popular culture, invoking Star Wars as the ultimate setting for the online war he had waged against the *Gutmensch*:

> I'm on the side of the Empire. Not when I was a kid really . . . but then I realized that actually the resistance are terrorists . . . and the soldiers of the Empire are dehumanized . . . the resistance kills them and doesn't seem to care at all but when they take off their helmets you see they are human. The emperor is this angry old white guy [which he jokingly identifies with], and besides, they [the Empire] were just cooler.

The reference to the Empire was metaphorically as close to the reality as it could get. In taking the side of the "old white guy," our interlocutor indexed a historically continuous political culture in which racially marked aggression ramps up and draws upon contemporary forms of gamified online fun and popular culture, repowering the hate ideologies of white supremacy.

Logics of Coloniality

To return to Ahmed's evocative analysis, hate—as viewed through forms of extreme speech in our analysis—does not move about in all directions. Greased as it may be with experiential autonomy, observability, algorithmically mediated polarization, and fun within the participatory condition of the digital, hate is not a free slide. As she forcefully reminds us:

> The transformation of this or that other into an object of hate is over-determined. It is not simply that anybody is hated: particular histories of association are reopened in each encounter, such that some bodies are already encountered as more hateful than other bodies. Histories are bound up with emotions precisely insofar as it is a question of what sticks, of what connections are lived as the most intense or intimate, as being closer to the skin.[91]

Following Nicholas de Genova, we could define these historical conditions as "postcolonial metastasis."[92] Assertions of aggrieved power common among white supremacists and their expression online in the form of exclusionary extreme speech emerge not only out of structural subordination under oppressive market conditions but also by a sense of dethronement, a product of far-reaching racialized processes of the global legacies of the Empire. Crucially, through nation-state relations canonized by colonialism, aggression wrought by imaginary wounds unfolds *within* different national and subnational contexts as racialized relations of majoritarian belligerence. Hindu nationalists in India, Sinhalese nationalists in Sri Lanka, Han nationalists online in China, the Sunni majoritarian politics around blasphemy in Pakistan, Rodrigo Duterte's trolls in the Philippines, and online nationalists in Nepal are some examples, and so are the meme makers in northern Chile who seize the mashup cultures of internet memes to portray migrants from Bolivia and Peru as "backward, unhygienic, uneducated, plunderers of limited resources and contributors to cultural degradation."[93] In an important review, Bronwyn Carlson and Ryan Frazer have highlighted research that has revealed that "Indigenous peoples experience cyber-bullying at higher rates than non-Indigenous populations" in Australia.[94] Such exclusionary discourses—against immigrants (a category that emerged from the nation-state distinction between inside/outside), minorities (a category that emerged from the nation-state distinction between majority/minority), and Indigenous communities as part of the violent settler colonial histories—are rife with racialized portrayals.

Colonialism reproduced hierarchy and difference as intrinsic features of the modern nation-state, and this process of racialization of social relations within the newly stabilized structure of the nation-state was *global* in scope.[95] To follow the argument advanced by Arjun Shankar, colonialism as a *global* process created "several interlinked racialization processes, which cannot fit neatly into a single national racial formation project."[96]

The ethnographic vignettes and analysis of vitriol discussed throughout this chapter reveal how online extreme speech—arguably the most striking symptom of affective digital communication—is part of the longer *global* process of colonial-modern relations that unfold both within and as external forces in different social and national contexts. A decolonial critique developed in this chapter suggests that it is only when *close contextualization* of proximate contexts—of media affordances in use or situated speech cultures—is developed in conjunction with *deep contextualization*—to account for grave historical continuities and political economic structures unfolding on a planetary scale—that a fuller understanding of extreme speech and its entrenched coloniality comes to view. This kind of decolonial critique of extreme speech impels us to imagine thick connections across contexts as a global liberatory project, a point we have highlighted in the introduction and that we will return to in the coda. In the next chapter, however, we will delve further into the coloniality of the current conjuncture by deepening our focus on the political economy of global data regimes beyond the particular effects around extreme speech they have helped coalesce.

3

Capture

The Coloniality of Contemporary Data Relations

> In villages, everyone knew everyone's secret. Then cities
> made us anonymous. We moved to digital & now anony-
> mous knows everyone's secrets.
> —Kannan Gopinathan

"You know, never before in history have fifty designers—twenty- to
thirty-five-year-old white guys in California—made decisions that
would have an impact on two billion people," fumes Tristan Harris
with his characteristic candor, as Netflix's instant-hit docudrama, *The
Social Dilemma*, wraps his angst with eerie music, typing sounds, and
indistinct chatter, catapulting his moral rage onto the global stage as
a pivotal crisis facing humanity.[1] The American docudrama's incisive
criticism of data monetization, addictive qualities concealed within the
design architectures of internet communication, the mounting threat
of artificial intelligence (AI) to human autonomy, the dangers of digital
disinformation for liberal democracies, and so on resonated strongly
with skepticism about internet communication shared by a section of
English-speaking net-savvy publics. Some reviews contended that the
film was so impactful that a number of viewers considered discarding
their mobile phones into the dustbin in panic.[2] The docudrama not only
held a mirror to the gloomy public mood, following similar dystopic
visions portrayed by popular cultural productions such as the British
television series *Black Mirror*, but it also timed its release around the
US general elections in 2020, aiming to undercut social media-led campaign frauds and populist propaganda.

Without doubt, with an engaging narrative that magnified its popular
appeal, the docudrama did offer a trenchant critique of the psychological and political fallout of data monetization. It highlighted how big tech

firms have imbedded polarization as part of the business model, driving democracies to the danger point where animosities are hardwired into the business models of mega corporations rather than spilling out as unintended effects. In the film and on various other forums, Harris has indicted the big tech corporate sector for deliberate profit-oriented polarization, pointedly describing this market-led decadence as "radicalization by design," as we highlighted in the previous chapter.

While laudable for stirring public consciousness around the pitfalls of internet communication—at least among its audiences—the film nonetheless diverted attention from the diverse stakes of the political economy of digital capitalism. At the outset, by reproducing the white, male, tech elite as the central moral subject and eventual savior, it reinstated the terms of debate within the European-Enlightenment racial paradigm of the reflexive interiority of the white subject as the bearer of the authoritative view of the world and concomitant curative capacity. By pinning the focus on well-meaning white guys whose passionate creation has now transformed into Frankenstein's creature beyond the original intentions or control of its creators, the film, despite its title, ironically had little to say about "the social"—the entangled complex of histories, institutions, interests, and mediations—that compose the actual grounds on which technology emerges and expands, in turn deepening and disrupting the grounds that seed it. As Aabid Firdausi sharply argues, the "prodigal tech-bro" narrative of the docudrama deliberately leaves out the sociological question, avoiding the need to answer "what is actually social about the social dilemma."[3]

In the previous chapter, we have shown how online extreme speech cannot be explained as "simply the expression of transhistorical prejudices and hatreds"[4] but a specific conjuncture of digital affordances and affects that have allowed colonial histories of racialization, religious majoritarianism, and ethnic divisions to impinge on and violently shape the present. In this chapter, we delve into the *socio-technological*—rather than the merely profit-driven technological—conditions for inequalities and dispossession by locating them within the emerging global political economies of digital capitalism.

The first critique we offer sheds light on a curious and disturbing continuity. Global data relations that aim to extract and monetize "behavioral surplus" share affinities with problematic anthropological-colonial tropes around capturing the natives in their natural environments. The liberal moral alarm over data surveillance practices, we argue, has ignored the historical trajectory of these practices and how they were tied to the colonial control of the "others of Europe."[5] We further demonstrate that the self-absorbed Western liberal contemplation around digital capitalism fails to fully address the vastly uneven ways in which mechanisms of digital capitalism have unfolded globally. We take up algorithmic racism and differentiated labor relations as evidenced in the global asymmetries in online extreme speech moderation as gateways to interrogate this unevenness and the structures of dispossession it depends on and perpetuates. We examine them as the material conditions for the unsettling affects of the digital and as a manifestation of the racialized, geospatial hierarchies of risk and labor shaped by colonial histories. In the final section, we situate the materialities of digital unsettling in relation to specific structures of domination shaped by colonial, imperial histories within a nation-state context by briefly discussing digital practices aimed against religious minorities in postcolonial India.

In these analytical moves, we operationalize the concept of *capture* as a way to anchor the political economy of contemporary digital capitalism in the historical *longue durée*, which has problematic parallels with how anthropology emerged as the science of the colonizer. The opening quote of Kannan Gopinathan, a former Indian administrative officer, sharply puts the imagery of the Indian village and the city on this predicament: the journey from the village, where no secrets can survive, to the city, where anonymity is guaranteed, but again into the digital, where "anonymous"—the data machine—knows everything. Through the analytics of capture, we take a cue from this backward journey, extending the debate about digital exploitations beyond what is commonly described as data surveillance and loss of privacy into excavating a range of content extraction and labor practices of digital capitalism and how they intersect with, emerge from, and shape geopolitical and national-political regimes in uneven ways. Capture, as we employ the concept here, signals processes of appropriating and disciplining labor, time, meanings, and bodies for digital capitalist accumulation, by laying a recursive trap of continuous online engagement that is observable, traceable, plottable, and in historically specific ways, manipulable. We thus advance a decolonial framework that pushes for historical awareness and attention to global unevenness in the materialities of digital unsettling, turning a critical eye not only to the mechanisms of the market but also to the limits of liberal critiques that have appropriated current skepticism about the internet by projecting particular experiences of the transatlantic West as a universal grievance affecting the whole of humanity in the same way.

Anthropological Capture and Data Relations

(Sahana) When I first came across Kannan Gopinathan's tweet, I saw the haunting imagery of moving from the village to the city to the world of data as traces of a pervasive trap. It is a trap of exposure—a condition of being exposed to others without one's knowing or approval, over which one had little control even when one complied or acquiesced. My mind moved across scenes, instantly evoking my recurring memories of visiting Oxford for the first time as a PhD student from India and walking out of the Pitt Rivers Museum. I had learned some theories and methods in anthropology and had absorbed the idea that any serious student of the discipline would include anthropological museum visits on their compulsory itinerary when they travel abroad. From inside, the museum was unlike anything I had known before. It was stuffed with rows and rows of items—canoes, carpets, clothes—some encased behind glass and some exposed to the thick indoor air. As I walked through the aisles, I struggled to see the reason behind these collections, and I felt a gnawing unease. I strolled around but stopped in front a small glass cabinet, gazing at what was inside. It was an ornate betel nutcracker. The edges of the two blades had a fine floral motif, and the little piece shone in a mild beam of light. "It is from my village," I protested silently. It was exactly the kind my grandmother back in the village used to crack the betel nuts that were grown in the *adike thota* (betel nut garden). I had seen the soft husk of the betel nut falling on the ground as my grandmother skillfully placed the nut between the blades and gave one hard press to crack it into two pieces, repeating the action several times until the nut broke down into chewable shreds. What odd sequence of events had come together to bring these all the way to the Oxford museum? Why were they in the glass case? Memories of wading through things that my ancestors could have actually used—to crack a betel nut or cover themselves in the rains or perhaps craft different kinds of callous magic against their rivals in the worlds they lived—resonated with Kannan's allusion to the rural-urban-data trap and the condition of being exposed and archived without one's approval. The gushing memories and associations raised the question: What are the blind spots in critical appraisals of contemporary data relations, and how do these appraisals ignore the historical antecedents of data as capture?

The roaring success of *The Social Dilemma* came close on the heels of another blockbuster that had set the stage for a critique of the internet, namely, the much-appraised magnum opus *Surveillance Capitalism: The Fight for a Human Future at the New Frontier of Power*, by Shoshana Zuboff. In a tone that would later be matched by the high-pitch rendition of the Netflix docudrama, Zuboff raised the stakes of the critique by stating that "Surveillance capital derives from the dispossession of human experience, operationalized in its unilateral and pervasive programs of rendition: our *lives are scraped and sold to fund their freedom and our subjugation, their knowledge and our ignorance about what they know*."[6] Surveillance capitalism, following Zuboff, unilaterally claims human experience as free raw material for translation into behavioral data. Some of this data is applied to product or service improvement, but the rest is declared as proprietary *behavioral* surplus, fed into advanced manufacturing processes (machine intelligence), and fabricated into prediction products that anticipate consumer behavior. "Right now we are at the beginning of a new arc that I have called information civilization," she cautions, "and it repeats the same dangerous arrogance. The aim now is not to dominate *nature* but rather *human nature*. The focus has shifted from machines that overcome the limits of bodies to machines that modify the behavior of individuals, groups, and populations in the service of market objectives."[7]

Similar to Zuboff's assessment, several studies have drawn critical attention to the workings of big tech, in particular the emergence of AI as the technological face of data capitalism and the dangerous prospect of losing human autonomy to the increasingly intelligent machine.[8] While critics of AI and surveillance capitalism are reclaiming humanism against the onslaught of the global data machine powered by data capture, we suggest that such criticisms do not recognize the historical trajectory of colonialism in which capture was the key modality for imperial capitalism and its conceptualization of humanity, as the European Enlightenment project sought to racially classify human, subhuman, and others.[9] How then do we map the historical stakes of capture?

At the highest level, we might recognize that the very institutionalization of widespread market rationality as forms of capture—of land, labor, bodies, and meanings—evolved with the colonial project. In its latest manifestation as digital capitalism, market rationality has threatened to usurp life for data extraction, subjecting life forms to a relentless machine of categorizing, slotting, plotting, and predicting behaviors to serve market interests. Nick Couldry and Ulises Mejias argue that the scale and ruthlessness of subjecting life to data extraction are akin to the ravaging effects of historical colonialism:

> Data relations enact a new form of data colonialism, normalizing the exploitation of human beings through data, just as historic colonialism appropriated territory and resources and ruled subjects for profit. Data colonialism paves the way for a new stage of capitalism whose outlines we only glimpse: the capitalization of life without limit.[10]

While on the one hand, Zuboff ignores the longer colonial histories that inform contemporary data extraction practices, locating her critique in a Western humanist tradition of lamenting growing capitalization (mechanization) and the loss of human autonomy, Couldry and Mejias's helpful invocation of colonialism as a way to signal structural continuities, on the other hand, leaves several questions around pinning down the precise parallels between contemporary digital capture and colonial knowledge production.[11]

Capture, we suggest, was the very modality through which the terms for seeing the "primitives" and the non-West as bounded entities that could be observed and deciphered through data collection, collation, prediction, and modification were braided with the colonial logics of power in the nineteenth century. The formative years of anthropology as a discipline in this period crystallized and institutionalized the ambition and acts of capture through systematic data collection *without* the approval of observed peoples. Such emergent stakes are vividly illustrated by the disciplinary history of British social anthropology. In 1898, when A.C. Haddon organized what came to be known as the Cambridge Anthropological Expedition to Torres Straits, he chose W. H. R. Rivers to "carry out the first systematic attempt to apply the 'new' experimental psychology to a 'primitive' population."[12] Rivers was originally trained in medicine and then moved to neurology, psychology, and anthropology. Around the same time, anthropologist James G. Frazer gathered "genealogies to discover whether or not those who were closely related resembled one another in their reactions to the various psychological and physiological tests."[13] Rivers was equally excited about the "sociological potential" of the genealogical method. Although he "continued to carry out important psychological researches" among the "primitives," he "devoted much of his energy in the decade after his return from Torres Strait to further ethnographic fieldwork."[14] What emerged out of these explorations in terms of the genealogical method is beyond the scope of this chapter, as are the fissures between the diachronic and synchronic approaches, or between evolutionism and diffusionism, within the diachronic tradition that appeared in the following years.[15] The ways in which these early experiments led to the structural functionalist tradition within anthropology are also not directly relevant to the discussion here. We instead draw attention to the *trap* of what is now called "data" that is spread onto peoples and their lands, lives, relations, and rituals, set within environments seen as unmediated and uncontaminated. Early anthropologists defined them as "the natural settings" and repeated the rationale of colonial science that all observations of people in this so-called natural environment would be for the greater good of progress that knowledge could bestow on their (imperial) societies. In the institutional history of anthropology, it occurred at a time when anthropologists rejected the skepticism that "human feelings . . . [are] unobservable for scientific research" and began to consider social actions as objects of study.[16]

Capturing the "primitives" in their "natural" environments for knowledge creation and political dominance emerged directly from the conditions of colonial rule and the prevailing intellectual atmosphere in the British Empire that nurtured a utilitarian view that knowledge was something that could be "used to manage the nation's empire's] resources of people and land."[17] As the historian of anthropology Henrika Kuklick writes, "Throughout its formative years, anthropology was conceived to be a useful scholarship."[18] It drew intellectual inspiration from classics, biblical studies, and philosophy but marked its distinctiveness more as a type of natural history, "one of the species of a class of knowledge—also including geology, botany, zoology and geography."[19] Early anthropologists, she writes, "believed in the utilitarian potential of science" and directly contributed to colonial administration and tailored its findings "in support of various policies within Britain."[20] In the colonial empire, academic anthropologists saw a "field for the practical applicability of their knowledge."[21] In these years, strengthened by the belief that anthropological knowledge had a utility value for the empire, the practice of observing people in their "natural settings" settled as the central methodological principle of anthropological ethnography.

Even in the later years—as late as 2011—practical guides for social science research defined ethnographic research as "studying groups in *natural settings*."[22] An online reading guide on research methods starts with the observation that "anthropological research is very different from laboratory-based experimental research," and adds:

> The problem with studying people who are not brought up in a Western culture is that they do not have the same values or schema. Putting them into a laboratory could result in fear responses or other reactions that destroyed the experiment. Even a simple interview can be distorting when there are large cultural and linguistic gaps between researcher and the researched. The only solution, it seems, is to study such people in their *natural environment*.[23]

We could here cut to the scene of Silicon Valley "social physics" documented by Zuboff.[24] In a detailed exegesis, Zuboff shows that the "high priests" of data science serving data capitalists today had come up with the idea of "unobtrusive wearable sensors" measuring communication, voice tones, and body language that would "automatically measure individual and collective patterns of behavior, predict human behavior from unconscious social signals, identify social affinity among individuals working in the same time and enhance social interactions by providing feedback to users of our system." The crux of this social physics experiment was "reality mining" that developed from data gathered through "ubiquitous infrastructure of mobile phones and combine those data with new streams of information from . . . wearable behavioral monitors."[25] Zuboff goes on to argue that these experiments and "inventions" led Massachusetts Institute of Technology computer scientist Alex Pentland and his collaborators to launch a company called Sociometric Solutions, with an ambition to realize behaviorist B. F. Skinner's "longed-for instruments and methods" to study, predict, and modify people's behaviors. Zuboff documents that Pentland's collaborator Nathan Eagle told *Wired* magazine that the reality-mining study represented an "unprecedented data set about continuous human behavior" that would revolutionize the study of groups and offer new commercial applications. He was confident that "It is now possible to actively instrument human behavior to collect detailed data on various dimensions of social interaction." Zuboff elaborates:

> The authors signaled their aim to employ MacKay's cardinal rule of unobtrusive surveillance for effective monitoring of herds, flocks, and packs, acknowledging that the continuous pervasive collection of human behavioral data could succeed only when conducted outside the boundaries of human awareness, thus eliminating possible resistance, just as we saw at Facebook. As the researchers enthused, "Electronic sensors can be used to complement or replace human observers altogether, and while they may convey a slight sense of surveillance this perception is likely reduced as sensors get smaller and smaller, and consequently less obtrusive." They concluded that "minimally invasive ways to instrument human behavior" would enable comprehensive data collection in "*naturalistic settings.*"[26]

Deeper into this inquiry, a study titled "Tools for Studying Behavior and Technology in Natural Settings," published by a team of MIT researchers in 2002, promised "three tools for acquiring data about people, their behavior, and their use of technology in natural settings."[27] These included "context-aware experience sampling tool, a ubiquitous sensing system that detects environmental changes and an image-based experience sampling system."[28] Such efforts tried to find a technological fix for realizing the desire to map human behaviors onto predictable models, foremost by capturing them in "natural settings."

Looking from the lens of anthropology's formative years during which research was conceived primarily as capturing the primitives within observable natural settings secured by colonial conditions—

conditions that ensured that the observed peoples offered least (or no) resistance—it becomes clear that the ambitions of data capitalists (and technocratic research studies) resonate with a similar idea of capturing online users in the presumed unmediated state of nature, as these users express, dodge, confront, collude, buy, and aspire through millions of online posts and networks, leaving behind digital traces that can power up their digital doubles. What is more, electronic sensors attached to bodies or social media affordances would ensure that users were either unaware or offer least resistance. In other words, the aspired digital petri dish of observable behaviors is the replica of the colonial-anthropological petri dish that was aimed at capturing the native in a state of nature.

The logics of capture is now cast much wider, beyond the Others of Europe. One might speculate that the moral panic voiced by transatlantic scholarship around capitalization of life without limit has emerged precisely because it is no longer limited to the periphery but has squarely hit the gut of the metropole.

To be sure, there are significant differences between colonial knowledge practices of capture exemplified by anthropology and today's data practices. Data capitalists, for the most part, do not approach their consumers as exotic subjects that require a civilizational lift, nor have they employed direct forms of physical violence to extract resources, labor, and time. Recognizing the arrogance of imperial capture as forms of knowledge should not lead to trivializing the actual violence that accompanied historical colonialism. By extending the metaphor of colonialism into the Western metropole, the kind of analysis advanced around data colonialism runs the danger of losing sight of violence as the site of physical capture and containment of slave/subject in imperial colonialism and the capture of land in settler colonial contexts.[29] The later sections in this chapter will discuss the geopolitics of uneven digital dispossession and data relations that intersect with postcolonial fissures as ways to pin down such specific structures of domination. But the point we highlight here—that is, the striking parallels between colonial anthropological capture and social physics practiced by the high priests of the Silicon Valley—reveal that not only has there been a historical precedent to contemporary forms of digital capture, albeit in a vastly different technological setting, but also that there is a continuity in terms of the sensibilities and ambitions powering them. The imperial, utilitarian utopia to accumulate knowledge for what John Stuart Mill articulated as the "faith in progress" and the greater good of the nation and resources has reincarnated in the digital world, with AI emerging as the new paradigm to articulate these reinvigorated desires.[30]

Perhaps there are none as exemplary as Silicon Valley pundits such as Alex Pentland, who have expressively articulated their ambitions to subsume independent thought within the social physics models for the greater good that is believed to serve everyone's best interests. In these imaginations, inspired more by the models of behavioral psychology rather than the unacknowledged traces of colonial anthropology and its overlaps with experimental psychology we have discussed here, AI is a potent technology to generate the best decisions and realize the ambitions of prediction and modification of human behavior. AI's far-reaching capacities are assumed to emerge from a promised trajectory of technological advancement where the inherently neutral machine-learning model will only become more robust, training itself with more and more data—data gathered in the "natural settings"—in an onward march toward perfecting social physics.[31] There is thus a shared logic of capture intrinsic to colonial logics of knowledge and the ambitions powering AI as a means for data gathering and analysis.

Algorithmic Racism

While data gathering in the digital age replicates the imperial logic of capture, the practices of classifying, sorting, ranking, predicting, and processing data have not affected everyone uniformly in a presumed post-political state of brute oppression. Building on the foundational arguments that raciality involves both signification and materiality, recent studies have shown that the materialities and politics of AI technologies reproduce racialized processes. The inputs of labeling, which is still done by people, routinely inject the machine with racialized categorizations of the world, arguably beyond the intentions of coders and annotators. As Ed Finn has emphasized, there is no such thing as "just code."[32] Algorithms are always the product of social, technical, and political decisions and negotiations that occur throughout their development and implementation.[33] Challenging the assumption that AI can be a solution to human bias, Constance de Saint Laurent has argued that "since choosing what information is relevant in taking a decision is never neutral . . . AI can only learn to reproduce existing classifications and thus can only be as fair as humans have been in the past."[34] Tarleton Gillespie clarifies further that data always need to be "collected, readied" and "sometimes excluded and demoted" before an algorithm can process them.[35] "Being part of databases means more than simply belonging to a collection of data," elaborates Taina Bucher. "It means being part of an ordered space, encoded according to a common scheme."[36] Providing further analytical clarity, Bucher cites Philipp Vannini to suggest that algorithms are not just codes but rather "hybrid assemblages with diffused personhood and relational agency."[37]

These human agencies and assemblages, we reemphasize, are shaped by the longer historical processes that derived racial power from the material conditions and logics of colonialism. In his incisive decolonial critique of the foundations of computing and information systems, Syed Mustafa Ali has highlighted the "persistence of certain 'sedimented' colonial ways of knowing and being—that is, colonial epistemology and ontology—based on systems of categorization, classification, and taxonomization and the ways that these are manifested in practices, artifacts, and technologies [of modern computing]."[38] In relation to commercial social media companies and search engines, Ruha Benjamin has demonstrated that while tech companies are busy designing marketing campaigns that showcase Black celebrities to "represent AI as empowering, forward-thinking, cool—the anti-thesis of anti-Black discrimination," precisely through these "positive" portrayals and opaque AI decisions, "tech developers, like their marketing counterparts, are encoding race, ethnicity and gender as immutable characteristics that can be measured, bought, and sold."[39] In her book *Algorithms of Oppression: How Search Engines Reinforce Racism*, Safiya Noble, focusing on Google's monopoly over search engines and information infrastructure, has shown that coders' decisions within commercial algorithm development have reinforced discriminatory social relations and racial profiling.[40] Crucially, this architecture of power, to follow Ruha Benjamin, is not only a "top-down story of powerful tech companies imposing coded inequity onto an innocent public. This is also about how we (click) submit, because of all that we seem to gain by having our choices and behaviors tracked, predicted, and racialized."[41] The tech industry has banked on and stirred this palate of consumer 'choices," as algorithmic sorting continues to toy with various permutations of categories and variables.

Critical inquiries have called into question technocentric assumptions about the neutrality of AI systems as they unfold not only within but beyond the tech spaces, revealing how governance practices of state welfare decisions to state surveillance are distorted by or draw on racialized categorizations embedded within the AI systems. Such technologies that range from facial recognition software to credit-worthiness indices have cemented a new infrastructure for control and disciplining of spaces and bodies while also impacting access to critical resources and basic conditions for safety and survival. In their study on "datafication and discrimination," Koen Leurs and Tamara Shepherd have documented the ways in which governments have used "automated social sorting" to surveil and control "undesired migrants" at the borders:

> For those privileged subjects carrying desirable passports, e-borders and iris scans sustain liquid flow across borders and planetary nomadic mobility as an effortless normality. By contrast, undesired subjects have to provide fingerprints—a genre of biometric data with a long history of criminal connotations—to be cross-referenced among a host of other identifiers in data-based risk calculations.[42]

For refugees and asylum seekers, welfare, protection, and the very prospect of entering safer places hinge on agreeing to gathering data about them, a process over which they have no say or little control. Sandra Ponzanesi elaborates further:

> While systems of measurement and classification are not a recent phenomenon (think of physiognomy, anthropometry, and phrenology), they have now become commonplace and give cause for serious concern when applied on a mass scale, without agential choice or clear consent, to vulnerable subjects such as refugees and asylum seekers, who have no control over how their data are stored, safeguarded, and shared.[43]

In such data-gathering and surveillance practices, refugees, asylum seekers, and minoritized publics are not only observed but also evaluated through racialized categories of automated systems. Such categories have emerged from oppressive state policies or are embedded as opaque classifications that draw in longstanding prejudices with little critical scrutiny. In her influential work, Simone Browne shows how digitally enabled surveillance practices in North America are shaped by the long history of racial formation and by the "methods of policing black life" in the "enduring archive of transatlantic slavery and its afterlife."[44] Although racialization processes and racial logics underpinning the state-market nexus and its latest artefact, AI, have received much attention in the US and European contexts—vast and valuable scholarship that we do not intend to summarize here—far less attention has gone into documenting the geopolitics of data capture in terms of the exploitation of uneven data-protection regimes in different parts of the world or the spatial politics of digital labor that runs the engines of data capture, including arrangements that dispossess workers in the Global South from the value they generate for the global tech companies.[45] While only signaling to the vast body of scholarship on algorithmic bias and critical race studies in this section, we hone in on one particular strand of this extractive and exploitative economy: forms of labor arrangement that digital capitalists have raised to keep the data pipeline running. Rather than approaching the pipeline as a problem of facilitating more data generation (which constitutes a significant part of the logics of data capture), we somewhat invert the focus to draw attention to the scum that gets removed from the pipeline—the kind of scavenging work that is relegated to the lowest rungs banished from caste society in India, and now in the global hierarchy of digital labor, to the Global South or the peripheralized corners of the metropole. These arrangements, to follow Sareeta Amrute's argument, reveal the overt and "latent correlations between race and labor" and a racialized hierarchy of labor that "distribute[s] risk unevenly and shape the lives of populations across the globe."[46] Specifically in relation to the global tech industry, she argues that racialized global labor is shaped by a broader "sorting of race in tech [that] knits the industry together across nations by creating the human-technical units it needs to function, from labor force, to clients, to markets."[47] Building on these insights and picking up the strands from the previous chapter on extreme speech, we inquire into online extreme speech moderation as a specific site that brings into sharp view the colonial encoding of data capture.

Differentiated Exploitation

"I found myself in a factory world as part of a global digital proletariat," wrote Burcu Gültekin Punsmann, a former employee of a content moderating contractor for Facebook in Berlin, in a feature story published by a major German newspaper in 2018. "I was part of a cohort of more than 700 people, in a closed environment with no communication with the outside world," she recounted. "My productive time and breaks were precisely calculated, I was stuck to my workstation, could only leave the production line for several minutes. I don't know whether we were producing anything, but I got the sense that we were helping to keep a multi-billion [dollar] industry running."[48]

Punsmann's article went on to describe, in a succinct prose of hard facts and candid reflections, the stressful three months she spent inside Arvato, a local company that was contracted by Facebook for online content moderation. Assigned to the 'Turkish market'—that is, the task of moderating content flowing from Turkey—she saw her monitor quickly filling with continuous "reports" (instances of violations of Facebook community standards reported by users) that required her decision to remove or retain the content. She estimated that globally, there were on average 6.5 million reports per week that continued "seven days a week with almost no interruption." After three months, Punsmann, a young mother, found it difficult to strike the work-life balance or keep her mind calm. Although she quit the job shortly after, she could see why the company still found people who were ready to take up the arduous task despite the hardships. "The system is based on migrant and young workforce," she pointed out, "and [it is] located in a city with draining [sic] well-educated multilingual cheap labor all over the world." The average age of her colleagues was twenty-eight years. She noticed that all her colleagues were migrants.

In 2019, Casey Newton, journalist at the *Verge*, exposed the "secret lives of Facebook moderators" by publishing the traumatic experiences of US-based content moderators employed by Cognizant, which offered content moderation services to Facebook. He reported:

> Collectively, the employees described a workplace that is perpetually teetering on the brink of chaos. It is an environment where workers cope by telling dark jokes about committing suicide, then smoke weed during breaks to numb their emotions. It's a place where employees can be fired for making just a few errors a week—and where those who remain live in fear of the former colleagues who return seeking vengeance.[49]

Before these investigative and personal reports became public, in 2014, *Wired* journalist Adrian Chen had drawn attention to the "soul-crushing world of content moderation, where low-wage laborers soak up the worst of humanity and keep it off . . . [the] Facebook feed."[50] His findings were based on extensive investigative reporting about the tech industry's outsourced content moderation sweatshops located in the Philippines. The same report cited a former chief security officer of MySpace who estimated that "the number of content moderators scrubbing the world's social media sites, mobile apps, and cloud storage services runs to 'well over 100,000'—that is, about twice the total head count of Google and nearly 14 times that of Facebook."[51]

In 2018, Mark Zuckerberg announced that by the end of the year, the company would have twenty thousand people working on content moderation. However, in 2020, *MIT Technology Review* reported that Facebook had fifteen thousand content moderators. A large majority of these moderators, or "mods" as they came to be called, were not full-time employees of the company. "The whole function of content moderation," reported *MIT Technology Review*, "is farmed out to third-party vendors, who employ temporary workers on precarious contracts at over 20 sites worldwide."[52] A study published by the NYU Stern Centre for Business and Human Rights in 2020 estimated the number of content moderators working for big tech firms: "15,000 workers, majority of those employed by third-party vendors, moderate Facebook and Instagram; 10,000 moderators moderate YouTube and other Google products; Twitter has 1,500 moderators."[53] Confirming media investigations, the report noted that content moderation has been outsourced to third-party vendors such as "Cognizant, Genpact, Accenture, Majorel, Competence Call Center, etc. in the Philippines, India, Ireland, Portugal, Spain, Germany, Latvia and Kenya."[54]

The tech industry has framed outsourcing of speech moderation to countries such as Turkey, the Philippines, Mexico and India as a scaling strategy, but the drive for cost benefits can hardly be overlooked.[55] Newton, for instance, quoted Facebook's vice president of operations, who claimed in a blog post that "the use of contract labor allowed Facebook to 'scale globally'—to have content moderators working around the clock, evaluating posts in more than 50 languages, at more than 20 sites around the world." Newton pointed to the cost arbitration logic that lurks behind scaling ambitions:

> The use of contract labor also has a practical benefit for Facebook: it is radically cheaper. The median Facebook employee earns $240,000 annually in salary, bonuses, and stock options. A content moderator working for Cognizant in Arizona, on the other hand, will earn just $28,800 per year. The arrangement helps Facebook maintain a high profit margin. In its most recent quarter, the company earned $6.9 billion in profits, on $16.9 billion in revenue. And while Zuckerberg had warned investors that Facebook's investment in security would reduce the company's profitability, profits were up 61 percent over the previous year.[56]

Joining media reports and the acclaimed documentary film *Cleaners*, directed by Hans Block and Moritz Risewieck, which have exposed various facets of the shadow and outsourcing industry of digital cleaning, a small number of academic studies have documented the underside of takedowns and content removal. Politically vested interests within specific national and regional polities that control the shadow industry play an important role, but the kind and conditions of labor enlisted through exploitative arrangements of multinational social media companies cut across the specificities of regional political scenarios. In a pioneering study on digital disinformation in the Philippines, Jonathan Ong and Jason Cabanes found that evidence about outsourced "digital sweatshop" political work was hard to gather.[57] However, they have exposed the precarious labor conditions of disinformation workers who serve political clients by engaging in project-based digital work characterized by race-to-the-bottom work arrangements.[58] They further note that casual workers are forced to cope with stressful work on their own, "in the absence of clear guidelines, psychosocial support systems, or remuneration."[59] In a recent study on commercial content moderators, Sarah Roberts has shown that workers who sift online content for violation of community standards and illegal content for Silicon Valley corporations are made invisible and forced to operate under opaque conditions of work.[60] Commercial content moderators operating in outsourcing destinations such as the Philippines and India are not only low paid but also rendered as low-status workers within the hierarchies of global corporations, partly since Silicon Valley avoids talking about "distasteful" work that has not yet found a "full-on computational solution."[61] The NYU Stern report made a similar observation that major social media companies "have marginalized the people who do this work."[62] Forbes did a quick calculation and pointed out that "Facebook employs about 15,000 content moderators directly or indirectly. If they have three million posts to moderate each day, that's 200 per person: 25 each and every hour in an eight-hour shift. That's under 150 seconds to decide if a post meets or violates community standards."[63] Such observations have sharpened the significance of personal accounts of content moderators like Punsmann, who precisely recalled that "at the end of the ramp-up process, a moderator should handle approximately 1300 reports every day which let him/her in average only a few seconds to reach a decision for each report. The intellectually challenging task tends to become an automated action almost a reaction. Repetition triggers a sense of frustration and alienation."[64] Echoing a similar appraisal, content moderators based in India have highlighted hyper-accelerated work routines that link compensations and incentives to calculated metrices of work performance indicators: "Some of the mods view as many as 6000 images over the course of a workday," revealed a moderator. "The average time to make a judgment call: 4.5 seconds. . . . Sania [pseudonymized content moderator] reviews 5700–6000 images per day. She can take longer than 4.5 seconds if required but at the risk of not meeting her targets, which in turn reduces her efficiency."[65]

Documenting several such accounts that have emerged from diverse destinations of outsourced, underpaid, and contracted work, the NYU

Stern report called for ending outsourcing, urging Facebook to provide secure employment to content moderators and to bring content moderation practices under the oversight of experienced executives. Following mounting public pressure, Facebook agreed in principle in May 2020 to "pay US$52 million to compensate current and former content moderators who developed mental health issues on the job."[66] However, media reports in countries like India, which houses several outsourcing centers for the global tech companies, have pointed out that the lawsuit covered only people who have worked for Facebook through third-party vendors in the US (estimated to be 11,250 people from 2015 to 2020), leaving out vendors dispersed around the globe from this corporate policy cover.[67] And while social media giants such as Facebook and YouTube have regularly issued public statements to affirm their commitment to protecting content moderators from psychological stress—even while faltering on delivering on such promises—Indian media reports have highlighted that content moderators working for smaller platforms such as TikTok, LIKEE, and Bigo Live that are newly popular for their short and live video sharing do not have the "luxuries like counsellors."[68]

As the global asymmetries in the manual labor for extreme speech moderation bears evidence, digital capitalism has continued and has amplified the logics of flexible accumulation and transnational commodification of information, processes that began when the post-industrial Western economy looked to the promise of spatially flexible knowledge services, and spatial disaggregation of business became a key strategy for capital mobility and capital fluidity.[69] Content moderation arrangements follow two decades of consolidating outsourcing work as the quintessence of networked flexible accumulation powered by digitalization. This kind of work ranged from pink-collar jobs such as those at call centers to low-level technology jobs such as business process outsourcing (BPO) that were shipped to low-cost destinations in the Global South, placing demands on cognitive, emotional, and cultural labor on unequal terms.[70] The information and communication technologies facilitated the vertical disintegration of the production process within large companies, which was reaggregated through dispersed global production centers providing "dematerialized" or "textualized" work.[71] In an insightful anthropological study of the IT outsourcing and call center industry in India, Carol Upadhya showed how in the 1990s, India became a "major outpost of the global economy," providing economic and cultural opportunities for upward mobility for workers employed in the new economy sectors while also normalizing new workplace precarities often glossed by industry executives as "voluntary" and "involuntary attrition."[72] Closely following the success of this outsourcing industry, which was also highly vulnerable to the vicissitudes of the "global commodity chains of service provision," content moderation emerged as a new area for the BPO industry that prided itself on its process-oriented professionalism, a key value proposition in the global marketplace. In a detailed report published in 2020, Indian newspaper *LiveMint* highlighted that "Content moderation is arguably the most important task that BPOs in India perform today, fulfilling outsourced contracts for social media giants ranging from Facebook and TikTok to LIKEE and Bigo Live, among others."[73]

On the one hand, because of the territorializing effects of content moderation that require linguistic competence and knowledge of local cultures, global tech corporations have been forced to engage local companies, including those located at the global metropolises with migrant and casual labor, rather than shipping them away to the lowest possible cost destination. On the other hand, as AI-assisted automations and cultural training become more widespread for economically powerful languages, these jobs are likely to be moved back to dispersed locations and the lowest bidders who provide far fewer safeguards for workers in terms of contractual and working conditions. As *Wired* magazine reported, "Many companies employ a two-tiered moderation system, where the most basic moderation is outsourced abroad while more complex screening, which requires greater cultural familiarity, is done domestically."[74] Even when the jobs are retained within economically advanced countries, outsourcing labor is drawn from precarious and casualized migrant workers in the big cities, as the Berlin case bears out.

Shoshana Zuboff describes global companies that rely on dispersed outsourcing arrangements as "hyperscale firms" and points out that such firms have become "emblematic of modern digital capitalism."[75] She has documented that in 2017, "24 hyperscale firms operated 320 data centers with anywhere between thousands and millions of servers (Google and Facebook were among the largest) . . . with industry concentration, and monopoly."[76] Rejecting industry arguments about efficiency, she argues that digital capitalists who "operate at hyperscale or outsource to hyper-scale operations dramatically diminish any reliance on their societies as sources of employees," except when chasing highly skilled data science labor in their own countries.[77] At the same time, she nostalgically recon-structs the lost "reciprocity" between capitalism and communities in the earlier phase of Fordist capitalism, since they at least promised jobs to the local populations. Neither her criticism of industry concentration nor the surprising nostalgia for the reciprocity of Fordist capitalism sufficiently documents the vastly uneven ways in which de-territorialized digital labor operates in the present day. As Andrew Ross, Tiziana Terranova, and others have documented, digital labor is dispersed and decentralized, often on highly unequal terms and conditions.[78] If "forced labor and labor camps were the engine that ran European capitalism," digital capitalism today relies on underpaid labor in the digital assembly lines and remote call centers, the grey zones of the clickbait industry, as well as the disposal of toxic e-waste chemicals and metals in non-Western countries, rais-ing concerns over the health hazards of rapid cycles of market-induced technological obsolescence and the dangers of seeing internet-related technology as ecologically benign.[79] For instance, Orish Ebere Orisakwe and colleagues have observed that "large quantities of e-waste end up dumped in low income countries, where second-hand materials come mixed with broken parts," leading to massive e-waste recycling in Afri-can countries posing a "serious public health threat."[80] Highlighting the human/subhuman distinction of the European Enlightenment project that underpins the very conception of computing, Syed Mustafa Ali inti-mates that "the push to establish a global Internet of Things is historically founded upon a prior Internet of Things. . . . the international network of land, resources, and enslaved humans as objects (inhabitants of Fanon's 'zone of nonbeing') situated in a colonized periphery constituted by colo-nizing human subjects situated in the 'core.'"[81]

Digital capitalism's exploitation of the Global South and peripheral-ized Souths in the Global North both as destinations for low-cost and under-protected labor, e-wastelands, and ambitious movement toward the internet of things follows from histories of non-waged, casualized, indentured, and surplus populations constituted through colonial dif-ferentiation. On casualized tech labor—a particular strand of differentia-tion in this global hierarchy—Sareeta Amrute observes that racialized tech labor in the digital capitalist order is "tied to the long history of creating migrant casual workers in colonial and later periods where casual labor was used to replace slave labor on colonial plantations in the British Empire, and as quick labor to reconstructed bombed-out German cities through the guest worker program."[82] As Arun Kundnani has argued, "Differentiation of workforce as much as homogenization can be derived from capitalism's core dynamics," which refutes the Marxist orthodox anticipation that capitalism will create a universal proletariat subject.[83] Recognizing the enduring structures of coloniality in the global hierarchies of labor is also the means to imagine a decolonial thinking around digital labor and to bring to question the varied strategies of expropriation and exploitation that have served as critical elements of market inflected technological innovation and obsolesce. Pushing for a "decolonial turn" in digital labor studies, Antonio Casilli has stressed that "the material dimension of the manufacturing of data, services, and content is decisive to establish continuities between structural elements of 'immaterial' digital labor and the everyday working conditions of multitudes of nameless click farmers, content moderators, and offshore gig workers."[84] Building on Richard Maxwell's work, he has highlighted how the "occupational opportunities of these subjects moved from traditional factory, agricultural, and extraction work to vulnerable self-employment and internet-mediated precarious on-demand jobs."[85] Digital labor—including content moderation labor—reflects and augments such forms of differentiated exploitation.

Here, we might open up another related area of differentiated exploitation that concerns the uneven allocation of corporate resources for hate-speech moderation globally. Facebook's hate-speech moderation practice offers a telling example. The company has consistently evaded demands for transparency around resources allocated to detect and remove extreme speech content, while also keeping the principles guiding its newly instituted oversights board away from thorough academic scrutiny. If lack of corporate transparency in institutional measures calls for sustained regulatory intervention, the vast disparities and discrepancies in how social media companies are moderating extreme speech in different parts of the world stress the need for critical examination since such arrangements directly impact what is allowed, amplified, curated, or blocked in the digital pipeline.

In a detailed news report, *Time* magazine revealed that Facebook increasingly relies on AI to detect and remove hate speech, but machine learning competency is currently limited to a handful of languages.[86] In the third quarter of 2019, Facebook claimed that it removed seven million instances of hate speech, an increase of 59 percent over the previous quarter. Over 80 percent was detected by AI. In the report, journalist Billy Perrigo points out that this seemingly impressive figure "conceals a structural problem: not all hate speech is treated equally." This gap has emerged because Facebook's AI systems are not trained equally for all the languages spoken in the world. Citing the hate campaign by the Assamese-speaking Hindu majority against the Bengali-speaking Muslim minority in Assam in India, Perrigo shows how messages that described Bengali Muslims as "parasites," "rats," and "rapists" and viewed at least 5.4 million times were not picked up by Facebook, because it did not have an algorithm to detect hate speech in Assamese.[87]

In an investigative report, human rights advocacy group Avaaz highlighted the gravity of the problem: "In the Assamese context, the minorities most directly targeted by hate speech on Facebook often lack online access or the understanding of how to navigate Facebook's flagging tools. No one else is reporting it for them either."[88] A senior campaigner at Avaaz cited in the *Time* report described this as a "huge blind spot" of Facebook. In response to a global outcry about the Myanmar crisis, Facebook expanded its resources and increased the number of Burmese language speaking human moderators to contain the online hate campaign against the minority Rohingya Muslims.[89] However, efforts to close the "blind spots" around the globe have been neither uniform nor transparent. Facebook's algorithm is better equipped to handle the content in English, Spanish, and Mandarin, allowing the company to respond to the spread of racial or religious hatred more efficiently within developed countries and large economies. The *Time* report points out that "languages spoken by minorities are the hardest-hit by this disparity."

Turning the focus on Ahmaric spoken in Ethiopia as an example of one such underrepresented language, computer scientists Zewdie Mossie and Jenq Haur Wang have highlighted that "apart from the common use of machine learning, majority of the detection tasks have focused on English tweets because of the availability of English corpora and the widespread use of the language. However, the available English corpora do not cover every possible context of offensive and hate speech. Therefore, offensive and hate speech detection have suffered setbacks in unpopular contexts like [the] South Africa domain."[90] They have further noted that it is difficult to protect ethnic groups from online hate speech whose languages have fewer computational resources because artificial neural networks need annotated training data for learning speech patterns.

The NYU Stern report voiced a similar concern that "Facebook's failure to ensure adequate moderation for non-Western countries has resulted in its platforms, including WhatsApp . . . [becoming] vehicles to incite hatred and in some instances, violence." In a report on hate speech and disinformation in India, advocacy group Equality Labs warned that "an estimated 350 million+ Indian caste, religious, gender and queer minorities [are] at risk from online hate speech in India."[91] The group complained that Facebook did not act on several instances of "reporting" objectionable content. Based on a set of Facebook's internal documents leaked by a whistleblower (which came to be called "The Facebook Papers"), the *New York Times* reported in October 2021 that "eighty-seven percent of the company's global budget for time spent on classifying misinformation is earmarked for the United States, while only 13 percent is set aside for the rest of the world—even though North American users make up only 10 percent of the social network's daily active users."[92] While the company spokesperson claimed that the "figures were incomplete and don't include the company's third party fact-checking partners, most of whom are outside the United States," the very lack of transparency around the allocation of resources and the outsourced arrangements around "third party partners" signal the severely skewed structures of content moderation inside global corporations.[93]

While outsourced labor and wide disparities in hate-speech moderation provide two illustrative, if limited, cases for the differentiated nature of exploitation in digital capitalism, data extraction practices of social media companies that seek to take advantage of the disparate privacy regimes globally have prompted a recent United Nations report cautioning that "developing countries risk becoming mere providers of raw data, while having to pay for the digital intelligence generated using their data."[94] Data extractivism as the new social order shaped by longer historical processes of colonialism has thus led to highly uneven distribution of the costs and consequences of data-as-dispossession. Data regimes not only depend on and perpetuate extractive labor practices, but through data hungry digital communicative practices around extreme speech, they have also cocreated the material conditions for exclusionary political cultures, as we have argued in the earlier chapter.

Analysis of labor and data extraction practices provides a critical lens to examine the political economy of global digital capitalism, but the full force of a decolonial critique follows when digital political economies are situated in relation to the social-political structures of domination shaped by colonial histories. What then are the implications when digital data regimes intersect with postcolonial fissures shaped by the colonial rule of difference? In the next section, we turn to an ethnographic case study from India to open this critical window.

Data Relations and Postcolonial Fault Lines

In December 2019, the Indian government amended the Citizenship Act of 1955, establishing religion, for the very first time, as a criterion for citizenship under Indian law. The Citizenship (Amendment) Act (CAA) of 2019 provides a legal path to citizenship for persecuted religious minorities that include Hindus, Buddhists, Jains, Sikhs, Parsis, and Christians who migrated to India from the neighboring countries of Pakistan, Bangladesh, and Afghanistan (before 2014). The act conspicuously omits Muslim minorities from the list. In August 2021, following the Taliban's takeover of Afghanistan, the government promised to prioritize taking in Hindu and Sikh refugees from the embattled country, but by leaving out Muslims from the visa priority program, the announcement drew criticism for echoing the discriminatory premise of the controversial CAA legislation.[95]

A policy move related to the CAA has sought to enforce compulsory registration for all Indian citizens through the National Register of Citizenship (NRC), placing demands on Indian residents to prove their citizenship with identity documents. Insufficient documentation entails the threat of deportation. Since the CAA extends the pathway for citizenship only to non-Muslim minorities, the NRC exercise, if fully implemented, would effectively target millions of undocumented Muslim families in India with the threat of statelessness, while also leading to a chaotic penetration of the state into the everyday existence of all others. The implementation of the proposed NRC relies on the state digital infrastructure of enumeration and identification facilitated by related policies of biometric identification for all Indian citizens.[96]

Such governmental policies replicate the colonial practices of capturing populations through enumeration and tracking, even as the state reasoning has emphasized greater efficiency in welfare delivery and protection of national borders from illegal immigration as grounds for implementing such measures. The controversial legislations of CAA and NRC sparked wide protests in India and the diaspora, driving students, women, children, non-residential Indians, public intellectuals, and professionals into the streets and onto social media to demand immediate withdrawal of the controversial legislation.

As protest videos circulated on social media, the ruling power aimed to redirect online circulations in favor of the CAA and NRC policies and to override criticism. Aside from large social media platforms such as Facebook, whose public policy head was later found to be directing her employees with internal memos to align their content moderation decisions with the specific interests of the ruling party, news media reports highlighted how the China based video sharing platforms such as TikTok with an estimated 119 million users (and banned since 2020 in India) and Bigo Live with over 200 million users in India, were also given instructions to manage and moderate the content flowing through their channels.[97] As Indian newspaper *LiveMint* reported, "When the protests against the Citizenship Amendment Act (CAA) first began in India in December 2019, moderators at Bigo Live were asked to 'reduce visibility' of videos involving [the] protest. Eventually, the platform told its moderators to ban all content around the protests altogether. It instantly changed what 200 million Indians could see or perceive."[98]

In a detailed report, *LiveMint* uncovered Bigo Live's content moderation operations, spotlighting "a handful" of moderators who worked out of the company's office in Gurugram, a major IT and BPO outsourcing hub in Northern India.[99] A moderator for Bigo Live, cited in the report, revealed that the company did not "allow content which includes topless men, people smoking on the platform etc. For political content, the tolerance is even lower. If the government says a Shaheen Bagh [anti-

CAA] protest has to be banned, it will be banned." Political scientist Buddhadeb Halder revealed that the ruling party's IT cells spent huge sums of money on social media campaigns (Facebook advertisements), missed-call campaigns, and a nationwide awareness campaign (Jan Jagran Abhiyan), including clickbait methods, "to generate public support in favor of CAA."[100]

Closely following concerted actions to dissipate CAA protest messages circulating online, the COVID-19 pandemic sparked a misinformation and disinformation campaign targeted at Muslim minorities in India, which stood out as a distinct strand in a shifting mix of theories ranging from Indigenous medicine as an absolute cure to COVID-19 to false news about the period of lockdowns during different waves of the pandemic. To contain the spread of COVID-19 during the first wave, the Indian government announced a complete lockdown in March 2020. The hastily announced and ill-prepared rollout of the lockdown led to thousands of migrant laborers stranded in horrific conditions when the police stopped them from returning to their villages. Small businesses were shut down, and millions were confined to their homes and exposed to police brutality even when they stepped out for essentials. The crisis was compounded by Islamophobic messages on social media that peddled rumors, conspiracy theories, and lies about Indian Muslim groups waging a "Coronajihad" against the country. One of the targets of Islamophobic outrage was Tablighi Jamaat, a Muslim religious organization, whose members had congregated for a religious meet in Nizamuddin near Delhi on March 13–15, 2020. Legal advocacy organization Article 14 documented the "22 days of fake-news frenzy" sparked by profiling Muslim minorities "cascading into hate speech and crimes against Muslims."[101] Despite very low rates of testing that made contact tracing difficult or even impossible, the Tablighi meet was framed as a "major national Covid-19 source." "Once the profiling was done," Article 14 reported, "a tsunami of fake news followed." A social media video on the coronavirus showed an unrelated video of Muslims licking utensils and claimed that Muslims were licking utensils to deliberately spread the virus.[102] In another video posted on Facebook, a Sufi ritual was portrayed as Muslims sneezing in unison to spread the virus in India. Debunked later by fact-checkers, this video was viewed more than twenty-four thousand times.[103] Article

14 described the Islamophobic fake-news cycle as mutually reinforced remediation across media forms:

> The fake-news cycle was clear: print and television media and social media were feeding off each other. Social-media users picked manipulated, exaggerated or fake news, spun it further, sometimes; in turn, the media picked up such posts and spun them as news.

Efforts to contain online discourse as evidenced during the anti-CAA/NRC protests and online campaigns against Muslim minorities during the pandemic illustrate the ways in which online speech moderation practices of social media companies that we highlighted in the previous section comingle with online propaganda and discursive strategies of control adopted by a majoritarian regime, even as several other political parties have scrambled to secure their voices and tactics to gain traction online.

In a multiyear ethnographic study, Sahana has shown that online nationalist sentiments and allegiances have emerged from the multifarious activities of a dispersed network of Hindu nationalist volunteers, who are known in popular media as internet Hindus, and an organized top-down propaganda structure from the ruling party that involves social media management strategies of its "official IT cell" and paid election campaigns run by professional data science and advertising teams.[104] Competing with other political parties who mobilize similar tactics, the party's "front stage," comprising the official IT wing, feeds and relies on an "unofficial" substratum run by contractors who gather and analyze social media data, ramp up the party's ideological line through gray practices of planted content, and subcontract online publicity and surveillance work to a sundry mix of clickbait brokers. These practices that both reflect and augment the official policies of the ruling regime have transformed the digital into a formidable frontier for religious nationalist politics.

From a historical point of view, the significance of religion—as forms of moral discourse, structures of community and categories for statecraft—evolved in the context of colonial governmentality and orientalist knowledge production that universalized the category of religion by bringing heterogeneous traditions under the rubric of "Hinduism" and "Islam" in South Asia.[105] Census and other modern practices of the colonial state deepened religion as a political identity, which was not always antithetical to national belonging.[106] Among other things, religion provided the ideological means for nationalist fighters to resist colonial rule, spawning new religious-political institutions led by Hindus and Muslims, at a time when participation in colonial political institutions was denied to the local populations. Leading up to the partition of British India, this colonial historical moment created the enumerable categories of majority/minority, in turn inscribing Hindus, Muslims, and other religious groups as majorities or minorities within the newly created nations of India and Pakistan.[107] In other words, the nation-state form that emerged from the colonial/modern matrix instituted the majority/minority distinction as a form of power, imbuing religious groups with specific kinds of political capital (or lack thereof) and frames for affective attachments to the nation that simultaneously drew an insider/outsider paradigm (a point we have highlighted in the "Extreme" chapter).[108] Differentiated exploitation of data relations in these cases has reached toxic levels precisely because of their intersection with racially coded distinctions between religious groups and the majority/minority difference sanctioned by the nation state form.

Capture and Crevices

A brief discussion of religious majoritarian politics in India holds a mirror to the tyranny of digital data regime when it intersects with postcolonial fault lines. What is seen in these contexts is a dangerous interweaving of racialized religious politics with the data infrastructure of extreme speech, biometrics, and digital surveillance. In an overview of scholarship on digital surveillance, Claudia Aradau and Tobias Blanke show how critical studies on surveillance practices under repressive regimes in diverse national or regional contexts have made similar observations:

> Critical analyses of algorithmic security and digital surveillance have . . . focused on techniques and devices that produce 'data doubles' through data patterns and associations. These have emphasised the work and profiling and normalization that produce categories of 'undesirables' and

risky selves to be monitored, corrected, or excluded based on the anticipation of future behaviours, while 'normal' citizens are integrated within
the flows of capital.[109]

Repressive data regimes thus underwrite and unfold within relations
of exclusion and exploitation canonized by colonial power in the nation state form, now brutally perpetuated by regimes at different levels—
global, national, regional, and local. China's surveillance practices on its
own citizens have led to the recognition that both within the nation-
states and on geopolitical levels, the extraction of data for commercial
and political purposes has reinvigorated colonial practices of surveillance and exploitation of land, resources, and bodies.[110] In a detailed
investigation of China's application of behavior-recognition technologies, British digital rights watchdog Article 19 has shown that behavior
recognition applications are based on the controversial claims of American psychologist Paul Ekman's "basic emotion theory" formulated in the
1960s.[111] AI-powered technologies that claim to recognize emotions are
deployed to assess a wide range of critical areas: credit worthiness and
criminal behavior, as well as student attentiveness inside the classroom.
The emotion recognition market, they conclude, are "built on the basic
assumptions about emotional expression . . . [as independent of human
perception and cultural context] . . . despite these assumptions being
rooted in dubious scientific studies and longer history of discredited and
racist pseudoscience."[112] The turmoil, as Catherine Walsh and Walter
Mignolo convincingly argue, has thus erupted at different levels, across
different epicenters, and along different axes of difference:

> By the 1990s, decolonization's failure in most nations had become clear;
> with state in the hands of minority elites, the patterns of colonial power
> continued both internally (i.e., internal colonialism) and with relation to
> global structures. . . . The turmoil is now at once domestic, transnational,
> interstate, and global.[113]

As we pointed out in the "Campus" chapter, these developments related to digital transformations reveal the durability of the world systems, ideologies, and fantasies that colonial and imperial conquest built
while laying the grounds for new mechanisms of differentiated exploita-

tion and dispossession. In this chapter, we have explored these mechanisms by highlighting digital data-gathering practices, digital labor in extreme speech moderation, and intersections between data relations and postcolonial fault lines.[114] The material and political consequences of these developments continue to be felt in the Global South and among the racialized Other in the metropole. Precisely for this reason, the material conditions of data relations have also been recognized as critical resources for resistance and reimagination. For instance, Indigenous communities in Oceania, the US, and Canada have pushed for sovereign rights not only to the lands but also to the airwaves and airspace that are critical to the telecommunications infrastructure.[115] As Marisa Elana Duarte has discussed in her illuminating thesis on network sovereignty, Indigenous communities and open-technology organizations in the US and Canada have advocated for open high-speed internet that could be harnessed for Indigenous rights, while also articulating sovereign rights to aerial and underground fiber-optic cables and wireless spectrum.[116]

Similar movements have gained pace among the Indigenous islander communities in Oceania, as they have mobilized efforts to establish community-based broadband networks that can challenge and counter restrictive and subsidized telecommunications monopolies. Duarte also observes that digital informational infrastructure has been critical for native organizations to craft self-governance and decolonization movements, revealing how the historical forms of material-infrastructural inequalities have also been brought to question with greater access to internet technologies and the potentiality of online informational flows to unsettle hierarchies and structures of dispossession. Efforts to cut through the capture, in other words, have pushed for alternative visions of the internet and have used the very digital means that are opened by the market to spread the data net as widely and ramp up data creation from as many users as possible. In the next chapter, we dive deeper into a specific strand in a vast canvas of contestation—efforts that have carved out crevices in the machinery of capture by attempting to upturn the logics of colonial data relations toward equitable knowledge relations.

4

Knowledge/Citation

The Production and Curation of Counter-Knowledge

I am an Africa-based scholar who has chosen to publish
most of my thinking on queerness and especially queer Africa on a publicly available blog as an ethical and political act
that refuses academic gatekeeping as the price one must pay
to be legitimized as a scholar.
—Keguro Macharia

In 2016, Keguro Macharia wrote a piece for *GLQ* that he titled "On
Being Area Studied: A Litany of Complaint." Pushing back on the
endurance of Cold War–era studies formations that delimit knowledge to prescribed geographies, Eurocentric renderings of queer
life, and the cloistered "behind the paywall" structures of academia,
Macharia introduced his readers to his blog, *Gukira*, as another means
to think with others and share one's ideas. Macharia describes the
blog as an intellectual space for fugitive thinking and blogging as an
"ethical and political act that refuses academic gatekeeping."[1] Macharia is not alone.

   In the last decade, there has been an influx of online knowledge
production by Black, queer, Indigenous, and otherwise marginalized
scholars who have trained in US, continental European, and British
academies. Blogs, podcasts, YouTube videos, Instagram accounts, websites, and Twitter threads have become vehicles for these scholars, who
experience being made peripheral by the colonial university, to articulate critiques and offer theoretically rich and empirically grounded
takes on current and historical predicaments. This compendium of
digital content creates what Mbembe, in his Abiola Lecture on Future
Knowledges, describes as "extra-institutional knowledge" that is "unbounded, uncontainable, and easily searchable."[2]

For many of these scholars, online sites of production and dissemination enable a political engagement and an interface with broader publics and specific networks in ways that sidestep the willfully naïve geopolitical orientation of the formal academy that continues to rank people and regions in racially configured geographies—thereby containing particular ideas and experiences in bounded forms while making others fugitive.[3] Moreover, the internet enables scholars to push against and altogether refuse formal disciplinary conventions regarding form, subject, method, and theory. Digital platforms, with all their multimodal and affectively charged potentialities, enable scholars to articulate theoretically rich insights that do not necessarily resort to what Barbara Christian describes as Western forms of abstract logic.[4]

These sites and infrastructures of digital knowledge production, as they are created by those affiliated with and trained in the formal spaces of the academy, are, at least in part, a response to the glacial pace of academic publishing and the gatekeeping mechanisms, as Macharia points out, that keep particular knowledges submerged and critiques silenced or, at the very least, slowed down and trapped behind paywalls. They are a mechanism for speeding up a response and speaking directly to calcified formations of knowledge/power. The production of digital forms of undisciplined scholarship are also a push to rethink form, not only to move beyond particular registers of academic writing but also to think beyond the written word itself and incorporate sound and image, voice and movement, to more fully articulate submerged epistemologies.

We might see these expressions of digital intellectuality that exceed the accepted means of form, production, and dissemination as a response to the growing precarity that humanities and social science scholars in North American and European universities face as they complete their terminal degrees. This is particularly true for students who in a previous era would have had difficulty accessing the university— particularly the elite universities of the Global North—and who come to realize quickly that the promise of entry and belonging within a particular disciplined mode of thinking, being, and producing will no longer guarantee an institutional future. The undeniable uncertainty that awaits those being trained as future social scientists and humanities scholars pushes those already on the margins of the academy to articulate against the grain and in the channels they have available. If they are unlikely to find institutional homes, why bother disciplining their modes of production to fit into one?

We should recognize these forms of expression, articulation, and theorization, since they come into being in the spaces of the digital as "subjugated knowledges," namely, those forms of knowledge production that in the words of Foucault have historically been "buried or masked in functional coherences or formal systematizations" in academic institutions. These forms emerge in a flood at a moment when the means of production enable thought and otherwise distanced relations of knowing to become visible.[5] These kaleidoscopic transnational formations, as they course through the digital, pick up on previous counter-ideological and anti-colonial movements of the twentieth century to reframe what counts as theory, what is validated as knowledge, and what is legible as critique. In Chela Sandoval's words, their powers can be thought of as "mobile—not nomadic, but rather cinematographic: a kinetic motion that manoeuvres, poetically transfigures, and orchestrates while demanding alienation, perversion, and reformation in both spectators and practitioners."[6] The cinematographic qualities of online knowledge production—as it puts the critical thought and experiences of those marginalized by the academe into conversation—might be described as a montage of potentiality, another means to link, amplify, and collectivize academics who find themselves on the peripheries of the colonial university.

These counter-hegemonic knowledge projects that are produced by those on the margins of academia are joined by the projects of those who do not have formal affiliations or informal connections with institutions—universities, think tanks, and so on. Here examples abound, but to briefly illustrate, we point to the efflorescence of Indigenous media production and their digital circulations in the last decade. As Faye Ginsburg notes, these (digital) media projects, built on the work of previous Indigenous media formations cultivated over the last several decades, and are important examples of a "self-conscious means of cultural preservation and production and form of political motivation."[7]

This chapter engages with these digital counter-hegemonic knowledge projects inside, on the borders of, and beyond the academy to think through how the digital facilitates an unsettling of disciplined knowledge formations. Here we mobilize *digital unsettling* to engage with the ways in which these knowledge projects interact with, disrupt, and potentially transform university-based research, teaching, and publishing, even as they challenge mainstream media representations in their travels in online spaces. In our return to the university and its campus as a site of digitally enabled rupture, we touch on the ways in which these sorts of projects broadly impact the social sciences and humanities, paying closer attention to anthropology as the discipline struggles to recalibrate and reimagine its project in light of its own ongoing crisis of legitimacy.[8] For anthropologists and scholars in related social sciences and humanities disciplines, these knowledge formations and the archives they generate online emerge not as an object of potential study but rather as an invitation to produce knowledge differently.

These formations, however, also are perceived to pose—and in some cases, do pose —a threat to systematic, disciplined knowledge production and the borders of expertise it generates. In part, this is because of the ways in which the digital affords the possibility of fashioning a combination of textual, visual, and sonic materials that are affectively charged, aesthetically appealing, intimate, immediate, and more easily circulatable than disciplined, institutionalized knowledge, which continues to sit behind paywalls. Moreover, the digital creates opportunities for different genres of writing that otherwise do not find purchase in conventional academic publishing. While the digital turn in the humanities and social sciences has been underway over the last decade and has pushed for a reimagining and legitimizing of a broader array of scholarly production—evidenced in increasing numbers of academic journals that publish podcasts, short films, photo essays, and creatively written scholarship—there remains a strong commitment to forms of legitimation that keep certain ideas, people, forms, and politics on the peripheries of institutions. Even with the turn to open access publishing and the labor-of-love approach that some have taken up to produce a more considered and inclusive knowledge commons, we have a long way to go in realizing, as Anand Pandian points out, what the full potentials of the "open" in open access might offer us.[9] The knowledge projects we touch on in this chapter remind us of the urgency to reimagine academic publishing in terms of what form scholarship can take, the time it takes to publish, who can publish, and who we might imagine our audiences are for the scholarship we generate.

As we attend to these emergent knowledge formations and their capacities to disrupt knowledge/power matrices linked to traditional academia, we think through the citational politics that these variously situated projects take up. We argue that an attention to (digital) citation allows us to see the kinds of legitimating and reflexive intertextualities that develop as these texts, in the broad sense of the term, circulate. Here we draw on recent theorizations of citation that recognize that its power lies in its capacity to reanimate, to breathe life "into an event of discourse through another discursive act that, in one way or another, re-presents it."[10] We point to the kinds of reanimations that emerge in and through citationality, whether the evocation of figures, speech fragments, images, or historical moments, and examine their reflexive potentiality and capacity to congeal and legitimate ideas as they are entangled with and in opposition to formal domains of knowledge production. In so doing, we build on our previous discussion of hashtags and images of protest in chapter 1 and extreme speech in chapter 2 to point to the ways in which citation plays an integral part in temporal and cross-border affirmations in various knowledge projects that seek to disrupt colonial orders.

Of course, it is important to recognize that the potential for a disruption of normative knowledge formations and the emergence of a counter-knowledge archive in the digital comes at a price. The extractive and unequal resource extraction and labor expropriation that is required to maintain the digital systems that allow for exchange—as we discussed in the previous chapter on capture—should give pause to any overly celebratory push to imagine a rupture in empire embedded within its techno-scientific workings. Moreover, it is important to recognize the ways in which the euphoric potentials of expression, articulation, and cumulative and collective knowledge creation on sites like Twitter, Facebook, Instagram, and so on are being monetized. As Cassius Adair and Lisa Nakamura argue, "Even online writing that feels like pleasure or resistance contributes to corporate-owned sites, which in turn produces profitable site traffic."[11]

The potential for profit extends to those who generate content for these sites. In other words, formations of counter knowledge, as they are produced and circulate in the "always on, ambient" spheres of the digital, offer content creators the potential to accrue various forms of capital—social, institutional, academic, and cultural.[12] This last point is crucial, as it suggests that knowledge projects, which in previous historical moments were unable to find the light of day, dwelled in in-between places, and are what Jack Halberstam describes as "low theory," are not simply disruptive of the status quo; when they circulate in the digital, they become ways for individuals and institutions to accrue cultural, political, and social capital. The potential for (individual) accumulation and institutional reprieve as a result of the production and circulation of what might be described as decolonial knowledge in digital worlds complicates a simple valorization of its emergence. This potential for individuals and institutions to create capital through their claims to unconventional, undisciplined, and critical thought risks watering down the political potentials of various projects and fracturing tenuous solidarities and opportunities for productive rupture that the digital facilitates in its capacity to facilitate transnational decolonial cultures.

Finally, it is not only counter-hegemonic knowledge that is being produced and disseminated in and through the digital. There are numerous examples of knowledge projects that have taken shape on the internet, whether Hindutva in India or right-wing white-supremacist formations across Europe and North America, that support the status quo or actively promote an upturning of the liberal order in favor of a virulent nativist national imaginary. These formations rely on a sleight of hand that masquerades violent, populist ideas as subaltern, embattled, and/or invisible within institutionalized knowledge formations, in some cases mobilizing decolonization to do so. The internet, as such, emerges as a site where knowledge that is founded in conspiracy, half-truths, whispers, and mythologies can flourish. Annunciations of right-wing embattlement are being taken up by actors in academia or on its margins, for instance, in Gad Saad's podcast, *The Saad Truth*, which we discussed briefly in chapter 1. These sorts of mediations are also being produced by actors who have no formal connections with institutions. Indeed, right-wing social movements have invested heavily in building digital knowledge infrastructures to promote their own pedagogical goals. We touch on these developments in our final section of this chapter to reiterate the ways the digital unsettles in ways that reinforce hegemonic power.

Algorithms as Culture and the Curation of (Counter) Knowledge

(Gabriel) I would not have encountered Keguro Macharia's scholarship—whether their blog or their academic publications—if I hadn't first come across them on Twitter. Macharia, like many scholars inside and outside the academy, have used Twitter to nurture and straddle various publics through the amplification of experience and thought and to curate their larger intellectual and creative projects. My encounter with Macharia's thought and writing on Twitter was inevitable. While the complex, reflective, and predictive algorithms that drive platforms like Twitter, as we discussed in the previous chapter, have the potential to capture, they also perform another function—to congeal networks of affinity through the communicative coordination of ideas and affects. As Illana Gershon has argued, to communicate is to coordinate.[13] Twitter certainly demonstrates how communication in the age of algorithmic recursion can become a tool to direct and coordinate affinities. Macharia, no doubt, appeared in my feed because the people I follow—scholars, activists, artists, and thinkers spanning at least three continents—pointed me toward him. The predictive capacities of the algorithm that drives Twitter placed his tweets on my timeline because there was a good chance—based on my articulated interests, as evidenced by my follows and those who follow me, my likes, and those who have liked my tweets—I would also be interested in what they had to say. In turn, over the two years I have followed Macharia, they have pointed me toward other thinkers, writers, and makers on Twitter and in the digital sphere.

In this sense, algorithms can be productively thought of *as* culture. Nick Seaver, drawing from the well of contemporary anthropological theory, pushes us to consider a socio-constructivist understanding of technology to better apprehend the complex role of algorithms in our daily lives. Algorithms, he writes, are not "stable objects interacted with from many perspectives, but as manifold consequences of a variety of human practices."[14] An *as culture* approach to algorithms and the platforms they drive recognizes the collective fashioning of thought, ideas, and practices and the recursive role the algorithm plays in making these collective ideas visible and in conversation with one another.

The algorithm, in this sense, is compositional, revealing, as we have argued throughout this book, the impulses, ideas, affects, histories, and politics that have shaped relations since the colonial period. The upshot of this, of course, is that networks that are recursively produced in online platforms like Twitter are reflective of a collective aspiration to a shared politics and set of cultural beliefs that are not technologically determined but, rather, historically wrought. As such, these platforms are deeply social spaces where desires and longings for seeing and being seen are channeled through techno-socially structured forms of textual and audio-visual communication, producing novel arrangements of knowledge and disruptive takes on stable epistemes. The dark side of this development, as we noted in the "Extreme" chapter, is an amplification and concentration of extreme speech as fun and the very real potential for practices of participation, whether in Germany, India, or the US, to slide into the reinforcement of hegemonic, fascist ideologies within and across national contexts, ideologies fomented in the socially bonding experience of an exchange of essentialized notions of culture and biologized notions of difference. However, an algorithm-as-culture approach also makes visible how anti-colonial, decolonial, abolitionist, feminist, and queer thought is being articulated in ways that create persistent connections across contexts.

We must, of course, keep in mind that the corporations that develop the algorithmically driven social media platforms do not create equal opportunities for the circulation of ideas or, for that matter, the conditions for unbiased representation. As Ather Zia notes, Facebook has been notoriously consistent in blocking the posts and pages of activists working in Kashmir and Palestine and argues that the multinational corporations' vested interests in maintaining access to nation state contexts like India pushes them into complicity with these states to erase or silence critique of settler colonial violence.[15] We might also think of the kinds of algorithmic reproductions of racialized hierarchy that Twitter has recently been found to reproduce. Recent reports of Twitter's visual cropping and blurring of darker phenotypes while centering white appearing faces and bodies reminds us of the ways in which algorithms *as* culture also reproduce dominant understandings of racial difference and are reflective of expropriative projects of the state.[16]

Yet even with this in mind, it is still important to recognize that the speed of connection and recursion that the digital facilitates across and between locations and actors in worlds offer the means for those producing this knowledge to bypass and effectively call into question traditional models of knowledge production and dissemination and to accelerate the formation of a decolonial digital culture that is productive of particular forms of resistant knowing. Speed, argues Bifo Berardi, is the hallmark of post-Fordist production and is epitomized in the digital's capacity to break all boundaries of private/public divides.[17] Digital speed, even as it offers emergent ways to connect and resist together, has the tendency to put the soul to work. In other words, it makes us all prone—through our digital devices—to processes of insistent subjectification. Another consequence of the speed of the digital age is that it encourages free labor on the internet.[18] Simply put, we become prone to building, creating, and generating ideas and infrastructures online that ultimately benefit those who actually control the means of production.

While these arguments, which point to the subjectifying tendencies of the digital, are certainly undeniable, the rapidity of exchange and networking potential of the digital—even though it is built on corporate-owned undersea cables that link continents—offers something else: the capacity to link individuated struggles to broader ones across geographies that have been cordoned off into areas since the Renaissance and that reinforce epistemic divides in institutionalized centers of knowledge production.[19] Scholars, artists, and activists across sociohistorical contexts struggling with colonialities of the present have the possibility of coming into contact with each other more readily and easily through iterative communicative practice on sites like Twitter and the production of alternate archives of thought in online spaces.

As such, Twitter (and other social media sites) function as a means to facilitate and curate speedy connections between and draw attention to submerged or otherwise less visible scholars, cultural producers, and collectives' bodies of work. It is a space of encounter, an opening that has the potential to foster a more meaningful engagement with another way of thinking and another location of thought between scholars, thinkers, artists, and activists who seek affinities in shared difference and together recognize the limits of institutional knowledge production. Social media, in this sense, facilitates a kind of algorithmically curated waywardness, a Benjaminian potential for taking a digital stroll through Twitter's curated content with the hopes of accidently running into signposts that direct one to unanticipated but important insights and, potentially, to actors who stand in solidarity.

This sort of digitally manifest wayward potentiality has its analogue precedents. Take, for instance, the 1981 book by Gloria Anzaldúa and Cherríe Moraga titled *This Bridge Called My Back: Writings by Radical Women of Color*. When it was first published by Kitchen Table: Women of Color Press in the early 1980s, it quickly became a countercultural canonical reading, circulating widely in various forms. Cassius Adair and Lisa Nakamura trace *This Bridge Called My Back*'s ongoing circulation on social media and its continued impact among minoritized reading publics in the US, arguing that digital social media–enabled networks offer ways to think about how networks more broadly can perform a pedagogical function. Affinity networks point those who are draw to them to books, films, or other kinds of content to learn differently while providing the potential to connect to others who are on similar (decolonial) journeys.[20]

Below, we touch on a few examples of the kinds of projects that Twitter (and other social media platforms) have pointed us to over the years as scholars within a particular networked culture of counter-hegemonic thought—projects that offer examples of how ways of knowing that emerge outside or on the interstices of formal knowledge production can take shape and produce affinities in and through the digital while offering particular critiques of coloniality in the contemporary.

Africa Is a Country (AIAC) is a web-based publication that features short pieces from scholars, artists, and activists who are deeply engaged with the politics of the continent.[21] Professor Sean Jacobs, who is currently at the New School for Social Research, founded the website in 2009 because he felt strongly that mainstream media coverage of Africa was, in his words, abysmal. Jacobs wanted to showcase perspectives that "introduced leftist perspectives on African affairs and undercut dominant media narratives about Africa."[22] While being fully aware of the limits of the digital, Jacobs also recognizes its potentials. He writes:

> I am not naive about the internet (we all know it is a cesspool of rightwing propaganda and misinformation), but the ability to self-publish,

has vastly contributed to democratizing the public sphere. I also know that despite our best efforts most Africans still source the news they read about themselves or other Africans elsewhere on the continent, via non-African sources. Nevertheless, I am very proud of the work we have done. I think we have managed, particularly in our early work, which was mainly media criticism, to make foreign correspondents think twice about the way they portray Africa. We have also created space for over 1,000 contributors, including a number of first-time authors, to write to a global audience. More recently, we want our work to be seen in languages other than English and we are keen to produce more visual media.[23]

As Jacobs argues, AIAC has provided a platform for first-time authors to produce and circulate their critical understandings of the world order and, in particular, to push back against problematic renderings of Africa and Africans. While many of the pieces written for AIAC have been produced by a diverse range of thinkers from the continent, a number of the pieces on AIAC are written by scholars who inhabit the European, British, or US academic worlds. The potential to articulate differently and to a different audience opens alternative opportunities for academics within Euro-Western institutions to write critique in ways that potentially would not be legible in the formal publishing spaces of the academy, would take too long to get published because of the various gatekeeping mechanisms in academic journals, and even if they got published in academic journals, would not have the potential of reaching multiple publics or to create shared spaces of political affinity. AIAC represents an explosion of online publishing platforms that offer academics from various disciplines the opportunity to destabilize academic convention, broadly, and disciplinary convention more specifically to directly engage with the colonial legacies of knowledge production and, in the case of AIAC, a specific critique of what counts as knowledge about Africa.

Like Jacobs, many of the creators of academic adjacent writing projects in the form of blogs, web-based publications, and so on describe their efforts as a labor of love rather than a means for individual gain.[24] These projects push against the notion that all labor in digital spaces is subject to being disciplined by capital or that they put the soul to work in a way that suggests its capture. For many who work in these spaces, the potential for writing differently and for different audiences creates a rupture in stable workings of academic knowledge production, and that rupture, as it creates new relations and ways of being, is enough. However, it is important to note that the financial stability of a tenured academic position and the access to the resources it facilitates is oftentimes crucial to the set-up and creation of platforms like AIAC. Even though websites and blogs are not so expensive to develop and maintain—particularly if they focus on writing rather than the more labor-intensive production of audio-visual material—they still require labor time and have fixed costs. While there are examples of online decolonial knowledge projects that do not rely on institutional support but rather maintain themselves through personal commitment, crowdfunding, and the like, these projects are precarious and potentially short lived.

It is also worthwhile to note that while academics who create platforms for exchange or personal blogs to articulate what they might not be able to in formal publishing spaces with no ambitions for personal gain, these types of projects have a tendency to make those who create these spaces visible in ways that potentially create new possibilities for them precisely because it allows for a different sort of writerly possibility. Writing differently (in relation to academic convention), of course, can mean many things. In the case of AIAC, there is a clear mission to write against problematic depictions of Africa and Africans. In other cases, it might mean pushing back against disciplinary conventions as they relate to colonial forms of knowing and being. Take, for instance, the volunteer-run web publishing platform Footnotes. In their "About" page, they state that their mission is to "offer a space for scholars, content, and expressions of that content that challenge the status quo in anthropology, which includes Eurocentric theory, methods, publishing conventions, and other forms of knowledge production, as well as structures of power in academia, colonialism, Whiteness, and capitalism."[25] Footnotes joins several other alternative web-based publishing platforms and blogs in anthropology. However, unlike the others—which also provide budding and established anthropologists an opportunity to write (and create) differently—Footnotes specifies its mission as one of rupture. They use the term *footnotes*, as opposed to one of the more fetishized method/theory concepts in anthropology, *fieldnotes*, to refer to the notes at the ends of texts that are some of what Zoe Todd calls the "juiciest bits" of academic writing. The editors argue that like academic footnotes, this group-anthropology blog supplements the disciplines' main texts "as a multimodal, anticolonial, and iconoclastic project."

The taking up of footnotes as a mode of writing suggests a particular relationship with conventional scholarly production insofar as it aims to stay in close conversation with it rather than depart from it altogether—toward providing substantive critique. As such, the citation practices that we observed in our readings of some of the blog entries rely on a reanimation and critique of conventional anthropological texts and their renderings of cultural worlds. They also take up anthropological texts that live on the margins of the discipline to offer another way to imagine the discipline's canon. In a recent blog post about reflexive anthropology and Black women's performance hosted on Footnotes, a PhD student, Carolina Nvé Díaz San Francisco, looks carefully at the work of Black women anthropologists and the ways in which they animate questions around reflexivity in the discipline. Drawing from Zora Neal Hurston, Lyne Bolles, and Irma McClaurin, San Francisco produces an alternate citational field that foregrounds Black women as the center rather than the periphery of the discipline.

In this sense, San Francisco picks up on the broader push across disciplines to #CiteBlackWomen, a campaign that anthropologist Christen Smith started in 2017. Smith began by printing T-shirts with the simple slogan "Cite Black Women" and selling them online. The campaign eventually extended to social media and has since generated a website, a blog, and a podcast of its own. Smith says that originally, the "idea was to motivate everyone, but particularly academics, to critically reflect on their everyday practices of citation and start to consciously question how they can incorporate black women into the CORE of their work. Although we are intellectually prolific, we are rarely the ones that make up the canon."[26] #CiteBlackWoman, especially in relationship to San Francisco's blog post on Footnotes, demonstrates the fluid links between social media presence and campaigning, online publishing, and other forms of multimodal production, and the ways they are generative of persistent decolonial digital cultures that foreground reflexive citation within and outside of disciplinary spaces as a key mode for disruption.

Scholars who write outside of conventional spaces on websites like AIAC or in Footnotes form one pathway to engage with a broader cultural push to decolonize knowledge production. In addition to these writerly endeavors, we might think about the various multimodal projects—podcasts, short videos, live events, digital syllabi, and so on— that social science scholars are involved in (often in collaboration with artists and activists) as a means to challenge academic convention and colonial ways of thinking about space, people, and ideas—and the promise these experiments hold in terms of creating disruptive circulations of thought. #CiteBlackWomen, for instance, has a bi-weekly program that "feature[s] Black women inside and outside of the academy who are actively engaged in radical citation as praxis, quotes and reflections on Black women's writing, conversations on weathering the storm of citational politics in the academy, decolonizing syllabi and more."[27]

In the UK, the *Surviving Society* podcast is another grassroots, ground-up venture taken up by early career Black scholars to think against scholarly convention by animating what they call a public sociology. They introduce *Surviving Society* with the following statement:

> We are Chantelle, Saskia and Tissot, and we are fed up with the mainstream conversations taking place around politics and current affairs. Every episode, we each pick a topic that has made us angry, either from the news or from our daily lives, and talk about why it matters from a sociological perspective. Through public sociology, we want to challenge common-sense understandings of "race," class, and gender, and to show how entrenched inequalities shape both political conversations and individual experiences.[28]

Projects like *Surviving Society* seek to involve the public in discussions that nominally take place in cloistered academic settings and have recently become visible as a result of historical conjuncture.

The move by academics or academics-in-training to produce and engage beyond academia has coincided with and undoubtedly contributed to several digitally enabled pedagogical innovations. Since the 2020 Black Lives Matter uprisings, there has been an explosion of online syllabi focusing on abolition, anti-capitalist, and anti-colonial thought. "Curriculation," as Kelly Gillespie has described these online initiatives taken up by politically minded academics and those they are in conversation with outside of the academy, "has as its orientation a collective project, explicitly sharing our thinking as a way of passing it on to others in conversation."[29] Projects to create shared and popular online syllabi have brought together scholarship otherwise obscured in formal academic settings—like the *Surviving Society* podcast, for instance—and put them into productive relationships with one and other. They have also put recognized scholarly works produced by academicians into conversation with writings and audio-visual work produced outside of the academy. These popular syllabi offer opportunities for putting our academic thinking into conversation with a broader array of knowledge and in the hands of people outside of the university. As importantly, it offers a new model for teaching and learning in the university—particularly in the social sciences and humanities—that places academic works in direct engagement with materials produced on its margins and in the digital sphere. As they circulate, these heterogenous reading lists (which also include audio-visual material) shape how critical questions of the moment are being thought through by students and taught by professors. As a result, what students engage with as knowledge shifts toward a broader array of possibilities in terms of form and epistemic potential. Scholars in the academy, in a kind of recursive feedback loop, are encouraged to deepen their engagement with forms of thought circulating online that exceed academic knowledge production.

The digital knowledge projects from outside academia that appear on these public syllabi are varied. We offer a few examples of experimentations with audio-visual and non-conventional writing that have been taken up outside of academia and represent worlds of knowing that are not mediated by academics. Our examples, again, emerge out of our own situated experiences in offline and online networks of relation, connection, and thought inside and outside of the university. One example is the collective Isuma.tv, an offshoot project of the Nunavut-based Inuit collective, Igloolik Isuma. Isuma.tv is a web platform that brings together Indigenous media broadcasters and makers from across the globe to share content, in multiple languages and forms. Isuma.tv offers a means for Indigenous people across the world to produce and share ideas, experiences, thoughts, and representations of their inhabitations of contemporary life with each other and other interested audiences through audio-visual representation while pointing to their shared struggle against settler colonial states' ongoing violence against them.

Each user who registers on Isuma.tv can design their own space, or *channel*, to reflect their "own identity, mandate and audience."[30] Foregoing a distribution model that privileges accumulation, IsumaTV shares its work freely and widely online. A broad array of publics can access some of IsumaTV's content. To access the site in its entirety, one has to become a member. To become a full member, one has to state their tribal affiliation. Audio-visual production and circulation become the means for Indigenous communities to engage with one another while creating contemporaneous figurations of Indigenous lives for others. Isuma.tv presents us with an example of an Indigenous media formation that has taken advantage of digital infrastructures to expand its network and circulation. In the current moment, Indigenous, diasporic, First Nation, and queer mediations circulate in digital worlds of making, come into contact with one another, and create powerful cross-pollinations of thought and access to worlds otherwise invisible under the colonial gaze.

We might also think with the project Dalit Camera. Dalit Camera, founded by Ravichandran Bathran in 2011, is a collective of Dalit media makers who have created a digital strategy in the form of a website and a YouTube channel that, "captures narratives, public meetings, songs, talks, discussion on Dalits."[31] Dalit is a category that B.R. Ambedkar popularized during the anti-colonial movement to organize oppressed groups who have been rendered Other in Brahminical Hindu society for time immemorial.[32] Dalit Camera offers an example of a digital unsettling that recognizes coloniality is tangled in structures of power that precede European colonization but was amplified by it. They creatively use various media forms not only to generate an archive of engagement with Dalit thought, activism, and cultural practice to make visible Dalit life but also to show the violent and unequal position Dalits hold in the Indian postcolonial state.

Dalit Camera is an example of a knowledge project that crowdsources and curates its content. Visual media is a central component of Dalit Camera's project. The audio-visual content is only partially produced by Bathran and volunteers who work with Dalit Camera; much of the content on the website is crowdsourced. Makers from across India submit their work via a Google form for review by the editorial team. This allows Bathran and others who work on Dalit Camera to take up their project as a curatorial one, foregrounding audio-visual work produced across the country that offers a visceral and direct engagement with Dalit voices otherwise not seen or heard in mainstream media or in academic knowledge production. As with Isuma.tv, the audio-visual self-representations that are curated on Dalit Camera offer a more visceral, affective, and immediate presence and experience than what the textual alone can bring. While these audio-visual renderings of Dalit political life are no doubt mediated, the possibility for publics to hear the voices and see the faces of people as they fight for dignity and their rights in the postcolonial state produces a rupture of media and scholarly depictions that speak for the marginalized or make them invisible altogether.

In this sense, Dalit Camera operates as a para-ethnographic project. Para-ethnography can be described quite simply as ethnography produced by non-anthropologists. It has been theorized in recent anthropological literature as part and parcel of a move that has attempted to reimagine the work of twenty-first-century anthropology as an explicit opportunity for creating collaborative knowledge and undoing the colonial anthropologies project of translating the Other. By identifying para-ethnographers who produce ethnographically rich work that is being produced by non-academics, the idea is that anthropologists can develop productive collaborations through the coproduction and shared analyses with counterparts who have equal footing and stakes in the project.[33] In anthropological accounts of these collaborations, however, there is a distinct sense that the counterparts who produce anthropological knowledge should inhabit adjacent expert domains. They are artists, designers, or planners who have been trained in the Western academy and have access to various forms of metropolitan capital.

Dalit Camera and Isuma.tv rupture this colonial configuration of collaboration, offering us a way to imagine different counterparts whose curatorial projects produced by political communities open another way to see ethnographically rich work that is being generated for political ends. We will discuss the possibility for a different anthropology that centers different counterparts and collaborators in more detail in the home/field chapter. But suffice to say that for this chapter, Dalit Camera and Isuma.tv, to name two of many important ground-up knowledge projects that circulate in online spaces, rupture disciplinary conventions, and unsettle knowledge production in the academy in ways that have pushed the question of open access publishing to the forefront. An attention to these projects sharpens questions regarding the relationship between knowledge, form, and circulation in the context of the digital and, we suggest, creates new ways to imagine a different kind of collaborative possibility.

Twitter and Insta as a Sites of Knowledge Production

Twitter and other social media platforms are, of course, more than just means to point elsewhere, to an individual's or a collectives' blog, podcast, or website. They are mechanisms by which knowledge is produced and institutional power is negotiated and, in some instances, disrupted. Here we turn to academic Twitter, which hails overlapping and distinct publics shaped by national, linguistic, and political categories, to think about the ways in which the platform serves as a site for alternative knowledge production within and outside institutional contexts and the kinds of disruptions they work to produce.

Academic Twitter describes a loose community of practitioners who engage in, but exceed, conversations related to disciplinary, institutional, and departmental concerns on the platform. As Bonnie Stewart suggests, academic Twitter should be best thought of as a "phenomenon in which oral and literate traditions—and audience expectations—are collapsed, creating a public that operates on very different terms from those of academia."[34] These "different terms" are shaped by the kinds of conversations the platform enables. Academic Twitter is crosscut by Twitter counterpublic formations—Black Twitter, Dalit Twitter, and so on. Like a Venn diagram, these overlaps create opportunities for dialogue when tweets by academics invite critical engagement in the form of direct responses, subtweets, and the like from those who normally would not have access to academicians. Academic Twitter also enables junior scholars to directly address senior scholars in ways that would not be possible within normative academic spaces of contact and exchange. As such, academic Twitter creates a space for encounter and friction that, in of themselves, are generative of new forms of thought and potential connection.

Much has been written about academic Twitter and the way in which scholars and aspiring scholars use the platform to articulate their branded selves. For Alison Hearn, the branded self is "an entity that works and at the same time points to itself working."[35] What Hearn points to here is a meta-pragmatic practice on Twitter where knowledge is reflexively and sometimes anxiously produced in short bursts of texts such that hierarchical structures that enable and constrain them are kept in view. This reflexive engagement is indicative of a broader set of practices on Twitter that disciplines users to "traverse from private to public . . . from the personal to the political, or the individual and the collective, and back."[36] What this means, if we begin to think about Twitter as a site of knowledge production, is that it is generative of a particular genre of knowledge, one that is reflexive to the conditions that produce it and is sensitive to the entanglements between affect and reason. In this sense it can be, in its most cynical reading, a literal rendering of the academic "soul" at work.

In this rather bleak framework, academic Twitter—for those located in some national contexts, the US in particular—has become almost as important a site for building one's personal brand as a CV.[37] By offering scholars the opportunity to create followers across various publics, Twitter enables those who can master tweeting as a craft an opportunity for academic Twitter fame. This potential for self-promotion, of course, is steeped in existing social, cultural, and institutional capital and has the potential to reproduce hierarchies of various sorts within academic worlds. Those who can master Twitter as a genre of practice and thereby gain followers have the potential to gain better access to institutional power. One simple reason for this, of course, has to do with the kinds of citational networks one can generate on a platform like Twitter.

These citational networks, as they link established scholars to up-and-coming ones, create new conditions and practices for networked advancement based on existing gendered, racialized, and classed hierarchies toward the mobilization and subsequent accumulation of cultural and social capital. Here, citation on Twitter, indicated through the use of the @ function and the retweet, is generative of networked relations within established and interlocking academic worlds. Beyond networked relations within and on the peripheries of academia, scholars who are successful on Twitter manage to create a following beyond formal institutional settings. This audience, evidenced in numbers of followers, likes, and so on, can translate into a form of capital within the institution.

While Twitter has become one tool by which savvy academics who mobilize their existing capital can build a career within academia, it also provides an opportunity for those inside and outside of academia who can wield the platform effectively to disrupt academic hierarchies and disciplinary formations.[38] These two possibilities are, of course, not so easily separable. Sometimes, careers in academia are built on disruptions that find the right balance of disorienting and reproductive. This has been one of the pitfalls of engaging with any politically resonant development in academia and has become viscerally felt with regard to the evocation of decolonization in university spaces. As Bhakti Shringarpure notes in a recent article in AIAC, universities have taken up tokenistic diversity strategies and rebranded them decolonizing initiatives, and certain scholars have recognized the self-branding potentials of a discursive claim to "decolonize"—on social media and in other public venues in this current climate—and have sought to maximize them.[39] Even for those scholars doing substantive theoretical work under the banner of decolonization, writes Shringarpure, this work is often being done behind the paywalls of academic journals or within the ivory towers of institutions. From our perspective, then, it is critical not to get caught up in the term *decolonization* as it is instantiated in social media spaces or in institutional ones. Rather, it is important to instantiate what counts as disruptive knowledge by following the way digital platforms enable productive disruption of coloniality in specific instances.

Disruptive forms of knowing are not always created by individuals, and in Twitter worlds, they are often the most instructive and impactful when they are collectivized. Collective disruption relies on the production of affectively charged thought in the form of multiple, unique tweets. One possible way tweets accrue as multiples, offering a different way of reading, understanding, and knowing, is in response to an event. These accruals, as they form a body of critique and mobilize a compendium of experience, can effectively work to puncture existing understandings and arrangements of knowledge production. To provide a quick example in anthropology worlds, the recent critiques of the open access journal *Hau: Journal of Ethnographic Theory* by precarious, junior anthropologists played a great part in creating the conditions for a reckoning of the journal. Here, our discussion of hashtags in the "Campus" chapter reemerges as salient, but this time in the discussion of knowledge production. The tweets, as they were individually generated by junior and precarious academics within the worlds of #AcademicTwitter and #AnthroTwitter, used the hashtag #HauTalk to point to deeply problematic labor practices and incidences of gendered abuse and violence in the management of the journal. These tweets also questioned the founding premise of the journal in its stated attempts to make the discipline great again.[40]

#HauTalk also raised important questions about the underlying logics of open access publishing, which has been imagined as a means to liberate important critical scholarship and link it to ground-up resistance. Because Hau, founded in 2011, touted itself as a fully open access anthropology journal, its problems, in terms of the way in which staff were treated, served as a space to critique the potential for open access to produce arrangements that changed very little in terms of whose success or prestige was enabled and the labor conditions that undergirded it. If open access publishing, in its efforts to create a different form of access and retrievability of disciplinary knowledge, reproduced the capitalistic and colonial arrangements of labor, what was it worth?[41] The critiques leveled against Hau regarding labor arrangements and abuses of power on Twitter were bolstered by an open letter that was written and circulated on various social media sites by a collective of Indigenous and settler scholars from Aotearoa (New Zealand). Mahi Tahi, a collective working "under the auspices of the New Zealand national anthropology association," directly questioned the ethics of care and misappropriation in Hau's use of Maori concepts like Hau and of Indigenous knowledge, more broadly. This digital letter, in its circulations, linked the critique from precarious scholars from Anglophone worlds to an Indigenous critique and created a body of knowledge that put into conversation questionable power dynamics and labor practices in the journal, with key debates in anthropology concerning the ethics of relationships between anthropology and Indigenous thought. These digital exchanges, we can surmise, created the conditions for crises and reevaluation of the journal's direction among its board of trustees.[42] They also opened up an important public discussion on the state of the discipline in the twenty-first century.

Another way Twitter enables the potential for critical public discourse—beyond unique tweets and their multiples—is by enabling single "authors" to create threads comprised of a series of 280-character tweets. The thread reader application, which composes tweets into PDFs that are archivable and shareable off the platform, enables scholars to disseminate thought in novel ways. Circulations of Twitter threads in digested PDF form extends the potentials of Twitter as a site for knowledge production and dissemination that extends beyond the platform. Rather than (or in addition to) publishing an argument and evidence in a conventional journal, one can create a condensed version and publish it on Twitter. As the thread circulates, a Twitter user can summon the thread reader app to create a PDF digest. The algorithm of the app responds with a salutation—a thank you in one of ten different languages—and proceeds to create a document for circulation. These PDFs represent an organic open access production of knowledge. In recent online syllabi projects, thread PDFs have increasingly made their appearances and sit adjacent to other, more formalistic, forms of textual knowledge production. Twitter threads, for the purposes of this chapter, reveal a counter-knowledge formation that has the potential to directly challenge disciplinary knowledge production.

One example of this centers around a controversy that erupted as a result of the publication of an image of Margaret Mead. In March 2020, a photograph of Margaret Mead smiling as she held the human remains of Indigenous people from Papua New Guinea became the cover image for a special issue on white supremacy in *American Anthropologist*, the flagship journal of the American Anthropological Association. As people began to share articles from the special issue, the image, as a thumbnail, began to circulate on social media, largely disconnected from the contents with which it was associated. In the weeks that followed, Twitter exploded with critiques of the visual depiction and circulation of Indigenous human remains, the lack of Indigenous and First Nations representation on the *American Anthropologist* editorial board, and the way this image reinforced the idea that anthropology's audience continues to be imagined as white.

This mobilization on Twitter had an immediate impact. The editor of *American Anthropologist* responded with a retraction of the image, and eventually, an apology was published on the journal's website. Key to this retraction were the threads written by Indigenous and First Nation anthropologists, who scrutinized the image, the decision to include it, and the politics of representation that undergirded the controversy. The critique generated on Twitter in this instance reveals how Twitter (and Twitter threads) can shape disciplinary trajectories. For academics on the peripheries, Twitter threads (and collective Twitter responses) can become powerful ways to rapidly publish critique that directly addresses unfolding events and, potentially, changes their outcome. Of course, this compulsion to direct speech amplifies the danger of obscuring context. In the case of the *American Anthropologist* controversy, the context of the issue's contents, which anthropologically addressed white supremacy and the specificity of problematic Pacific Indigenous representation (rather than Indigeneity more broadly), was minimized in favor of broad issues pertaining to anthropology, Indigenous representation, and the question of making visible human remains. This tendency encourages Twitter users to narrow their use of phatic and metaphoric speech to hail specific intersecting publics they seek to engage and traverse.

Citation as such becomes central to a Twitter mode of address. In the short bursts of characters that typify the platform, users create recognizable and aesthetically informing speech through the evocation of other speech acts, speakers, and so on. Mastery of Twitter, as such, relies on a user having a sense of cultural sensibilities of the overlapping communities of practice they wish to reach and the styles of communicative practice they need to do so. Style, then, becomes crucial to making one's ideas engaging on Twitter. As Constantin Nakassis argues in his theorization of style, to find the right speech and semiotic deployment requires a careful calibration of citation. If the choices are over the top, if speakers slip into what Nakassis describes as "overstyle," they can lose credibility.[43] To linger on style recognizes that how we communicate matters as much as, if not more than, what we are trying to say and that in the worlds of Twitter, where there is an interest in garnering likes and gaining followers, stylistic forms of citation become central to produce an aesthetic of rupture.

Equally important, of course, is the frequency/regularity in which things are said on Twitter (and other social media sites). The more regularly one tweets, the greater, ostensibly, will be the potential for reaching targeted (and incidental) publics. It should come as no surprise, then, that Twitter tracks the number of tweets an individual user produces and prominently displays this information at the top of the user's personal feed. Of course, these individual tweets that are counted in this aggregate number are not necessarily new, unique tweets. Retweets—the reposting of other peoples' tweets—also count as part of this number. Retweeting, as citational practice, recognizes particular ideas, positions, and experiences as important and valid.

Retweeting is also a mechanism by which one identifies oneself through others. By retweeting particular figures who articulate and argue specific positions, one creates an intertextual legitimacy, as we have described in earlier chapters. One can offer a sense that what one is saying is also being said by others or that what others are saying is linked to what one thinks or says. Retweeting to identify oneself through others does not just rely on an engagement with tweets that align with ones' views but is also a technique to point out the flaws/problematics in other positions. Retweeting with comment, in this case, allows one to generate the distance between oneself and what is cited. It creates the space where citation is used as a form of critique rather than agreement. Similarly, subtweeting, where one comments on a tweet or on someone's Twitter activity, more generally, but does not include the original tweet as a referent or an @ to bring the person who is being critiqued into the conversation, is yet another way to cite someone while maintaining distance or clarifying difference. Only those who understand the contextual clues of the subtweet and what, specifically, it is speaking to can understand its relevance.

All these citational practices of alignment or distancing can of course be misread or in read correctly but to the detriment of the Twitter user. We must therefore recognize that Twitter critique produces the potential for backlash. Recall our chapter on extreme speech, where we discussed how academics who make critiques on Twitter not only become public targets and face vile abuse in social media spaces but are also subject to potential retribution in the institutions where they work. Twitter, as we have suggested, can flatten analysis that on the one hand initiates an immediate response (as was the case with the *American Anthropologist* controversy) and on the other hand potentially short circuits a more complex discussion of what is at stake in a particular event. Finally, Twitter opens the possibility for individuals, through intertextual mobilizations that are generative of and point to particular ways of knowing, to participate in and make themselves visible to a cultural formation, whether counter-hegemonic or otherwise. Without belaboring each of these potentials, the point we are making in this chapter is that these articulations of critique in social media spaces should not be seen as merely communicative acts but, as we suggested earlier, as actions that coordinate thought and—as we are suggesting here—actions that are generative of thought itself.

The potentials for creating (and coordinating) counter-hegemonic thought on Twitter (and the consequent danger of flattening analysis) extends beyond the ways in which academics on Twitter wield its potential. Take, for instance, activists' projects that emerged during the 2011 Jasmine Revolution in Tunisia. As Zeynep Tufekci argues, Twitter and blogging became the way to not only communicate and organize but also to breathe intellectual life into the 2011 Tunisian uprisings.[44] Or take the recent uprisings in Puerto Rico. In the wake of Hurricane Maria, Yarimar Bonilla argues that Twitter and other social media platforms played an important part in creating a "leaderfull" movement driven by an autonomous organizing impulse that rejects a sovereign future if it is to be built within the same framework that reproduces a lack of economic power in a capitalist world system.

Bonilla pushes us to think about how street art and online memes that emerged during the street protests of 2019 and eventually outed the governor of Puerto Rico, Ricardo Roselló, circulate on platforms like Twitter and Instagram and create a space to collectively theorize an otherwise and to develop a political imagination that attempts to decolonize sovereignty.[45] Visualization of an otherwise through the circulation and/or production of images, memes, and street art becomes a critical site where beyond-colonial-thinking emerges. The role, in particular, that images and their circulations play as a site for knowledge formation—whether in Puerto Rico or in Tunisia—become central when we think about the potentials of (shared) knowledge production on social media toward the disruption of stable arrangements of power. Images, as Walter Benjamin wrote, are not simply illustrative but are the basis for flashes of insight, of what he describes as the "now of recognizability."[46] Images, such as the ones Bonilla or Tufekci describe, are generative of a way to recognize the relationship between the past and the future by engaging deeply with the present and push us to recognize the specific ways in which the right to look—a claim of counter-visuality in the face of hegemonic productions of seeing—emerge as knowledge in online spaces.[47]

With this in mind, we touch on the social media platform Instagram, with its focus on image production and circulation, and the opportunity it offers those outside of academia to create alternate sites of knowing and sharing that push against normative, hegemonic formations and attempt to collectively imagine an otherwise. Take, for instance, the Queer Muslim Project, founded by Rafiul Alom Rahman. The Queer Muslim Project uses Instagram to produce what Rahman calls an opportunity for "subversive self-expression."[48] Rahman curates materials submitted to the site from across the world, balancing the struggle to ensure safety of the participants with the need to create political visibility. Here, Rahman recognizes visibility is at once a trap, a potentially harmful or dangerous space where vulnerable subjects become known, and a space for disrupting conventional ideas around what it means to a Muslim.[49] In a similar vein, we might think of the art that the artist known as Queer Habibi circulates on Instagram.[50]

By producing visual representations of queer life in Arab worlds, Queer Habibi seeks to create an archive of possibility and to disrupt ideas of conservatism and oppression ascribed to Arab lifeworlds by Euro-Western interests.[51] The illustrating of queer desire on Instagram—with their playful citation and subversive reimagining of "Orientalist" ways of seeing and clichéd signs of modernity—offers another example of the ways that images are generative of knowing differently. Queer Habibi recognizes that by making these desires visible, there is a danger of backlash. Becoming visible might invite violence and suppression. However, Queer Habibi, like others who use the space of social media to push for different way of seeing, suggests that this risk is worth the potential that an image creates in its capacity to make visible ways of being in the world that are otherwise mobilized by liberal states to perpetuate, at least in this case, an Islamophobic world order.

Right-Wing Mobilizations of the Decolonial—Some Final Thoughts

(Gabriel) In December 2020, I scrolled through my Facebook timeline and noticed that a participant from an ethnographic project I conducted from 2012 to 2018 and with whom I have maintained a relationship had posted a YouTube video critiquing Sikh Punjabi farmers involved in the farmer protests against the Indian government's new agricultural reforms that opened the agricultural sector to private investment.[52] This video is produced by String, a Hindu nationalist collective that states that its mission is "about establishing a network among individuals who are working toward uplifting the culture and spiritual ethos of this country."[53] I clicked the link to the video, wincing at the title: *Future of Sikhs: Bootlicking Amarinder Singh.* As I started watching, I was surprised that the video was in English. I stopped the video and quickly went back to String's YouTube channel. In addition to their English content and channel, there were Hindi, Telugu, and Kannada content/channels under their banner—suggesting a well thought-out project that seeks to engage multiple linguistic publics inside India and across its diasporas.

I then went back to the video in English that my former participant and friend had posted and watched it in its entirety. In the video, the host, a young mustached man with a crimson tilak on his forehead and wearing a dark red kurta, argues that the chief minister of Punjab, Amarinder Singh, who has been supportive of the farmers' strikes, is antinational and is from a family of anti-nationalists. Mobilizing historical "evidence," the speaker uses nineteenth-century documents to indict Amarinder Singh's grandfather, Bupender Singh, of consorting with the British. What is more is the tone and language that the speaker uses to describe Sikhs and what the speaker describes as their eventual but inevitable extinction in India. The speaker begins by saying, "Sikhs in Punjab, get ready to die. Don't worry this will be a slow death, not the way you people died in 1919 in Jallianwallah Bagh," referring to what is more commonly known as the Amristar Massacre, when British brigadier-general Reginald Dyer ordered his troops to open fire on a large group of anti-colonial protesters. The host's violent speech, punctuated by dramatic music, suggests that the information indicting Amarinder Singh and his grandfather, Bupender Singh, has been kept hidden and that he is revealing the hidden agenda of Sikhs who, first in collusion with the British then with the Congress Party, have duped the people of Punjab for their personal gain and are doing so again by supporting the protests.

String's video is one of many examples that demonstrate how Hindutva is using digital media to create a narrative about itself as a kind of liberating force that is locked in an epic battle with anti-Hindu forces that seek to maintain colonial forms of power to protect their legitimacy. While other Hindutva digital media channels propose an alternative Hindu epistemology through Hindu philosophy, science, and the like—a means to reject Western ways of knowing and to teach young people an "Indigenous" way of knowing—String approaches its mission presumably to influence a younger generation of Hindus in India and abroad, by offering a historical indictment of corrupting anti-Hindu forces. To do so, they practice a particular form of citation that suggests that they are familiar with historical methods of research that mobilize archival evidence to make particular claims.[54] At one point, the host quotes Sir Michael O'Dwyer's praise of Bupender Singh as evidence of the family's long history of corruption and collusion with colonial forces and shows an image of the text from which the quote comes from (without adequate reference) to create a believable citational field of historical evidence.

We raise this example at the close of this chapter as a reminder of the ways in which the digital functions to advance hegemonic political projects by rendering them decolonial and "from below." In the case of India, we can see how YouTube channels like String's bill themselves as suppressed knowledge that ruptures the status quo and protects the Hindu state from attacks from within. These online efforts, as Akanksha Mehta reveals, are part of well-developed, long-term, and multipronged strategy to reshape the educational terrain in India. Through organizations such as the Vidya Bharati Akhil Bharatiya Shiksha Sansthan, the educational wing of the Rashtriya Swayamsevak Sangh (RSS), there has been a push to seize control of the "anti-Hindu" public university system, infiltrate teacher training and textbook publication, and reshape public consciousness through the publication and dissemination of Hindu Rashtra (nation) materials. Mehta points to the centrality of the digital in these projects, arguing that pedagogical materials produced by various Hindutva publishing houses "are circulated widely through organizations and *shakhas* and via YouTube, websites, social media, text messages and WhatsApp."[55]

This turn to the decolonial to describe majoritarian, populist, and right-wing ideologies as embattled, underdog forms of knowledge has taken root, albeit in different forms, across the world. Digital infrastructures are critical to the dissemination of these forms of reproductive knowing. Various platforms are being strategically utilized in ways that directly subvert universities by casting them as sites that reproduce secular Western knowledge projects that submerge or discredit other ways of knowing.[56] The liberal response within the university has been to buckle under sustained pressure and to turn to a freedom-of-speech argument to justify (re)platforming right-wing speakers in order to divert their critiques away from the institution. In so doing, universities have, whether strategically or naïvely, equivocated the positions of powerful, well-financed, and coordinated populist projects with the positions of those who continue to be systematically positioned outside of and subject to colonial forms of knowledge/power.[57]

The digital turn in knowledge production thus signals a broader struggle (some of which we have touched on in the chapter on the university campus) regarding the relationship between knowledge, power, and being and the ways in which institutions, disciplines, scholars, and various other actors, marginal or otherwise, position themselves within it. It is a terrain that is imbued with affective intensities and temporal resonances that signal and materialize the colonial as it shapes epistemic projects linked to political ones. It pushes us to remember that even as the digital enables what Nvodlu-Gatsheni describes, in his writings on decolonial African knowledge projects, as a series of parallel and intersecting movements toward epistemic freedom, it also creates the conditions for a deployment of decoloniality that reinforces power dynamics that precede but were amplified by European colonialism.[58]

The digital turn in knowledge production also signals the potential to critically engage with (and rethink) the colonial geographies of imagination that dominate the social sciences. In the next chapter, we explore how home/field—a venerable spatial metaphor first articulated in anthropology and picked up in other adjacent disciplinary and development spaces—is being remixed and unsettled through the digital in ways that confound and collapse the idea that Europe and North America are always already home and elsewhere is always the field.

5

Home/Field

*On the Vulnerabilities and Potentials of Remixing
Colonial Locations*

I also recognize that *field* and *home* are dependent, not mutually exclusive, terms, and that the lines between fieldwork
and homework are not always distinct.
—Kamala Visweswaran

(Sahana) I had just finished the bulk of writing planned for the morning
and was ready to walk down the stairs for lunch at an old villa in Goet-
tingen in central Germany. The villa housed the Max Planck Institute of
Religious and Ethnic Diversity, which had been my employer for several
years. Back then, in 2013, my daily ritual was to put the desktop computer on the sleep mode each time I stepped out of the office, although
there was no reason to think that someone would step into my office
to peek at the screen let alone mess with the gadget or its glut of data.
Yet the ritual had to be followed. It was a habit of practiced caution that
came from an anxiety that the online world was not safe, especially for
researchers studying the belligerent right-wingers. Clicking the sleep
option, I stood up from the chair, took the smartphone, and moved
toward the door. Out of yet another compulsive—and on reflection,
annoying—habit, I instantly checked the new-messages notification
on the smartphone. This habit, as is widely acknowledged in literature,
came from an anxiety attached to digital consumption, the restlessness
to follow each update and received message at close intervals, almost
continuously, across gadgets, regardless of the diverse scenes dotting the
day. I was quite aware that I had just finished checking the mails on the
desktop and knew well that the smartphone would not deliver new messages that were different from the ones on the desktop computer. After
all, it was the same mailbox that was synced across the gadgets. New

media cultures are trenchantly compulsive, I told myself, clenching my teeth. However, the annoying compulsive habit revealed, on that day, something strange, something that shook me.

On the smartphone, the inbox of the non-official email account displayed a notification about a new message, which I again, compulsively, clicked on. The mail had just arrived from my official account. I checked the timestamp; it had been sent just a minute ago. I knew that I had not sent the message—not one minute ago and indeed not in the last few days. It must have been a freak accident, I presumed. The automated labyrinth hidden beneath the gadget's surface would probably have sent out the mail randomly because of a glitch, a misread software command, or botched-up wiring. Such things happen all the time, I told myself. The mail was addressed to my non-official email account but copied to the director of the institute. I was intrigued. The mail had an attachment and no text in the body. The attachment was a draft of the chapter on internet Hindus for an edited volume on religion in Asian cities, which was then in production. The attachment was the draft version with edits that I was expected to send back to the copyeditor in a separate email thread. The random mail didn't bother me much, but for the content of the attachment. After all, internet Hindus, right-wing religious nationalist supporters active on social networking sites in India and the diaspora, were known for their zeal to challenge "liberal" academics for their alleged pseudo-secularism and twisted accounts of India.[1]

I had met some of them in Mumbai just a week ago, and the conversation was thick with tension. It was clear that some of them did not want to be questioned by an academic like me, as they made clear that they resented an English-educated academic, now living abroad, asking them inquisitive questions. Since I was quite sure I hadn't sent that message, I started to think that these tech-savvy ideologues could have done something to my email account. Would they have hacked into my system? Was it a message warning me that I should stay out of researching internet Hindus? Yet I had also met and interviewed several Hindu nationalist online volunteers, many of whom were cordial during the meetings and willing to share their views. Was I then just paranoid? There was no way to tell. Back at the moment of discovering the bizarre email, I shuddered, and I changed the password instantly. I went to the institute's IT team to clarify the matter. It could have been a freak technological error, they suspected, but they couldn't be sure. Access to the official mailbox would be impossible without passing through layers of security and the administrator account, they explained, and there was no sign of such suspicious activities from the technology end they handled. I tried to probe more with some Google searches but soon left it as it was not leading anywhere. The email stayed on my system for a while with no trace of what might have triggered it. Whether the mail went out through an act of deliberate intrusion or an impersonal technical glitch remained an enigma.

Conundrum

The unresolved question of the freak mail opens a larger conundrum. The perpetual uncertainty haunting the digital space—of who spread the news, what is fake and rumor, who is followed and admired or stalked and surveilled—injects a sort of vexing vulnerability for researchers navigating and researching the digital. While the freak mail incident relates to anxieties around an extreme case of possible hacking of an email account, there are also several spaces—especially social media platforms—where researchers often feel they are on the (digital) edge of encountering pleasant, unpleasant, known, and unknown interlocutors in unforeseen ways. Such feelings are accentuated partly by researchers' own compulsive habits of staying online. In a broader sense, we might describe this as *networked exposure* that draws researchers into evolving, shifting, and haunting webs of connection that demand researchers' attention, agility, and quick reciprocal action. These vulnerabilities, of course, extend to those whose research does not necessarily have anything to do with the digital, unless one decides to stay away from digital social media networks for professional reasons or personal preferences.

As our research is increasingly available for public scrutiny, whether as descriptions of our research interests and projects on our institutional websites, examples of our writings on our private web pages, or digital announcements of our upcoming talks, researchers have become increasingly visible in digital spaces. This has implications for those doing ethnographic work, since our informants can easily search for us and find out what we are doing long after our fieldwork has concluded.

John Lester Jackson Jr., for instance, discusses his experience doing research with the Black Hebrew community in Israel and the ways in which his interlocutors would keep track of his public talks as they were advertised online and, in some cases, would show up to them years after his primary research was completed.[2] Similarly, Ed Simpson discusses how his online presence allowed Hindutva scholars to know when he was next speaking and to appear at a public talk he gave in London to refute his findings.[3]

The possibility for our interlocutors in the field to turn up at our talks or other public events has only increased in the age of the pandemic. As we grow increasingly comfortable giving Zoom talks that are publicly available, we extend our audiences to include those beyond our institutional spaces. These developments offer opportunities to recognize and more clearly articulate the ethical and political stakes of our projects, as well as our own positions across geographies and as historic subjects. If, as Jackson argues, the digital turn has allowed our informants a half a world away to look over our shoulders as much as we look over theirs during fieldwork, this signals a decolonial opportunity for us to clarify our commitments, goals, and ways of methodologically engaging as researchers.[4] This digitally mediated field offers a corrective to previous eras' extractive and disconnected research on the formerly colonized. Indeed, Simpson, whom we could imagine would have been mortified to see right-wing ideologues show up to refute his work and, as he narrates, to demand his firing from the School of Oriental and African Studies, argues that despite the negative attention and uncomfortable encounters we might face as a result of networked exposure, we should celebrate that fact that our scholarly work can be productively challenged in ways that incite critical public dialogue, particularly if we consider that anthropologists have been lamenting their waning influence and relevance in recent decades.[5]

Of course, the position that Simpson articulates—where one celebrates one's own exposure rather than grows circumspect because of it—is easier to argue if the location of one's research is far from home—affectively, spatially, and relationally. For many researchers, even if the digital collapses distance such that informants or other invested parties can track, contact, and even make life difficult for them, home provides some degree of safety, and ultimately, the possibility of changing ones' research program if things get too difficult is always an option. For each of us, as transnational/diasporic Indian anthropologists who research home while making our lives abroad as new homes, the proposition of doing research, particularly politically sensitive research, is trickier insofar as it immediately raises questions about the stakes of our work. The possibility of being scrutinized in uncomfortable ways in India or our new homes in Germany or the UK creates a particular challenge for those who have multiple homes.

In this chapter, we take a cue from our experiences of networked exposure and explore how it might take a form that is conducive to research in terms of enhancing reciprocity and mutual exchange between researchers and research participants or develops into a virulent form when connectivity becomes a vexing issue for researchers—particularly transnational and diasporic ones—who are engaged in exploring grim practices such as online cultures of contemporary right-wing movements at home. We push for a reading of an ethical research praxis that does not necessarily bifurcate these two effects but rather sees them as part and parcel of the consequences and potential opportunities that the digital produces as it remixes the home/field distinction along multiple vectors. In so doing, we extend what Gökçe Günel, Saiba Varma, and Chika Watanabe call patchwork ethnography—"an acknowledgement that recombinations of 'home' and 'field' have now become necessities," highlighting the digital as a key site where these recombinations take shape in ways that unsettle normative frameworks.[6]

In the first section of the chapter, we unpack networked exposure as a digitally mediated condition that has transformed some of the prevailing assumptions about the spatial, temporal, and epistemological distinction between the researcher and the researched. In exploring this, we use the anthropological trope of the home/field distinction, grippingly elucidated by Akhil Gupta and James Ferguson, as a key conceptual resource.[7] Digitalization, we suggest, has decoded the distinction between home and the field and associated ideas of distance and nearness, now and after, us and them. With the always-on character of digital social networks now entrenching the fields of anthropology and other disciplines, the metaphorical distinction between home as a site of calm academic reflection as opposed to field as a site where "alterity is discovered" appears not only untenable but also unfamiliar.

In the next two sections, building on our own journeys across multiple homes and fields, we explore the methodological implications of these developments for multidisciplinary research on the digital, especially how we might bring anthropological reflexivity to computational methods and activate digital networks toward collaborative research programs. We draw from our ongoing research projects on artificial intelligence (AI) and online extreme speech, and multimodal, collaborative research to illustrate these methodological potentials. We conclude by reflecting on the methodological principles to ground computational big data analyses of the digital with a critical historical sensibility and multimodal engagements. We suggest that these efforts might be broadly conceived as decolonial methodological moves. These moves that are attentive to home/field fluidities further articulate what we have described as montage, a methodological stance that productively embraces continuity and connection by recognizing the colonial legacies that link places, processes and people, and the digital technologies that help these relationships become visible.

Field as Network

In their influential formulation, Gupta and Ferguson draw a distinction between home and field, a separation that they argue is crucial for anthropological knowledge, since it shapes, if largely implicitly, the epistemological and ethical basis of the discipline.[8] Anthropological common sense prevails that "home is the place of cultural sameness and . . . difference is to be found 'abroad.'"[9] The journey between home and field enables the "discovery of difference." By framing knowledge as a discovery of difference achieved by a purposeful journey to "another" place, the home/field distinction thus serves as a powerful axis along which the colonial structure of marking and essentializing alterity is sustained. Furthermore, Gupta and Ferguson observe that the very construction of home renders some fields more anthropological than others because they are "more not home than others." They define this as the "hierarchy of purity" of field sites.[10] These purities directly affect prospects of career growth within the disciplines; for example, the further away the field is from the country in which the institution is located, the more likely the anthropologist is commended as a "true fieldworker."

However, these gradations also represent the unspoken and taken-for-granted hierarchies and demarcations of cultures and areas.

In the disciplinary history of anthropology, the ontology of the inferior non-Western other as constitutive of the European modern self (a point we discussed in the Extreme chapter) has been accompanied by the epistemology of the distant field, where alterity is discovered.[11] Methodologically, these tropes have normalized the exercise of constructing otherness via the trope of fieldwork. Even before the expansion of digital media and circulations, the trope of home/field came under intense scrutiny, foremost for its limitations in spatially circumscribing the sites of anthropological research as bounded wholes. Movements of people, ideas, objects, and capital across national, regional, and local geographical boundaries that accompanied the transformative processes of late capitalism prompted anthropologists to call for multi-sited fieldwork with a decentered understanding of interlocking locations rather than territorially and geographically bounded fields.[12]

These spatial tropes are further complicated as postcolonial subjects participate as social scientists in the global research community. Xiang Bao argues that "while scholars from the West roam the world, researching and doing battle with 'issues' in far-flung, non-Western countries, researchers from developing countries more typically specialise in 'home' topics—as 'local' scholars."[13] Bao describes his own experience in an elite anthropology PhD program in the US and how he resisted the pressure to do fieldwork in China, opting instead to conduct a project on transnational digital labor regimes by following the pathways that Indian cognitariat take as they are "body shopped" globally. In the narration of his journey and the pressures he faced, Bao suggests another wiring of home/field that imagines the postcolonial subject, educated in Western universities, as an elevated native anthropologist particularly capable and almost duty bound to conduct fieldwork at home—not taking into account the complex layers of difference and hierarchy that constitute any location.[14] The digital, both "as a means and sign of globalization," has heightened the need to reimagine fields as diverse, plural, and networked rather than as singular, bounded, and self-contained.[15] Specifically, the digital has redefined the home/field trope in at least three ways, which has implications not only for anthropology but also for other disciplines engaged in fieldwork.

In Gupta and Ferguson's conceptualization, the distinction between field and home in ethnographic knowledge is enacted as a "spatial separation."[16] It is spatial because data are gathered in one place and analysis and writing up happens in another. The influence of digital media networks on this spatial separation has been significant; for instance, researchers can no longer clearly demarcate their field from home while researching Twitter hashtags, online video games, or online activist movements, since these field sites simultaneously open up on their computer monitors and unfold in the places where they carry out fieldwork, and some of these networked actions might also circulate within what they would consider home. While the blurring of boundaries is especially pronounced for themes that are directly related to digital transformations, there is also a recognition that the ongoing digitalization of politics, society, governance, and cultures leaves no field untouched by these transformations, especially the ways in which the binary spatial logic of home and field is infused with the polycentric logics of networks.

The distinction between home and field as an anthropological trope is also temporal because the common assumption is that writing comes after fieldwork is complete. Here again, the temporality of social networking sites has radically reconfigured this sequential separation. Digital media's instant reaction loops have encroached on times reserved for analytical reflection, as neoliberal universities and funding systems put pressure on academic researchers to remain visible on social media platforms. Even as researchers struggle to find a balance between the pressure and allure of just-in-time commenting with a commitment to public engagement, the prevalence of spatially agnostic digital data has made it difficult for researchers to temporally demarcate data gathering from writing. Researchers increasingly find themselves simultaneously navigating the digital networks to gather data, write up research, and promote their work on social networking sites. These activities occur in iterative loops fed by system-driven feedback (comments, tags, and mentions), visibility scores (likes and followers), and the accumulation of more data. Admittedly, factors that interrupt these processes are the quality and availability of internet access, data access permissions, and the researcher's own conscious decision to stay out of the self-perpetuating cycles of data.

Even the form of writing that constitutes a separation between textually fragmentary fieldnotes that are close to field experience and ethnographic writing surrounded by theoretical texts and peer publications is
reconfigured in the digital age.[17] Internet Hindus, the focus of Sahana's
research, for instance, are active in throwing back snippets of theoretical
positions, arguments, and archival "evidence" that seemingly expose the
duplicity of Western-trained secularism. Researchers have to confront
these theoretical and "evidence based" arguments even while doing
fieldwork. In most cases, such arguments and confrontations constitute
actual field encounters.

Temporal succession, spatial separation, and contexts of writing have
thus been transformed by digital networks, altering the lives of academics and the styles of writing disciplined by conventions. The shift is also
seen in the other area of contrast that Gupta and Ferguson highlight: the
anthropological tropes of *entry into* and *exit from* the field. For scholars
studying digital media in particular, the looming question is when to
enter and, moreover, when to exit the digital worlds. When researchers
become part of a Facebook group or witness an ever-evolving hashtag
that hibernates for a while only to flare up later, what are the practical
and methodologically appropriate ways to exit the field? In many ways,
researchers navigating the digital are arguably never out of the field. The
exit points have to be consciously earmarked both spatially and temporally based on the research topic, since research analysis cannot happen
for infinitely expandable data, and moreover, even in the era of big data,
researchers should get a life!

Finally, of critical importance in the distinction between home and
field is the space of calm security that the home guarantees the researcher. In the colonial context, this security resulted from an entry
into and observation of the field that were enabled by the privileges and
power of the imperial home. The imperial home also provided ways
to impose the epistemological and evaluative perspectives on research
subjects, since these actions enacted in the name of research largely
went unchallenged in the violent context of colonial conquer, as we
highlighted in the "Capture" chapter. The digital has productively upset
the modalities of entry and exit, as well as the analytical and evaluative
perspectives shaped by the researchers' privileged home of calm security. Researchers' analyses are brought to question or at the least actively

negotiated by actors who are the subjects of research. The field, in other words, is constantly speaking back to researchers in and through digital media networks.[18]

In terms of the knowledge relations we discussed in the previous chapter, the implications of the erosion of the home/field distinction offers opportunities for subjects of research to challenge the findings of experts by offering their own accounts. For the less powerful and well resourced, as Gabriel's research on Delhi's youth hip-hop worlds suggests, the potential for producing self-representations in online spaces for transnational circulation and the refusal to engage with outsiders and their knowledge projects—on their terms, at least—forms another means to disrupt and erode the home/field distinction.[19] At the same time, researchers studying right-wing political cultures face the challenge of navigating hyper-nationalist actors who follow and expose academics online, attempting to affix researchers in a state of constant alertness and anxiety.

Such challenges are pertinent for anthropologists who view their discipline "as a field of knowledge [that] depends on fieldwork as the distinctive mode of gathering knowledge," but the deeply ambivalent effects of digital networks upon the home/field distinction have also become relevant for scholars engaged in fieldwork in other disciplines/subdisciplines such as development studies, information and communication technologies for development (ICTD), political science, gender and sexuality studies, and sociology, among others.[20]

In the next two sections, we turn to two methodological moves that reflexively utilize and scrutinize field-as-network, shaping our efforts to bring politics and perspective into computational methods, and extend the networking capacities of the digital toward developing multimodal methods for engaged research.

Technology, Data and a Fragile Home

The freak mail incident Sahana described at the beginning highlights a vexing aspect of the dissolving boundaries between home and field in the digital age. While digital networks have productively unsettled colonial privileges that bestowed home with the comfort that was underwritten by its extractive potential, this disruption has also provoked risks that are undesired, if not fully unexpected. As critical research-ers especially those studying oppressive politics increasingly become embedded within digital networks, the desire to find spaces that are free from oversight is nearly impossible to obtain. For instance, Indiafacts.com (now Indiafacts.org.in), a Hindu nationalist website engaged in ideological work online, published a regular column in their earlier ver-sion to "expose" what they considered as duplicitous academic research that deliberately maligned the country's rich heritage.[21] The targeted academics were English-educated scholars, largely from the disciplines of history and English literature and known for their left-liberal posi-tions and theoretical grounding in Marxist historiography. Ed Simpson, whom we mentioned in the introduction, discusses how the right-wing Hindutva scholars showed up to his talk with a book of their own, to counter his.[22] This is a very particular example, of course, as it evidences the ways in which powerful and resource-rich, state-backed ideological projects challenge the imagined spatial distance of metropole-periphery division through digital surveillance and air travel. Once one has located a "liberal academic" and tracked them in online networks, as long as one can pay for the air ticket between Delhi and London and obtain a visa to make the journey, one can disrupt otherwise stable knowledge arrange-ments by journeying to where they live and heckling them. Similarly, several cases of trolling, such as the UK nationalists' troll attack against an academic we analyzed in the "Extreme" chapter, attest to the growing fears that academic research processes are derailed, disrupted, or threat-ened by diffused and powerful groups of xenophobic actors online.

(Sahana) I have often said to myself that if fieldwork has to come in the manner of observing incidents of trolling, shaming, and shadowing people online and beyond, I might rather migrate to a different topic. While I have stayed on, a heightened sense of caution that haunts my research activities has also shaped the opportunity to imagine a different home/field relation, one that draws strength from one home to scruti-nize and reflect upon the actual conditions of safety in another home, as I see myself navigating multiple homes as a migrant and a researcher. The problem of multiple homes started when I moved to Germany after graduate education in India and stints visiting US universities, facing a sudden silence—also quite literally—when I felt that I had been air-dropped into the quiet streets and quaint office spaces in a small German town where even the drop of a pin or churnings in the stomach could be heard like a thunder. It was an unsettling realization that the social world around me had vanished overnight. The disquieting silence accentuated my intellectual inquiry—for that was what I had hoped to get there in the first place—but I feared that it would flatten the highs and lows of my activist noises back in India and all the affective charges they came bundled with.

The guilt of leaving home and civic-social engagements of different kinds half-way has haunted me ever since, and there is no way to reckon or reconcile it. At the newly embraced home of Germany, I weave projects around issues pertinent in India, Germany, and several more locations as they open before me as new homes. It is partly the work of the digital, I surmise, that brings the frontal attacks on progressive voices in Turkey, racist discrimination and continued impoverishment of the Romani people in Hungary, white supremacist denigration of immigrants in Denmark and Germany, the Hindu nationalist violence of rumor and lynching in India, and so on, as something I recognize and feel impelled to see together as an evolving conjuncture that besets my multiple homes, a feeling that also animates our research methodology of montage.

For sure, for the most part, aside from the digital, I have actually lived and worked in India, Germany and Hungary and visited other places mentioned here, but the work of the digital is also in bringing aggressive assaults on speech, dignity, and safety in these locations and elsewhere as viscerally palpable, immediate concerns. In such moments, I have often failed to see a field, a separation that marks the boundaries of here and there, now and after, us and them. Instead, I have been swept by the urge to keep my multiple homes safe from the harms of exclusionary speech and data capture and, in a narrower but vital sense, of keeping our research team and myself safe from the banal forms of surveillance that networked exposure makes possible.

And yet, even as I continue to take up emotionally taxing research topics and feel the regressive enclosures and threats across the locations I consider home, the public relations apparatus of my home university's central administration has tossed me up on their publicity plans, featuring me in their videos, interviews, and press releases. My research (and profile), like other grant winners whom the university has attracted, signals the new growth agenda of a centuries-old university to position itself on the leading edge of internationalization, global competitiveness, and research marked as cutting edge. The visibility conferred by the publicity apparatuses of the university and the EU-level grant bodies has offered a buffer that I imagine can fortify a safer home to raise and think through difficult questions, navigate oppressive regimes, and stay stubborn. This imagined safety is braided with the EU's grant-making rationale that frames valuable research as "high risk, high gain." Am I then not in a safe home that accommodates risk and prods its researchers to go look for it?

I have sought to make use of the resources gained in the wealthy Western academic system—actual money as well as publicity capital—to create opportunities that I could perhaps not have created otherwise. Set within the EU funding environment that generously supports in-depth, longer-term studies, my efforts to draw from different avenues, including consultations for the United Nations and access to elite German circles that I mentioned briefly in the "Extreme" chapter, have yielded possibilities to push research around grim research topics further, toward crafting social interventions that can bring thoughts and experiences of people and material resources together.

Such opportunities for assembly and partnerships have also helped to address another kind of vulnerability that digital researchers face: the rapid obsolescence of technical skillsets and the pressure to keep pace with the shifts in technology. This leads to a broader point about networked exposure. In as much as it emerges from the political fields and propagandistic interests in the form of banal or organized surveillance, digital vulnerability also stems from the technical side of research that places expectations of requisite technical knowledge and skill-upgrading on digital researchers. Skills such as software coding and data analysis (or collaboration with those equipped in these areas) might not only help researchers to better navigate digital attacks, but since the technological and the social are closely intertwined in digital formations, they are critical to carrying out research on digital cultures. Rahul Mukherjee describes this condition as "infrastructural imaginaries" that "lie at the intersection of structured state policy/corporate initiatives and lived experiences/affective encounters of ordinary citizens."[23] At the intersection of state, corporate, and everyday imaginaries and practices, the digital

continues to be a massive "transitory phenomenon," as digital mediations spread through fleeting and rapidly mutating platforms with forms
and styles of engagement that are always in flux.[24] Indeed, the very rapidity of changing platforms, constellations of data types (textual, sonic,
visual, spatial, and temporal), data access and data-protection standards
constitute a dynamic scenario that demands great agility and up-to-date
technological knowledge during fieldwork and writing. In other words,
as the field becomes a network, disrupting the distinction between home
and field, the technological, social, and political imaginaries come bundled in dynamically evolving forms, the ramifications of which could
be traced in their fullest possible scope when technical disciplines collaborate with social sciences. Conversely, while technical disciplines
might be equipped to technologically map, build, and examine big data
networks, the evisceration of the social in these studies could lead to
grave limitations in technology design and adverse sociopolitical consequences, as the problem of algorithmic bias we discussed in the "Capture" chapter vividly illustrates.

Addressing bias is a serious concern for various fields of digital transformation, but the problem is especially pronounced for extreme-speech
moderation as I witness vituperative and vitriolic online exchanges
threatening the safety of immigrants, religious minorities, and regime-
critical voices across my multiple homes on different levels, from everyday social interactions to legal, constitutional guarantees. By no means
can online speech be left alone in the hands of computational methods
and corporate initiatives. This has led me to design the project AI4D-
ignity, which has tried to address the immense problem of bringing
cultural contextualization to big data sets by creating a curated coding
space with fact checkers, ethnographers, and AI developers to detect and
label extreme speech.[25]

Aside from the gravity of the issue, what drove me to take up this collaborative project was the first-hand experience of labeling problematic
expressions online, when we realized how even the seemingly obvious
instances of extreme speech turned evasive and slippery for labeling on
closer inspection. Even with thoroughly dedicated student researchers
who were parsing the texts carefully, we encountered hurdles at every
step of annotation while mapping online discussions for problematic
content. The bulk of these discussions came from the data we gathered

from Twitter and WhatsApp during the Indian general elections in 2019, Twitter hashtag data for themes related to religious politics in India collected since 2015, and the Twitter troll attack against a UK-based academic analyzed in the "Extreme" chapter. During the two-stage coding process that involved primary coding (identifying concepts based on prior research work and close reading of the current pool of tweets) and synthesis coding (connecting concepts across themes), questions piled up over what strands of discussion should be placed under which category, what should be considered derogatory extreme speech (insults, offence, and ridicule), and what should be categorized as exclusionary extreme speech (direct or implied call for excluding the target groups from an imagined and/or institutionally backed ingroup).[26] Even before assigning the labels to expressions, defining the categories and drawing the gradation of severity were challenging tasks, as we navigated multiple typologies and definitions for hate speech circulating within the policy, legal, corporate, and academic discussions.[27] Questions were growing—whether ad hominem attacks should be considered derogatory extreme speech or exclusionary extreme speech, whether sarcastic insults should be grouped under derogatory extreme speech or left out of the list, if mocking the actions of political opponents counts as hate speech, and so on. The genre of perceived humor was particularly painful. A large number of GIFs that were shared in a sampled pool of online discussions prompted project research assistant Miriam Homer to wonder if these short clips that showed "reaction in a silly, sometimes funny way" should be considered in the category of "sarcasm with humor" or just "any other" (meaning no label can be assigned). I suggested that in the context of a troll attack, which was the nature of the sampled online discussion in question, there would be no innocent humor. Humor, in these instances, comes braided with aggressive messaging and collective celebration of vitriolic exchange. Questions and doubts, however, continued to flow, at times causing awkward moments that left me confused. Our student researcher once asked, "Would it be interesting for your analysis if I took a look at the skin colors of people who appear in the used media [mostly GIFs]?" I didn't have a ready answer. Where and how should we notice the color line in GIFs that had no textual content? Would the student researcher have proposed the idea were I not a person of color living in Germany? Even if we documented the skin colors of the characters in the GIFs that were shared during a troll attack, what kind of analysis would this lead to?

The two brief illustrative cases of humor and references to skin color (in images) in the extreme speech passages reveal how data comes loaded with intended, implied, and situated meanings that are relayed and absorbed as they traverse online posters, onlookers, and annotators. For instance, we decided not to pursue the "color mapping" of characters featured in the GIFs in content analysis, but the meaning of visuals, especially the mashed-up variety that were cryptic, indirect, allusive, and evasive posed a huge challenge in the annotation work. Such situated meanings that come coded with longer histories highlight the complexity of meaning and context that arises even during intense manual coding of online extreme speech.

AI4Dignity has emerged out of our efforts to navigate this complexity and do something about it. It follows from a recognition that the primary focus of machine-learning models and computational linguistics has been on detection and labeling of data, with insufficient contextual knowledge of actors, real-world networks, and cultural meanings underpinning hateful content. One example from the corporate world is the vastly publicized project Perspective API, a joint creation of Google's Counter Abuse Technology project and Jigsaw to evaluate toxicity of online speech instances.[28] The ambitious project has aimed to deploy the latest machine-learning models to scale up crowdsourced evaluations of speech. Perspective's aim to fine-tune machine learning models to detect toxicity in online discussions resonates across corporate and academic efforts steeped in computational methods. Premising that any dependence on human moderators comes with the risk of long response time, such efforts articulate the desire to bring scalability that can overcome the challenge of speed and volume in online hate speech moderation. Other implied or stated motivations for corporate-driven automations in speech moderation have been to reduce costs and decrease human discretion and emotional labor. For a significant section of the computer science community that has supported the corporate data industry with technological knowledge and research, the challenge to equip machine learning models with greater capacity to detect meaning and context that can also function *at scale* is attractively daunting. However, the problem of context and meaning looms large in AI-centric efforts, as does the problem of bias.[29] Internet discourses cannot be isolated from other media channels and communication forms or indeed from the broader structures of power that shape vulnerability and conditions of culpability for extreme speech.

Such cautionary notes about digital communication research do not mean that disciplinary traditions must compete to establish the uniqueness or greater value of their approaches, but they stress that digital research is better served when disciplines collaborate to advance a holistic, critical approach to social and cultural worlds within which digital circulations unfold. At a very basic level of content coding, interactions between computer scientists and social scientists could yield productive iterations. My interactions with the natural language processing (NLP) researchers in the AI4Dignity project might provide an illustrative vignette. During the course of this project, a computer science (NLP) scholar and I got into a lengthy discussion about the list of labels that should be used for annotating extreme speech. The first list I had proposed was rather long and covered derogatory or discriminatory expressions directed at immigrants, women, ethnic minorities, and sexual minorities, as well as expressions that relay or articulate racist expressions and conspiracy theories. Furthermore, following the theoretical focus on agonistic extreme speech, I included three separate labels: "criticizes mainstream legacy media in uncivil terms," "criticizes politicians in uncivil terms," and "criticizes the state in uncivil terms."[30] The NLP partner appreciated the intention to capture the granularity but was hesitant to include too many labels because he thought the annotation work would be too cumbersome. In addition, considering that we were requesting partnering fact checkers to take up the annotation work, the longer the list of labels, the more hectic it would be for our project partners. He proposed that the three categories of extreme speech aimed at the state, media, and politicians could be merged into one. This conflation could be incorrect, I pointed out, since merging criticism aimed at legacy media, the state, and politicians as "anti-establishment extreme speech" would evade the vast differences in national media systems with varying degrees of media freedoms. Extreme speech directed at the state and media, for instance, would have a different implication for contexts of state-owned media, compared to contexts of relatively independent media operating as critical watchdogs of the state and the political class.

On another occasion, the NLP researcher proposed one other way to reduce the complexity of labeling. "I am wondering whether the 'racist expressions' category should be expressed in a different manner," he said. "Wouldn't 'portrays racial groups in disrespectful terms' be clearer? Plus it would conform to the rest of the categories better. For example, racial slurs and slurs about sexuality shouldn't be treated differently in data collection, right?" While certainly appreciating their good intentions and the enthusiasm for clarity in the process of labeling, I nonetheless remarked, "Thanks, but there are no 'racial groups.' Race is a constructed category. Racialization or racial power operates through these constructions." After these iterations, we arrived at a list that retained all but three labels from the original version but with a better way to display them in the online annotation interface so annotators would not find it exhausting to navigate a long list of labels.

On yet another occasion, the NLP model that the team was working on to reduce bias in corpus-based datasets produced an output, "I hate black coffee," by automatically replacing (through machine intelligence) the word *people* in the original sentence with *coffee* in the corrected sentence. The model had thus debiased the sentence "I hate Black people" by turning it into "I hate black coffee." In the earlier version of the paper, the model had produced the output "I hate black cats" for the same sentence. As we were working on several versions of the paper, the coder on the team thought the sentence would be less biased if it referred to black coffee instead of black cats. When the draft came to my desk for the comments, I politely objected. "Both the versions are problematic," I remarked. "*Black coffee* can refer to the musician and would therefore be disrespectful, and *black cats* can be offensive, too." I asked if we could not have an example where we replaced the problematic sentence with "I hate black money" so the replaced word is *money* and not *coffee* or *cats*. Time was running out for submission. "In NLP, it's not acceptable to make up examples," our colleague clarified. "The examples must come from the actual behavior of the model, and it's time consuming to find the right examples," they said, while they also started tweaking the model further to arrive at more reasonable outputs.

These interactions yielded a healthy exchange of concerns between the two disciplinary perspectives, leading to a more coherent, if not perfect, set of examples in the final version of the paper. During these efforts, I was negotiating not only with researchers from a different disciplinary background but also, more critically, as a diasporic transnational female scholar who was baffled by and strove to unsettle naturalized categories around race and gender and to highlight processes that had escaped critical categorization in the "new home" of Germany. These reflexive engagements altered our relation to the digital datasets, allowing different researchers on the team to ask critical questions about how categories that are gleaned from digital expressions, and are variously tabulated, compared, and weighted in further analyses, always come coded with ossified modes of knowing, and how, therefore, they are in need of constant critical scrutiny and iteration.

Strides in computational and quantitative techniques are thus promising as well as necessary, considering the vast volumes of digital data generated each day and their systematic use by vested interest groups. However, if on the one hand, quantitative approaches are constrained by restrictions that social media companies have imposed on the availability of data for research and by high price tags for archived data and lack of transparency in data selection, a blinkered approach to online communication data, when available, might result from a lack of contextual knowledge— linguistic, historical, or cultural—and such limitations are arguably more common in computer science–based approaches.[31] While we have discussed bias and discrimination in corporate algorithmic systems in the "Capture" chapter, well-meaning academic efforts in computational sciences, as the extreme speech annotation efforts briefly illustrate, are also weighed down by limited contextual and reflexive knowledge. More critically, studies have shown that in these disciplines, including communication studies, non-white scholars continue to be "underrepresented in publication rates, citation rates, and editorial positions," mirroring the skewed demographics of the corporate technology sector that employs disproportionately fewer women and people of color in positions of decision making.[32] There is thus a greater need to forge interdisciplinary collaborations, and furthermore, to anchor them to processes of iteration shaped by reflexivity and attention to power as a point of convergence for history and culture. Reflexivity and critical attention to power have been the hallmarks of the post-1980s transitions and contestations in the field of anthropology, and they have also been articulated by decolonial efforts to reconstitute the discipline by unsettling its "overwhelmingly Western intellectual and ideological project."[33] Developing a reflexive position that is mindful of colonial histories as they shape anthropological research in the field is a critical step toward deepening contextual knowledge in multidisciplinary explorations of digital discourse and their political ramifications. As well, teaming up with computer scientists offers valuable means for ethnographers to navigate large datasets, speed up high level analysis through automation, and intervene directly in terms of bringing inclusive, reflexive datasets to AI assisted systems.

Aside from addressing the need for contextual knowledge in computational approaches, a related critical intervention in the AI4Dignity project has been to bring people-centric perspectives to computational methods. In this project, we have collaborated with independent fact checkers from Brazil, Germany, India, and Kenya as critical intermediaries in AI assisted models for speech moderation. Recognizing that human supervision is critical, the project has proposed the need for connecting, supporting, and mobilizing existing communities who have gained reasonable access to meaning and context of speech because of their involvement in online speech moderation of some kind. Building spaces of direct dialogue and collaboration between AI developers, ethnographers, and relatively independent fact checkers who are not part of a large media corporation, political party, or social media company is a key component of AI4Dignity.

Through such triangulation, the project has developed a *process model* with curated space of coding between communities and academics as a key approach to detect and categorize extreme speech.[34] The process model has laid out the procedural protocols and practical guidelines to create and replicate collaborative spaces for annotation and detection of extreme speech beyond the purview of the corporates and the technical-only focus of computational methods. In a policy brief, we have recommended that social media companies and governments should institutionalize people-centric frameworks by reaching out to communities and incorporating feedback to shape the future development of AI-assisted content moderation.[35] We have also stressed that beyond company practices, collaborative models for identifying extreme speech independent of corporate and government spaces need to be fostered and supported, while also recognizing that such efforts are very time consuming and resource intensive.

AI4Dignity provides one example for a possible productive synthesis of the benefits of scale and volume that computational big data and NLP methods might offer, and the perspective and contextualization that social sciences, especially those rooted in ethnography, could bring. Such collaborative efforts—when resources are made available—offer pathways to ground big data and computational methods with a critical sensibility to cultural difference, historical contexts, local practices, and meanings drawn by users themselves in everyday lived environments. They also offer ways to extend access to AI-related technological competence beyond the Global North for communities that are leading the efforts to ground digital discourse in democratic values. In the next section, we open up another way to engender collaborative research, one that mobilizes audio-visual modalities to disrupt distances marked by the home/field binary.

Multimodal Engagements—Home/Field Disruptions

In the last several years, there has been a turn in the social sciences, particularly anthropology, toward producing audio-visual, textual, and embodied forms of representation and analysis. Multimodality has been used to point to this turn, one predicated on the "centrality of media production in the everyday life of both anthropologists and our interlocutors," and is a recognition of the profound ways in which digital technologies of communication and representation can reshape how we might reimagine doing ethnographic research and what forms research outputs can take.[36] As such it has the potential to disrupt the home/field binary and offer a decolonizing potential to doing ethnographic fieldwork in a number of ways.

First, it opens up the possibility to initiate what Jean Rouch, over forty years ago in his filmic experiments with interlocutors, called a shared anthropology.[37] While visual anthropologists have experimented with making with others for decades, the possibility of entering into projects with collaborators who are on a more equal or, at the very least, familiar footing with the digital technology affords new possibilities for co-creation. Indeed, multimodal anthropology has been driven, in large part, by an ethos of collaborative making that recognizes the explosion of knowledge production underway in online worlds (see the "Knowledge/Citation" chapter for examples) and the deeply reflexive sensibility to production and circulation that these projects evince. As such, the potential for collaboration in the digital moment lies in the alternative forms anthropological research might take as it congeals into the production of shared representations.

Writing, as Gabriel and Isaac Marerro-Guillamón have argued, is not particularly conducive to producing shared knowledge with participants.[38] This is particularly true if we consider that disciplinary genre and specialized academese create persistent barriers to the pursuit of a shared anthropology or social science that is rooted in textual production. Thus, even if we are in close dialogue with our interlocutors in the field and exchange ideas with them in ways that are mutually fulfilling, once it is time to represent our engagements, we find ourselves alone in front of a computer, often writing to specialized audiences with jargon-filled descriptions that have little chance of being disseminated out of the ivory tower of the university. As importantly, writing solidifies the notion that the ideas being articulated are the author's alone—even if there are disclaimers written in the text that say otherwise. The very circulation of these texts in academic spaces reifies this notion of singular authorship/ownership and a separation between knowledge qua knowledge and so-called folk understandings.

Audio-visual production, on the other hand, offers a different opportunity. If our interlocutors already have experience as digital makers—producing videos, podcasts, and images for broader dissemination in online spaces—this creates a different kind of footing for the co-articulation and creation of shared projects. Here, the possibility for participants to determine the direction, scope, and query of a project predicates the sincere production of shared knowledge projects, as opposed to, say, a more developmentalist participatory audio-visual model where parameters have already been determined a priori by the researcher, and as a result, expert-novice binaries persist throughout the project.[39] To materialize an idealized shared research project, of course, requires a commitment from the researcher and their collaborators to reflexively tease out each of their positions in the interlocking worlds they cohabit and their respective relationships to the multimodal project they are undertaking.

Moreover, it is imperative that researchers and their collaborators discuss the ways in which expertise—technical, social, and analytical—is shared between those involved in the project, what the goals for circulation are for the project, and finally, the ownership of the content and outputs. If the researcher is decentered through an iterative process of dialogue (and disagreement) regarding shared ownership of a project and of its outcomes, there is potential for a collapse of distance between here and there insofar as extractive methods are replaced in favor of mutual ones. Unfortunately, as Stephanie Takaragawa and her colleagues have argued, "although the idea of multimodal anthropology may challenge dominant paradigms of authorship, expertise, capacity, and language . . . there is nothing inherently liberatory about multimodal approaches in anthropology." The potential for a decolonial anthropology instantiated through digital multimodal approaches can easily be disrupted by the *bad habitus* of a colonial anthropology that simply refines "the pseudo-science of appropriating Otherness."[40]

(Gabriel) Takaragawa and colleagues, of course, are right to be skeptical of techno-utopic approaches to ethnography. However, in my experience, this reproduction of colonial forms of appropriation and representation does not have to be the case, particularly if an ethos for critically thinking and making together toward mutually determined ends is the focal point for working with multiple modes of representation. When (ethnographic) encounter is reimagined and instantiated as collaborative *and* multimodal, "home" opens up more readily as a location where multimodal projects can be initiated that offers a means to creatively and productively engage in the politics of location on several different scales at once—the interpersonal, the local, the national, and the global. This offers an opportunity to recognize—through shared production—the multiple ways we as researchers are implicated in various histories of contact and contemporary inequalities.

When I started my journey as a PhD student in anthropology and education at the University of Pennsylvania, I grew immediately dissatisfied with the idea that I had to wait to enter the field before I could initiate any sort of meaningful project. I joined a like-minded group of PhD students from across disciplines/departments in the university and, with the support of key faculty, created a group called CAMRA.[41] Our goal was two-fold: to institutionalize non-textual forms of research in our respective disciplines, and to initiate collaborative research initiatives in the city where we lived and studied, including a media festival that we called the Screening Scholarship Media Festival (SSMF). SSMF, which had its ten-year anniversary in 2021, has for a decade invited junior scholars, media makers, and community workers to submit and screen their research-based projects to a wider audience. By including multimodal productions made by academics and non-academics alike—including films, web-based installations, and audio projects—we sought to democratize not only what forms counted as research but also who could do legitimate research on pressing social issues.

While we developed the model for SSMF, finished coursework, and prepared for the so-called field, members of the CAMRA collective also developed research projects with various community groups in Philadelphia and beyond. Our collaborative, multimodal research projects focused on topics that ranged from environmental justice filmmaking and digital archiving to the production of gallery showcases. All our work jumped off the page and was able to inhabit various locations—the gallery, the film festival, the web page—in ways that reached multiple publics. Through the digital and multimodal methods we employed, we made our home the field before we set out to conduct our official fieldwork.

Our move to engage with home as a field, in and of itself, was not new. Since the 1980s, anthropologists in the US have increasingly turned their attention to doing fieldwork at home; in so doing, they have opened up discussions about the future of anthropology that push against journeying to an elsewhere as a rite of passage to conduct long-term ethnographic fieldwork, instead committing to doing anthropology at home. Carol Greenhouse opines that doing anthropology at home is in some ways far more difficult than doing anthropology elsewhere. It requires that one explicitly engage with the familiar of home and find new ways to open up relationships that shake up what is already known.[42]

For many of us involved in CAMRA, however, this simple reading of home/field did not apply, as many of us who participated in the creation of this initiative were diasporic/transnational and racially marked subjects in the US. The US was home to us, certainly, but in complicated ways that continuously revealed our partial belonging and, as such, shaped a particular kind of reflexive attention.

We channeled this shared experience of not quite belonging into our ethos for CAMRA and the research projects that we decided to take on, before we undertook our dissertation research. Several of us initiated projects that explored the racial, gendered, and classed dynamics of Philadelphia. I, for instance, worked closely with Philadelphia Theater of the Oppressed (T.O. Philly), one of many T.O. groups around the world that take up Augusto Boal's embodied modalities to explore collectively how power shapes interactions. I brought my DSLR camera to T.O. workshops, which at the time were deeply invested in thinking through gentrification in the neighborhood of West Philadelphia, where many of us lived. I shot and shared my footage regularly with TO participants to initiate further discussions on what it meant for us to inhabit a fast gentrifying neighborhood and, for me in particular as an upper-caste, middle-class Indian immigrant, what it meant to have affiliations to an elite university that was a major driver of gentrification in a historically Black neighborhood.

Over the two years I worked on this project—prior to my departure to the field—I brought T.O. practitioners who had film experience into the project, slowly developing a film and archive of footage with them. T.O., with its embodied visual modalities for theorizing, teaching, and learning about power offered a "para-site" to create a multimodal shared project that enabled, for me and others, a deep engagement with the place we called home.[43] This experience shaped how I imagined, articulated, and shaped my dissertation research in Delhi, a city I had called home as a child.

My project in Delhi was decidedly shaped by the lessons I had learned in graduate school. In my research I, wanted to think through questions of urban change, economic inequality, and the role that social difference plays in shaping life trajectories of young people in India's booming urban centers. I decided to focus on hip-hop involved young men from migrant and working-class communities in Delhi, mainly because I intuited that I could find ways to support and, eventually, collaborate with the young men to produce hip-hop inflected audio-visual productions of themselves and the city. The collaborative production of music videos that I undertook with these young men enabled me to learn about the changing contours of the capital city of India, while offering them something tangible in return—a digital artefact that they could circulate toward their own goals for participation and accumulation.

The videos eventually led to two collaborative film projects: the first, a film with Somali refugees about the racialization of Africans in Delhi; the second, a film about hip-hop, masculinity, and aspiration. These films, which emerged out of the relationships I forged in the hip hop scene, allowed my collaborators and me to share in the production of research that could contain our visions in productive tension. My multimodal projects have taught me an important lesson: that long after the anthropologist has returned to their home, a conversation around existing shared audio-visual projects and the potential for new ones continues on social media. These long-term relationships evince how, through an embrace of network exposure, we might create different forms of reciprocity through the production and circulation of shared representational forms. Home/field—within these digitally enabled networks of reciprocity—collapse, and in their wake emerges a set of complex, scaled relationships to location.

Unsettling Methodologies: Some Final Thoughts

In this chapter, we have argued that the hauntings that the digital produces create an opportunity to develop decolonial methods for undertaking social research precisely because they vex seemingly stable geographic, temporal, and identificatory relationships that have persisted since the colonial period. In *Methodology of the Oppressed*, Chela Sandoval argues that if we start with a deconstruction of commonly held tropes of description linked to the colonial imaginary—home/field, in this case—we arrive at a place where we can "reconstruct theory and method to create a new vision and world of thought and action, of theory and method, of alliance."[44] We have described the methodological gains of computational methods when combined with a critical deconstructive sensibility to create new relationships between data and observer that rely on people to reflexively, with a careful attention to language, track hate speech and disinformation. Sahana's research in this area is suggestive of the ways in which complex navigations of home/field could bring reflexive approaches to unsettle naturalized categories that quantitative big data analysts use to train computing machines, as well as to highlight processes that require critical categorization. It also imagines an interdisciplinary and collaborative ethos to bring the distinct epistemologies of computational methods and ethnography into dialogue with one another to reach out to communities and integrate their perspectives into the design of algorithms (labels, models, variables) as a regular, open, accountable process.

We have also discussed multimodal and collaborative strategies in Gabriel's research that directly take up our participants' proclivities in digital worlds to create shared projects and outputs in ways that decenter expert-novice binaries and take up the potential of the digital as a site for producing alternate archives of knowing. While there is a danger in naïvely valorizing these methodological possibilities if we do not recognize the potential for them to simply reproduce ideas of racialized and hierarchical time, space, and personhood, we have argued for the potential of this approach when particular questions foreground its instantiation: How are all collaborators differently positioned in this shared endeavor? Given our positions, what are the questions we want to explore, the representations we want to circulate? How will this shared output benefit those involved? What is the possible risk of creating these outputs?

Finally, we have touched on the ways in which the digital haunts our fieldwork enterprises, creating an opportunity for experimenting with method even as it portends an increasing degree of vulnerability and exposure. We have argued that this vulnerability and exposure is not evenly experienced. For the diasporic and transnational researcher who has complicated relationships with multiple local and national contexts, digital networked exposure—particularly when one's research focuses on right-wing nationalist projects, but also when research deemed broadly political in the Western academy is increasingly under scrutiny—produces anxiety and the potential for backlash. These digital conditions and the affects they generate have pushed us to imagine new ethical frameworks for doing digital research. We conclude this book by offering several lines of flight on how one might initiate and inhabit these methodological possibilities, recognizing that our positionalities greatly shape the contours of possibility.

Coda

Reflections on Ethics and Method

2021. As we put the finishing touches on this book, the COVID-19 pandemic rages on. The uneven distribution and rollout of vaccines and the various digitally mediated measures for surveillance shaped by nation-state logics of division and demarcation are fitting reminders of the distances, degrees of separation, and unequal access to life and death that colonialism continues to mete out and the intricate power struggles that the contemporary moment has exacerbated.

This year has also made visible—in mainstream media representation and online social media discourse—a state-led and institutionally sanctioned backlash to last year's Black Lives Matter protests in the form of denouncements of critical race theory in the US and UK and against postcolonial, decolonial, and critical race theory in France. Dubbed the "culture wars" by liberal media—a metaphorical framing that problematically suggests an epic contestation between equal parties—these developments put critical and politically engaged scholarship and Black, Indigenous, and other scholars of color, at risk. These developments in the Europe and the US are mirrored by related developments in the postcolony. In India, we have paid close attention to the ways in which academic censure, the restructuring of public institutions, and the surveillance and online targeting of activists and academics accused of sedition continue.

We have also paid close attention to other colonial eruptions as their traces are etched online, including the discovery of mass graves of First Nation children in what were once Christian missionary residential schools in Canada and the multiple ongoing First Nation and Native American–led digital campaigns to demand that churches release the relevant records and the state takes responsibility by sponsoring a criminal investigation regarding these deaths and to initiate public pedagogical reckoning with settler colonialism and its genocidal effects on Indigenous peoples across the world. These developments, alongside a pandemic-enabled restructuring and defunding across various institutions and national academies, portend that across the globe, the university, and academic knowledge production more broadly, will become an increasingly unsettled and unsettling location in the years to come and that we must pay close attention to how the digital organizes volatile discourse and shapes affective distances and proximities to ongoing struggles for life, land, resources, and dignity.

Each of these more recent events and the iterative and overlapping discourses they generate on social media highlight the continued salience and impact of enduring colonial relations, stressing the import of what we have theorized as *digital unsettling*. For us, *digital unsettling* marks the potential of digital mobilizations to challenge colonial forms of relation across divided geographies and social locations. This affectively charged potential, as we have described and analyzed (in Campus, Knowledge, and Home/Field), is uneven, fraught, and always in danger of cooptation and diffusion through empty gesture and elision.

Moreover, as we have demonstrated in the Extreme, Capture, and Home/Field chapters, the solidarities and participations that social media technologies generate also enable the conditions for a retrenchment of colonial forms of extraction and violence and unsettling anxieties in the life worlds of critical scholarship. The networked possibilities of social media have laid the ground for a global revival of nationalist, xenophobic, racist, and anti-immigrant politics, as white supremacists and far-right and majoritarian actors take up cues and draw strength from one another across affective and strategic networks of social media, while simultaneously, algorithmic workings of the global tech industry, in the background, slot polarized sentiments for data-generative interactivity, pushing them to even deeper troughs of nasty confrontations, self-confirmation, and collective aggression. The large data capture machine that enlists and ramps up interactivity perpetuates the colonial logics to observe, track, and change behaviors, while reinforcing and drawing from a global hierarchy of labor constituted through colonial differentiation.

In either case, *digital unsettling*, as opposed to the liberal framings of a perceived crisis wrought by contemporary digital communication or the digital's capacious capacity to foster individual freedoms, calls for critical attention to the digital as a historically constituted field of power and to the specific constellations of struggle, rupture, and dispossession it has enabled in the historical longue durée of coloniality. This critical attention, we contend, offers ways to link struggles across sociohistorical contexts in ways that offer analytical and methodological opportunities for disruption and thinking otherwise.

As we have moved between examples that emerge in the spaces we inhabit as researchers and as subjects in the world and examples that emerge through our networks of connection beyond home/field binaries, we have attempted to articulate and make explicit our methodological moves and their orientations. We describe these moves as a stance that centers continuity and connection by exploring the colonial legacies that link places, processes, and people and the digital technologies that reinforce and help these relationships become visible. In articulating our methodological moves and political sensibilities, we have embraced centers unsettling both as an imperative to unsettle prevailing norms and ways of knowing as well as a recognition of the ways in which digital participatory flows shake up, muddy, or otherwise push against existing social, political, and economic orders. Unsettling suggests how we might approach researching life under these conditions in ways that are not only attentive to our own positionalities but that actively take up an ethics of decolonial sensibility toward the shifts and changes that digital unsettling portends.

We conclude this book with a brief discussion of the ethics of ethnographically grounded research on the digital. Discussions around ethics in anthropological research have in recent years linked questions regarding our ethical stance as researchers in relation to our perceptions and ideological investments concerning the morality of those we encounter in the field. As Carlo Caduff critiques, the received wisdom is that ethics offers a way we might free ourselves, as researchers, from the subjective morass of our own normalized moral positionings or from the disciplinary dogma of relativism.[1] He suggests that imagining ethics as a universalizing logic that enables researchers to avoid the pitfalls of cultural relativism, on the one hand, and our own moral positionings, on the other, doesn't quite get to the complex ways in which we are positioned and position ourselves in our research endeavors.

Indeed, as Veena Das notes, this tendency to think of ethics as somehow universal—a one-size-fits-all kind of model—takes us away from our experiences in the world and our positions in it. Das, instead, calls for an ordinary ethics that invests in the ethical "as a dimension of everyday life" where we "become moral subjects."[2] We push this idea forward by suggesting that an ordinary ethics—the way we relate in our everyday lives but also as ethnographic researchers—are shaped by the multiple and complex positions we inherit, the alliances we seek to develop, and the interactional frameworks we find ourselves in. This, of course, extends any engagement with the ordinary in "ordinary ethics" beyond the home/field binary. As we have explored in this book, our encounters not only with participants but also with colleagues, kin, students, and various other interlocutors online and offline are generative of various attentions, frictions, connections, and aporia.

For instance, our exposure to right-wing politics in intimate circles and the pressure to maintain ties with research interlocutors (including those with problematic ideologies) have raised difficult dilemmas. The middle-class neighborhood in Bangalore in southern India where Sahana grew up, for example, brought Hindu-centered politics as unmarked politics. The student wings of the right-wing party and some senior members of the RSS in the neighborhood began approaching her and her friends when they were finishing their secondary schooling by offering free tuition for the board exams and the morally laden promise of participation in social voluntary work for the benefit of the nation. Researching and writing about the political cultures of media, many years later, has entailed reflections on the intense feelings of participating and questioning the logics of right-wing organizations from within during the heydays of high school life. The spirit to resist was largely shaped by *vaicharikate* [critical thinking] of her ancestral village. It also inspired her college years, during which she developed a sharper voice against exclusionary politics and engaged in civic activism of different kinds, from protests against road widening projects to environmental activism around protecting the trees in the city. Her investment in critical reflection is also built on several years of experience of working as a journalist in the city when ideologues of different hues had to be engaged as news sources. The predicament that is part of being an ethnographer of digital politics has extended the journalistic necessity of maintaining cordial enough relations with diverse interlocutors, sparking ethical and methodological questions around when and how relations should be maintained, severed, or dodged. It has also, on another level, deepened the ethical commitment to advance critical analysis that is grounded in ethnographic inquiries built on relations and close engagements with actual people who make and remake such ideologies.

These experiences, taken individually and together when thinking about what constitutes ethnographic research broadly and ethnographic research on digital communications technologies specifically, have been a source of productive discomfort in ways that shape each of our ethical stance and our political commitments. This has extended into the ways we have navigated and learned from various encounters that shape this project.

We have, for instance, encountered harsh reactions to the very use of the term *decoloniality* in advancing this scholarly endeavor. Some scholars in the Euro Western academies we are employed in have cautioned us that this term could divide the academic community with "woke ideas" or have dismissed it as a "macro-historical mouthful"—echoing, in unexpected quarters, some of the backlash that has taken place in the wake of the Black Lives Matter movement in the US, Europe, and the UK. We had to think carefully about how to respond to this position, recognizing the burden to maintain decorum and respect placed on us, as former colonial subjects, and any strong response can be seen as indicative of irrationality that ultimately can be used to discredit our intellectual and political projects.

Other colleagues have expressed, and rightly so, a wariness around our deployment of *decolonization* (rather than some other concept or term) to ground our inquiries because of the myriad ways in which the concept has recently been used to elide or evade Indigenous struggles or, in some cases, any sort of material struggle related to colonial legacies at all. As we have written and revised this book, we have reflected on our social locations and how they shape our relationship with coloniality and decoloniality. Throughout, we have sought to make the relationships and connections between and across various struggles as they manifest in digital worlds visible—deploying our method of montage—even as we recognize and admit that our locations as researchers and subjects in the world and the encounters they have enabled draw us to engage particular concerns more deeply than others.

In our research for this book, we have also run across various appropriations of *decolonization* and *the resistance to white supremacy* as tropes to gain moral ground and legitimize corrupt regimes and exclusionary politics. We have become deeply aware of the problematic trajectories of its invocations as seen through instances such as the Gupta family's reference to "white monopoly capital" to whip up a distorted story of racial injustice and hide its corrupt deals in South Africa or Hindu nationalists decrying Twitter actions against their speech as white people of an American firm doing bad things to brown people.[3] We have worked to think through and analyze them as part of our project to engage carefully with digitality and the unsettling it makes possible.[4]

Finally, our geographic locations in the UK and Germany have also served as a determinant for how decolonization's multiple meanings position us. For instance, a colleague based at an institution in the Global South, responding to our invitation to speak at a workshop on media anthropology and decoloniality in Europe, remarked that we should better "understand . . . the political question of placing the only participant located outside the West in a decolonial section." Their articulation signaled a discomfort around invoking decoloniality—as we understood from the cryptic comment—as a new device for marking alterity and maintaining a separation between scholarship generated in the so-called Global North and Global South. The affective responses of our colleagues signal the polyvocal and contested nature of decoloniality that opens a generative and complex reading of the current political moment and the role of the digital in its unfolding.

These instances where admonition or concern have been expressed around the use of decoloniality as a concept have occurred at the same time as the universities or the disciplinary community we work within have sought to enlist us for anti-racism and institutional "decolonizing" initiatives. To add to this, our everyday efforts to offer critical perspectives on coloniality in our classrooms and, in Gabriel's case, to work closely with students pushing against the coloniality of the university have landed us in uneasy situations within our institutional spaces. These uneasy encounters—when seen in relation to our multiple and often contradictory subjectivities shaped by the privileges of upper-caste, middle-class Indian heritage and our status as immigrants of color with stable academic jobs in the West—highlight the complicated ways in which we are located in the institutions and places we call home. These various positionings, reactions, and concerns have—together—shaped our ethical positions and have engendered reflexive exploration of our relationship and investment to decoloniality as a concept in the analysis we have presented here.

The contradictions and frictions we have encountered have only deepened our commitment to our critical engagements within the university while also reminding us of the limitations of where we stand and what we can accomplish under its remit. This has pushed each of us, albeit in different ways, to build networks and connections between the academy and the world, making way for new encounters, relations, and the frictions they inevitably bring. These experiences shape the concerns we have been hinting at throughout this book, which we sketch below, in a somewhat schematic manner, as necessary elements of our ethical praxis and what lessons they might offer for others who seek to develop critical methodologies for the digital. These elements are not meant to provide a definitive guide or a tick-box exercise for how one might ethically engage in research. Rather, we see it as a way to offer some sense of the contours of our learning in the process of undertaking this project and to gesture toward a decolonial sensibility.

Global North and Global South

The terms *Global North* and *Global South* emerged in the 1980s as a shorthand to geographically indicate gaps in terms of resources and development between colonizing countries and their former colonies (not including the settler colonies of the United States, Canada, Australia, and New Zealand). These geographical terms have also more recently been utilized to problematically indicate or infer other markers of difference between these large geographic swathes of territory. Digital unsettling has pushed us to develop a comparative method, which we described as montage in the introduction chapter and have instantiated in different ways throughout this book, that envisions reading through

digitally mediated lived scenarios around the globe as intimately in relation to one another, rather than reproducing colonial and neocolonial
mappings of the globe on the hierarchical scale of rationality and emotion. This call for comparative and relational parity is starkly felt in the
analyses of several domains of the digital, from digital activist projects
for environmental protection to digital disinformation research. As
illustrated by online extreme speech research, we have suggested that
a decolonial methodological praxis involves upturning the schema of
the rational center (the self-understanding of the liberal West) and
emotional periphery (the rendering of the non-West) and comparing
instead online vitriolic cultures of different regions of the world as they
feed and animate one another, while drawing strength from specific
conditions of exclusion on the ground. The global comparative methodology we articulate—not as a set of prefiguring, universalistic rules
but rather as signposts for cultivating an ordinary ethics of ethnographic
engagement—is also a call for recognizing structures of domination and
dispossession unfolding on a planetary scale and inquiring into how
they are deeply shaped by the histories of global racial capitalism now
manifest as expropriation of digital labor, among others, within the
overarching logics of rendering "communication itself . . . [as] a value-
extractive process" in the contemporary systems of digital capitalism.[5]

Historical Awareness

Ethical methodological praxis thus involves situating contemporary
digital cultures in the historical *longue durée*, not only in terms of gaining clarity about the continuities and discontinuities in structures of
dispossession and conditions to challenge power but also, more critically, to avoid the fallacy of presentism and exceptionalism that declare
oppressive forms of contemporary digital circulations as a mere aberration to long-standing liberal norms. By the same token, any prognosis
of the emancipatory possibilities of the digital participatory condition
could slide into techno-optimistic arguments if it does not develop a
keen understanding of the colonial-historical conditions that enable and
limit "insurgent sensibilities of anticapitalist struggles" forged in and
through the digital.[6] Here we evoke (again) the idea that the essence of
decoloniality is, in Jamaica Kincaid's words, a "demanding relationship

with history."[7] These demands require that we develop a critical reflexive praxis around our own positionalities and how they shape our relationship with history.

Reflexivity

Ethical methodological praxis places digital research within an iterative process of reflexivity that impels researchers to not only examine and reexamine the outputs of qualitative and quantitative analyses but also the very categories they build on, as researchers work through their own positionalities in the iterative process of refining the analytical categories they deploy. This reflexive stance reflects the position developed in feminist science and technology studies that knowledge is situated, socially produced, and contingent. Circumventing the messiness of the social might appear as a convenient scaling strategy for quantitative and computational methods, but the often painful and elongated processes of excavating the social through reflexive modulations are critical for nuancing computational scalability with ethnographic attention to power.

Collaboration

Digital ethnographic praxis, as we have described in the previous chapter, foreground the possibility of the coproduction of knowledge and the shared invention of cultural worlds to imagine an otherwise. These possibilities hinge on an explicit and critical engagement with anthropology and its primary way of knowing—ethnography—as an always already collaborative venture, which could (but doesn't necessarily have to) include developing extra-textual representations with interlocutors. A digital ethics of shared making—under the rubric of multimodality and community centered data perspectives—interrogates power and embedded forms of colonial relation that precede any cheerful or hopeful notion of collaboration and pushes for an ongoing discussion with participants regarding the multiple routes of circulation and shared ownership of mutually developed work as central to developing equitable and mutually beneficial projects.[8]

A reflexive ethical praxis honed by what we might call a decolonial sensibility—some elements of which we have sketched above—is not meant to raise new divisions, whether across geographical boundaries or as a reification of the color line. Rather, it thrives on alliances—between researchers of different disciplines as a methodological practice, between researchers of different knowledge traditions as an epistemological practice, between researchers with related agendas and a shared impulse to unsettle the conditions of coloniality as an activist practice, and between researchers and research participants spread across lived, imagined, and adopted homes, now productively connected and ruptured by digital networks—to build a more just and equitable world.

ACKNOWLEDGMENTS

We thank all the research participants for collaborating with us and sharing their insights. We thank the amazing editorial team at the New York University Press—Jonathan Gray, Aswin Punathambekar, Furqan Sayeed, Adrienne Shaw, and Eric Zinner—who deftly shepherded this book to completion. We would like to thank all the reviewers who read drafts of this manuscript and offered sharp, critical feedback and words of encouragement.

SAHANA UDUPA
I thank the European Research Council, Henry Luce Foundation, Social Science Research Council, and the United Nations Department of Peace Operations for generously funding my projects; my student researchers, especially Laura Csuka, Miriam Homer, and Leah Nann for their valuable research assistance; and all the factcheckers and civil society activists for their trust and energy. My sincere thanks to Gabriel for making this exploration an enriching one. My gratitude to Sindre Bangstad, Peter Hervik, Max Kramer, Faye Ginsburg, Radha Hegde, Katrien Pype, Philipp Budka, and Ursula Rao for their warmth and intellectual support.

ETHIRAJ GABRIEL DATTATREYAN
I would like to thank Sahana, for inviting me to join her on the journey of thinking through and writing this book. This project helped to anchor me in a period of great flux and uncertainty, and for that, I am grateful. I am deeply appreciative of Patricia Alvarez Astacio, Elena Gonzalez Polledo, and Arjun Shankar for all their critical and generative feedback along the way.

NOTES

INTRODUCTION

1 Jayal 2019, 33.
2 For a commentary on the digital as a set of diverse technologies, interfaces, and devices, see Hilderbrand 2009.
3 Stalder 2018; Udupa 2016a.
4 Udupa 2016a. A fuller explication of this framework in relation to religious politics in India is available in Udupa and Kramer (forthcoming).
5 See Hu (2015) for an engagement with how white middle-class coders create and maintain the taken-for-granted architecture of the internet in ways that shape knowledge production and circulation and the potentials for data extraction.
6 Bonilla 2017.
7 Papacharissi 2014. We engage more fulsomely with Papacharissi's theorization of affective publics later in the book.
8 Schullenberger 2016. In this commentary, Schullenberger critically engages literary scholar and anthropologist of religion René Girard's theory of scapegoating and how it contributed to Trumpism in the US through the works of Silicon Valley venture capitalist Peter Thiel, a former student of Girard's, who adopted scapegoating as a "positive project." In this context, he discusses a Girardian theory of social media as a desire-producing machine that induces horizontal rivalries by rendering all users as competitors in "mimetic antagonism."
9 Schullenberger 2016.
10 Shirky 2011; Gillmor 2004.
11 For surveillance and expropriation, see Benjamin 2019; Noble and Tynes 2016; and Amrute 2016. For discourses of gendered racism, see Noble 2018. For politics of extreme exclusion, see Bangstad et al. 2019; Hervik 2019; McGranahan 2017; Nagle 2017; Phillips 2018; and Udupa 2017.
12 Schroeder 2018.
13 For *technopolitics*, see Gagliardone 2019; and Treré and Carretero 2018. For *cultural formations*, see Cody 2018; Coleman 2014; Dattatreyan 2020b; Gajjala 2004; Hegde 2011; and Mankekar 2015.
14 Blaya 2019.
15 See Berry 2014; Doueihi 2011; Bollmer 2018; Gere 2002; Negroponte 1995.
16 Fuchs 2011; Hindman 2009.
17 Stalder 2018.

18 Stalder 2018, viii.
19 Ibid.
20 Benkler, Faris, and Roberts 2018; Arazna 2015; Mejias and Vokuev 2017; Richey 2017.
21 Bennett and Segerberg 2012, 749.
22 Kavada 2015.
23 Brown 2018; Han 2017.
24 Udupa, Venkatraman, and Khan 2019; Margetts et al. 2016.
25 Benjamin 2019, 26.
26 Ibid.
27 Tynes, Schuschke, and Noble 2016, 26.
28 Ibid.
29 Ibid.
30 Hundle 2019, 298.
31 In a fine-grained study of twentieth-century decolonization projects, Adom Getachew shows that decolonization was not merely a moment of nation-building but that the "central actors of [decolonization projects] . . . reinvented self-determination reaching beyond its association with the nation to insist that the achievement of this ideal required juridical, political, economic institutions in the international realm that would secure non-domination" (2019, 2). We might notice a similar push for global articulations in contemporary decolonization movements, which have emerged in close connection with the technological condition of the networked potentiality of the digital. By the same token, the ambivalent relation between technology and twentieth-century nation-building projects of decolonization has continued to shape twenty-first-century enunciations around decolonial thought. If in the twentieth century, skepticism about modern technology as an instrument of imperial power stood in tension with programmatic embrace of technology as a pathway for modern development in postcolonial nation-building, twenty-first-century digital technology similarly represents an imaginary of disruption and a condition for the reproduction of colonial relations, as we argue throughout this book. For detailed analyses of twentieth-century decolonization movements in different anti-imperial contexts, see Getachew 2019; and Shringarpure 2019. For critical histories of technology, see Mumford 1963, 2010; de Sola Pol 1983; Headrick 1988; and Kumar 1988.
32 Betancourt 2016.
33 Shringarpure 2020.
34 Moosavi 2020.
35 *Survivance* is a term coined by Anishinaabe scholar and theorist Gerald Vizenor to describe Indigenous cultural projects that reject victimhood and claim an active presence; see Vizenor 1999. For critiques of the use of decoloniality that elides Indigenous struggle, see Tuck and Yang 2012, 3. We touch on Tuck and Yang's critiques in more detail later in the chapter.

36 Shringarpure 2021.
37 Udupa 2020. See also Mamdani 2020.
38 Shankar, n.d.
39 Thirangama, Kelly, and Forment 2018, 65.
40 See Ali 2016; Brown 2015; Mahendran 2011.
41 Mignolo 2007b.
42 Ginsburg 2018. See also Biddle 2016.
43 Here we draw from the pioneering scholarship of Faye Harrison, who advocates for a transformative anthropology that begins by recognizing the discipline as a historical project embedded in colonial relations and that seeks to engage with and struggle against contemporary conditions of inequality. See Harrison 1992, vi. For a contemporary engagement with the "decolonizing generation" in anthropology, see Allen and Jobson 2016.
44 Jackson 2013.
45 Mignolo and Walsh 2018, 6.
46 The phrase *situated knowledges* was coined by Donna Haraway; see Haraway 1988. In this highly influential essay, she critiques the ongoing romance with objectivism and the "view from nowhere" and an apolitical relativism to point, instead, to the knowing subject who comes to know through and despite the various structural power dynamics that constrain them.
47 See recent treatments of montage in visual anthropology and the ways in which early twentieth-century cinema—notably the work of Dziga Vertov—has shaped experimental forms of thinking about method, knowledge, and form within the discipline. See Russell 1999; Suhr and Willerslev 2013. We are interested in how these theoretical and methodological developments in visual/media anthropology can be productively utilized in digital anthropological studies where social media, with its idiosyncratic juxtapositions, meet our networked encounters.
48 Rosales 2016.
49 McKittrick 2021.
50 Tuck and Yang 2012, 3.
51 Liu and Shange 2018, 90.
52 Shringarpure 2021.
53 Tuck and Yang 2012.
54 Getachew 2019, 10.
55 Dattatreyan and Mehta 2020.
56 Jack Wong, "New Book Explores 'Concept of the Ordinary'—100 Words at a Time, *University of Chicago News*, August 6, 2019, https://news.uchicago.edu.
57 Mignolo and Walsh 2018.
58 See Couldry and Mejias 2019; and Milan and Trere 2019.
59 See Zuboff 2019. See also Weheliye 2014; and Wynter 2003.
60 Gupta and Ferguson 1997.
61 Ibid., 8.

1. CAMPUS

Epigraph: Ferguson 2017, 68.

1 Eve Fairbanks, "The Birth of Rhodes Must Fall," *Guardian*, November 18, 2015, www.theguardian.com.

2 Ahmed 2020.

3 As Achille Mbembe (2015) notes regarding Rhodes, "To those who are still in denial, it might be worth reiterating that Cecil Rhodes belonged to the race of men who were convinced that to be black is a liability. During his time and life in Southern Africa, he used his considerable power—political and financial—to make black people all over Southern Africa pay a bloody price for his beliefs. His statue—and those of countless others who shared the same conviction—has no place on a public university campus 20 years after freedom."

4 See Rhodes Must Fall mission statement, accessed November 12, 2020, https://www.facebook.com/RhodesMustFall/posts/1559394444336048/. This page is no longer available.

5 Gillespie and Naidoo 2019.

6 Mathew and Lukose 2020.

7 De Carvalho and Flórez-Flórez 2014.

8 #RoyallMustFall refers to a movement at Harvard University inspired by #RhodesMustFall that confronted Harvard's complicity in slavery, focusing on the brutalities of slaveowner Isaac Royal Jr., who is commemorated in the crest for the Harvard Law School. Accessed November 20, 2020, www.facebook.com/RoyallMustFall/. Johnson, Clayborne, Cuddihy, "Royall Must Fall," *Harvard Crimson*, November 20, 2020, www.thecrimson.com.

9 See, for instance, "Students across US March against Debt and for Tuition-Free Public College," *Guardian*, November 12, 2015, https://www.theguardian.com. See also the COLA movement, based in California, and their efforts to make the university radically accessible with the slogan "Decolonize, democratize, queer, and abolish the university"; see https://strikeuniversity.org/.

10 Mbembe 2016, 35; emphasis in the original.

11 In 2017, Raya Sarkar published a list of university professors in India and in the Indian diaspora who were accused of sexual harassment. The publication of this list and its subsequent social media circulation created a groundswell of both support and criticism for Sarkar's methods of using social media to publicly call out professors. For a discussion, see Gita Aravamudan, "#MeToo Campaign to Raya Sarkar's List: How the Feminist Movement Changed in 2017," *Firstpost*, December 29, 2017, www.firstpost.com.

12 Pillay 2015.

13 Ritty Lukose draws on Karl Mannheim's 1928 essay "The Problem of Generations" to discuss how young people come into contact, make sense of, and push against, the received knowledges of previous generations. See Lukose 2018.

14 For a discussion of the relationship between publics and networks and their increasing salience, see Varnelis 2008. We will delve further into counterpublics and networks a bit later in the chapter.

15 Abdul Khayum Ahmed 2019a. Ahmed discusses the various and complex disagreements among organizers who participated in #RhodesMustFall, a productive and sometimes painful internal reckoning that Gabriel has seen among students who organized the Goldsmiths occupation. Because they become public on social media, these internal struggles offer older progressive and radical observers the opportunity to dismiss the younger generation of organizers and their "woke" online politics. In Gabriel's experience, this is a mistake. Students today are developing ways to use available communication technologies to synthesize new political subjectivities out of disagreement. The publicness of the disputes they have with each other, we would argue, is a strength, not a weakness. However, the same bickering culture is also common among right-wing actors who mobilize through such disagreements (see also the "Extreme" chapter), revealing how online tactics alone cannot reveal the effects of digital unsettling, a point we have emphasized throughout this book by drawing attention to longer historical structures and entrenched forms of inequity.

16 Boggs et al. 2019.

17 Gopal, "On Decolonisation and the University," 875.

18 Ferguson 2017.

19 Castells 2012.

20 McIlwain 2020.

21 Meyerhoff 2019, 5.

22 This document, part of a larger archive that details GARA's actions and activities, elaborates on GARA's initial demands: https://docs.google.com/document/d/1l6Jn-q8TLqnZtEGiEjEtod_egF7oq2ENcOmwJyk5ulM/edit.

23 See the #MOVEME guide to social movements and social media, a project out of University of California, Berkeley, https://moveme.berkeley.edu/project/nodapl/#ftnt27.

24 King 2019.

25 Deloria 1988.

26 As a recent call for papers in the American Association of Geographers points out, Black, Indigenous, and feminist theorists point to a critical engagement with temporality where Euro-Western understandings of teleological unfolding are replaced with a deep attention to non-linearity, repetition, and endurance of the past in the present. Accessed June 3, 2021, https://docs.google.com/document/d/1a1jVvLGsZun4oNzW7xYoPgWWZcczduAfJSWgsQmanw/mobilebasic. The link is no longer functional.

27 Juris 2012.

28 Brown 2015.

29 Abidin 2020.

30 Rao 2020.

31 Weller et al. 2013.

32 Richardson 2017.

33 Bonilla and Rosa 2015. See also Mariam Durrani's discussion on the co-occurrences of hashtags that point to unfolding social movements in her example #ferguson and popular cultural phenomena and the intertextuality that emerges between them; Durrani 2015.

34 See Asif Agha's discussion of Bakhtin's concept of the chronotope. Agha argues that in social media frameworks, time cannot be separated from space. It is "textually diagrammed and ideologically grasped in relation to, and through the activities of locable selves"; Agha 2007.

35 Bruns and Burgess 2011.

36 Bonilla and Rosa 2015, 6.

37 See Cole 2015.

38 Newsinger 2016.

39 Mikhail Bakhtin introduced the concept of *chronotope* as a means to think through how "space becomes charged and responsive to the movements of time, plot, and history"; Bakhtin 1981, 84.

40 See Fraser 1990. See also Michael Warner's work on counterpublics (2002).

41 Gramsci 2007, 168.

42 See Lamont Hill 2018.

43 Ibid.

44 McKittrick 2006.

45 See Subramaniam 2019.

46 In the US, Equality Labs, a digital group of activists, academics, and journalists, who straddle India, the UK, and the US, have pushed to prosecute a caste-based discrimination suit in the US, discrimination that materially links the university to digital transnational labor formations. See Geetika Mantri, "Caste Is Part of the Silicon Valley Ecosystem: Equality Labs Director on Cisco," *News Minute*, July 6, 2020, www.thenewsminute.com.

47 Papacharissi 2015.

48 Gamedze 2020.

49 Sara Ahmed 2021. In her recent book, Sara Ahmed theorizes complaint, mainly within the context of the bureaucratized university, but also beyond it.

50 See Crawford 2009. See also Nick Couldry (2006) for a careful engagement with aurality.

51 See, for instance, the ways in which young women's campaigns to address gender violence through forms of naming, claiming, and shaming come under scrutiny in contemporary South Africa. Maluleke and Moyer 2020.

52 The most relevant of these lists, in the context of the university, was published in 2017 by Raya Sarkar on Facebook. Sarkar, who gathered the names through connections maintained through social media, named upper-caste male professors across national contexts as sexual predators. This list generated many conversations, including an intersectional engagement with feminism

and caste politics in India and its diasporas. See Apurva Vishwanath, "Raya Sarkar's 'List' Forced Difficult Conversations, but Due Process Got Lawrence Liang," *Print*, March 9, 2018, https://theprint.in.

53 Nivedita Menon, "Statement by Feminists on Facebook Campaign to 'Name and Shame,'" *Kafila*, October 24, 2017, https://kafila.online.

54 boyd 2010. Jenny Odell uses resistance-in-place to argue that escapism won't save us from late capital's attention economy but that rather, we must learn to cultivate strategies to resist from where we are located. We use *resist-in-place* to signal the ways in which racialized students push back against colonial forms of control, exclusion, and incorporation where they are—inside the university. Odell 2020.

55 For a discussion of how neoliberal policies racialize populations into deserving and undeserving subjects and reinforce the logic of exceptionality and merit in the UK, see Shilliam 2018.

56 Abolitionist University Studies, https://abolition.university, accessed February 15, 2021.

57 See also Georgetown's Digital Slavery and Reconciliation Project, http://slavery.georgetown.edu.

58 Partridge and Chin 2019. See also Flores and Rosa 2015, 149.

59 Coulthard 2014.

60 Hundle 2019.

61 Dattatreyan and Mehta 2020.

62 Sarah Kessler, "7 Ways Universities are Using Facebook as a Marketing Tool," *Mashable*, October 24, 2017, https://mashable.com.

63 Hundle 2019.

64 Dattatreyan and Mehta 2020.

65 Here are two examples of statements put out by universities, departments, and professional academic associations. These statements were circulated on Twitter and Facebook. Frances Corner, open letter, Goldsmiths, University of London, June 19, 2020, https://www.gold.ac.uk/news/racial-injustice; and "Society for Cultural Anthropology in Solidarity with Black Lives and the Association of Black Anthropologists," Society for Cultural Anthropology, June 10, 2020, https://culanth.org.

66 Wekker 2016.

67 Severin Carrell, "Glasgow University to Pay £20m in Slave Trade Reparations," *Guardian*, August 23, 2019, www.theguardian.com.

68 In May 2021, the German government formally recognized the atrocities against occupied people in Namibia as a genocide and agreed to offer €1.1 billion as reparation to communities affected by the genocide. See *Deutsche Welle*, "Germany Officially Recognizes Colonial-Era Namibia Genocide," www.dw.com.

69 See, for instance, the eruption of the COLA wildcat strikes in the University of California system by graduate school workers fighting for living wages. See "Colas Movement and Wildcat Strikes, accessed February 7, 2022, http://ga.berkeley.edu/news/ucsc-wildcat-strike/.

70 "Universities Must Be Decolonized to Address Silent Crisis on Campus," *Oxford Mail*, July 22, 2020, www.oxfordmail.co.uk .

71 Gebrial 2018, 22.

72 This short opinion piece in the *Atlantic* lays out the core arguments of free speech first adherents in the twenty-first century and the trouble with the left: Peter Beinart, "A Violent Attack on Free Speech at Middlebury, *Atlantic*, March 6, 2017, www.theatlantic.com.

73 Sam Harris, "#47-The Frontiers of Political Correctness: A Conversation with Gad Saad," October 6, 2016, in *Making Sense*, podcast, produced by Sam Harris, https://samharris.org/podcasts/the-frontiers-of-political-correctness/.

74 We can look to the case of George Cicarello-Maher, a tenured professor of political science at Drexel University, whose tweets were used as a lever by right-wing groups to pressure administrators to terminate his contract. Eventually, Cicarello-Maher resigned, stating that it was no longer safe for him to teach in the university. See Scott Jaschik, "Controversial Professor Quits," *Inside Higher Ed*, January 2, 2018, www.insidehighered.com.

2. EXTREME

Epigraph: Maurice McLeod (@mowords), "There's been an alarming rise in racist hate crime across London in the last few months. Sadly this looks like the feared backlash to the Black Lives Matter movement. When you're used to supremacy, equality looks like oppression, https://www.met.police.uk/sd/stats-and-data/met/hate-crime-dashboard/," Twitter, September 22, 2020, 4:51 a.m., https://twitter.com/mowords/status/1308373261248536576.

1 Bartlett et al. 2011; Brubaker 2017; Kramer 2017; Moffitt 2016; Postill 2018.

2 Brubaker 2017, 18.

3 *Deutsche Welle*, "Germany's Buzzword of the Year Takes Political Correctness to Task," January 12, 2016, www.dw.com; Hervik 2019.

4 Hallin and Mancini 2012.

5 Khanna 2020.

6 For more on the concept of extreme speech, see Pohjonen and Udupa 2017; Udupa 2017; Udupa and Pohjonen 2019; Udupa, Gagliardone, and Hervik 2021.

7 Edenberger 2019; Lee 2019.

8 Udupa 2017; Udupa and Pohjonen 2019.

9 Irvine 1993.

10 Penfold-Mounce 2010.

11 This analysis builds on speech act theory of John L. Austin (1975) that considers the situatedness of speech in terms of the illocutionary contexts and perlocutionary effects, within the realm of what Judith Butler (1997) defines as linguistic performativity.

12 Marwick and boyd 2011.

13 Udupa 2017.

14 Chow 2012; Féral and Lyons 1982.

15 Ferreira da Silva 2007, xviii.

16 Yu 2001, 6.

17 Asad 1973; Lewis 1973; Pinney 1990.

18 See Dhavan (1987) for a discussion on how the colonial framing of the empire's subjects as impassionate publics has remained as the core rationale for legislations to restrict media and speech in the postcolonial state of India. See Oldenburg 2020 for a discussion about hate speech regulations that are articulated within an international media development framing of African countries as "conflict societies" (and the related periodization of "post-conflict societies") and how they have also shaped domestic regulatory structures for media and speech. Such approaches that center social and cultural difference can also be traced in the normative assessments of speech and media in non-Western countries, for instance, as voiced by Oldenburg in the same chapter that "processes of social transformation and reconciliation" are difficult because their "social embeddedness is rather weak in the Rwandan context" (291). See also Frére 2007.

19 Chakrabarty 2000, 101.

20 Mignolo 2007b.

21 Asad 2003.

22 Rajagopal 2001.

23 Mignolo 2007b, 454.

24 Denis Ferreira da Silva (2007) observes that the spatial field of the racial is characterized by a constitutive overlap between symbolic spatiality (racialized geographies of whitenesss) and the material terrain of the world.

25 Bangstad, Berstelsen, and Henkel 2019; Brown 2019; Mazzarella 2020; Nagle 2017.

26 Mazzarella 2020.

27 Ibid., 14.

28 Ibid., 13.

29 Ibid., 14.

30 Ibid.

31 Lefort and Macey 1991.

32 Ahmed 2004.

33 Mazzarella 2020.

34 Brown 2019.

35 Brown 2019, 69.

36 Ibid., 70.

37 Ibid., 61.

38 Hervik 2021.

39 Hervik 2011; Bangstad 2014; Bangstad, Berstelsen, and Henkel 2019.

40 Hervik 2021, 141.

41 Ferreira da Silva 2007, 153–54.

42 Brown 2019.

43 Ibid., 61.

44 Ibid., 75.

45 Ahmed 2004 p. 57.

46 Ahmed, 2004, p. 57

47 Fanon 1986, 109.

48 Ibid., 112–13.

49 Fanon 1986, 112.

50 Das 1998.

51 Hardaker 2010.

52 Sahana thanks student researchers Miriam Homer and Pranav Raghupathy for their meticulous work in gathering the tweets and coding the themes.

53 Hall 1975.

54 Thematic categories were counted by the frequency of their occurrence in the tweets. A single tweet typically had more than one thematic category. Therefore, the total count of instances of thematic categories exceeds the total number of tweets in the sample.

55 Many tweets quoted here have been modified slightly by citing only a part of the tweet, by combining two similar tweets, or by replacing selected words with those with a similar meaning.

56 Brown 2019.

57 Leach 1964. For a critique of Leach's theory, see Halverson 1976.

58 Leach 1964, 39. The theory also proposes a homology between the social distance of edible/inedible animals and the permissibility of sexual relations between women and men.

59 Ibid., 29.

60 As Leach (1964) explains, "The English treat certain animals as taboo—sacred. This sacredness is manifested in various ways, partly behavioural, as when we are forbidden to eat flesh of the animal concerned, partly linguistic, as when a phonemic pattern penumbral to that of the animal category itself is found to be a focus of obscenity, profanity etc." (33–34).

61 Rogeres and Fandos 2019.

62 *Sati* was a practice of widow burning found mainly among the Hindus in the northern regions of modern South Asia. In a feminist historiography of *sati*, Lata Mani argues that despite the prohibition of widow burning in 1829 by the colonial administration, "a fascinated ambivalence toward the practice suffused official discussions" (25, 98, 161). She furthermore argues that the debate around *sati* supported the misconception that it was a voluntary act of "wifely devotion" (76, 189, 193). See Mani 1998.

63 Hervik 2019.

64 Ibid.

65 https://www.facebook.com/BasedBrahmanMemes/, accessed on October 13, 2020. This Facebook group is no longer available.

66 Murray makes this point in his controversial book, *The Strange Death of Europe* (2017).

67 Neyazi 2019; Udupa 2019.

68 Ganesh 2018.
69 Puschmann et al. 2018.
70 Langton 2018; Lewis 1979.
71 Langton 2018.
72 The poster is available online at https://www.afdbayern.de/wahlen-2018/themenpl
akate/#iLightbox[gallery_image_1]/1, accessed October 12, 2020.
73 "Unser Ziel ist die Schaffung einer patriotischen Zivilgesellschaft, in der Heimat-
liebe und das angstfreie Bekenntnis zur eigenen Identität wieder als Leitwerte des
sozialen Zusammenlebens anerkannt werden." Identitäre Bewegung, "MetaPoli-
tik," accessed 28 April 28, 2022, www.identitaere-bewegung.de.
74 Rietzschel 2018. See Kaiser 2021, 211–26; and Shoshan 2016.
75 Salzborn 2018.
76 Sindre Bangstad's comments at the EASA e-seminar "Decoloniality and Extreme
Speech," authored by Udupa, https://www.easaonline.org/downloads/networks/
media/65e.pdf. See Bar-On 2013; and Zúquete 2018.
77 Ahmed 2004, 44.
78 Ibid., 123.
79 Ahmed 2004.
80 The situation is worsened by changes in the political economy of professional
journalism that now relies more on "native advertising" (advertising unrecogniz-
able as paid), social media trends as news sources, and "clickbait media" in which
"legacy news organizations compete with low-cost, zero credibility upstarts who
attract large number of viewers"; McGregor 2019, cited in Freelon and Wells 2020,
148.
81 Barney et al. 2016.
82 Couldry and Mejias 2019; Milan and Trere 2019.
83 Kumar 2021.
84 Barney et al. 2016.
85 Zuboff 2019.
86 Coser 1961.
87 Udupa 2019.
88 Challenges, "'Ligue du LOL': Sur les réseaux sociaux, une violence bien ancrée,"
February 12, 2019, www.challenges.fr; See Dagnaud 2011.
89 "La lol culture, c'est se présenter avec autodérision, être prêt à se damner pour
un bon mot." Quoted in Challenges, "Ligue du LOL': sur les réseaux sociaux, une
violence bien ancrée," February 12, 2019, www.challenges.fr.
90 Ahmed 2004, 54.
91 Ibid.
92 Genova 2010.
93 Aguilera-Carnerero and Azeez 2016; de Seta 2021; Dennis 2017; Ong and Cabanes
2018; Schaflechner 2021. The quote about the portrayal of migrants from Bolivia
and Peru in the Chilean context comes from Haynes 2019, p. 3123.
94 Carlson and Frazer 2018.

95 Treitler 2013.
96 Shankar n.d.

3. CAPTURE

Epigraph: Indian administrative officer Kannan Gopinathan (@naukar-shah), Twitter, May 12, 2017, 11:29 p.m., https://twitter.com/naukarshah/sta-tus/863280067262021632.

1   The American docudrama *The Social Dilemma* was directed by Jeff Orlowski and written by Orlowski, Davis Coombe, and Vickie Curtis. It was released in 2020.
2   Tuohy 2020.
3   Firdausi 2020.
4   Kundnani 2020.
5   Ferreira da Silva 2007.
6   Zuboff 2019, 498, original emphasis.
7   Ibid., 515.
8   Bucher 2018; Gillespie 2014; Saint Laurent 2018.
9   Weheliye 2014; Wynter 2003.
10 Couldry and Mejias 2019, 336.
11 For other critiques of surveillance capitalism, see Doctorow 2020; Morozov 2019.
12 Stocking 1988.
13 Ibid.
14 Ibid.
15 For a detailed discussion on this topic, see Kuklick 1991; Stocking 1988.
16 Stocking 1988.
17 Kuklick 1991, 6.
18 Ibid., 6, 182
19 Ibid., 6.
20 Ibid., 5.
21 Ibid., 13–14. She adds, "Ironically anthropologists withdrew from public affairs just when state demand for their services was most intense. Britain was particularly eager to employ anthropologists in the post-World War II period, when officials hoped that anthropologists would help develop viable strategies for turning colonies into independent nations."
22 Curtis and Curtis 2011. Emphasis added.
23 *Changing Minds*, "Anthropological Research," accessed on November 20, 2020, http://changingminds.org, emphasis added.
24 Zuboff 2019, 418–19.
25 Ibid., 420; see also 421–32.
26 Ibid., 424, emphasis added.
27 Intille et al. 2003.
28 Ibid., 157.
29 For a critique of data colonialism as a concept to examine data surveillance and data extraction practices, see Segura and Waisbord 2019.

30 Kuklick 1991, 7.
31 See Zuboff 2019, 418–19. Studies have been skeptical about claims that AI is the potent tool that can achieve the goals of "social physics." Constance de Saint Laurent, for instance, argues that machine learning and neural networks as technical solutions are "still quite far from leading to the elaboration of a fully functioning artificial mind," (2018, 739).
32 Finn 2017.
33 Forlano, "Invisible Algorithms, Invisible Politics."
34 Saint Laurent 2018, 741–42.
35 Gillespie 2014, 169.
36 Bucher 2018, 5.
37 Vannini 2015, 5.
38 Ali 2016, 18. See also Chun 2009; de Sousa Santos 2010.
39 Benjamin 2019, 52 (e-book version).
40 Noble 2018.
41 Benjamin 2019, 72 (e-book version).
42 Leurs and Shepherd 2017, 214.
43 Ponzanesi 2020, 6.
44 Browne 2015, 11.
45 For an illuminating critical discussion on how racialization, sex, class, and culture shape digital technologies and how these "power relations are organized through technologies," see Noble and Tynes 2016.
46 Amrute 2020, 906.
47 Ibid., 922.
48 Punsmann 2018.
49 Newton 2019.
50 Chen 2014.
51 Ibid.
52 Jee 2020.
53 Barrett 2020, 3.
54 Ibid.
55 Caplan 2018.
56 Newton 2019.
57 Ong and Cabanes 2018, 15.
58 See also Rongbin 2015.
59 Ong and Cabanes 2018, 29.
60 Roberts 2019.
61 Ibid.
62 Barrett 2020, 1.
63 Koetsier 2020.
64 Punsmann 2018.
65 Banerjee 2020.
66 Whittaker 2020.

67 Rohan Seth, "Why India Needs to Be the Centre for Content Moderation Reform," *Deccan Chronicle*, May 27, 2020, www.deccanchronicle.com.

68 Banerjee 2020.

69 Harvey 1990. See also Castells 2000.

70 Castells 2000; Freeman 2000; Upadhya 2016.

71 Castells 2000; Zuboff 1988.

72 Upadhya 2009.

73 Banerjee 2020.

74 Chen 2014.

75 Zuboff 2019.

76 Ibid., 501.

77 Ibid.

78 Ross 2013; Terranova 2000, 33–58.

79 Maxwell and Miller 2012; Menon 2020. See also Forti et al. 2020; Libirion 2021.

80 Orisakwe et al. 2019.

81 Ali 2016, 21.

82 Amrute 2020, 907.

83 Kundnani 2020.

84 Casilli 2017, 3939.

85 Ibid.; see also Maxwell 2015.

86 Perrigo 2019.

87 Ibid.

88 *Avaaz*, "Megaphone for Hate: Disinformation and Hate Speech on Facebook during Assam's Citizenship Count," October 2019, https://avaazpress.s3.amazonaws.com.

89 Lee 2019.

90 Mossie and Wang 2020, 21479.

91 *Equity Labs*, "Facebook India: Towards a Tipping Point of Violence Caste and Religious Hate Speech," 2019, www.equalitylabs.org.

92 Frenkel and Alba 2021.

93 Ibid.

94 United Nations Sustainable Development Goals, "Global Efforts Needed to Spread Digital Economy Benefits, UN Report Says September 4, 2019, https://unctad.org.

95 Singh and Raj 2021.

96 For a critical anthropological discussion of biometric identification in India, see Rao 2013; Rao and Nair 2019.

97 *BBC*, "Ankhi Das: Facebook India's Policy Head Quits amid Hate Speech Row," October 28, 2020, www.bbc.com.

98 Banerjee 2020.

99 Ibid.

100 Halder 2020. Missed-call campaigns are a popular campaign tool used by political parties in India. People are encouraged to give the IT cell of the political party a missed call on a widely publicized mobile phone number, following which the call

will be returned by the party functionaries with campaign materials or targeted content. Missed calls also serve as recruitment drives; a simple missed call would lead to enlisting the caller as a party member. The report noted that the party spent between 1.5 to 1.7 million INR (US$23,000) between December 20, 2019, and January 23, 2020, on advertisements on its Facebook page alone when the CAA related protests and mobilizations had peaked. Amounts spent days before and after this window were negligible.

101 Jain 2020.
102 Chaudhuri 2020.
103 Chaudhuri and Sinha 2020.
104 Udupa 2019.
105 Hilal Ahmed 2019; Saberwal 2006; van der Veer 1994.
106 van der Veer 1994.
107 Chatterjee 1993; Dube 1998; Jaffrelot 1996; Veer 2001.
108 Mignolo 2007a,b.
109 Aradau and Blanke 2017, 6.
110 Couldry and Mejias 2019.
111 Paul Ekman, "What Are Micro Expressions," www.paulekman.com, accessed January 28, 2021. See also "Emotional Entanglement: China's Emotion Recognition Market and Its Implications for Human Rights," Article 19, accessed January 28, 2021. www.article19.org.
112 Article 19, 2021.
113 Walsh and Mignolo 2018, 6.
114 While the focus in this chapter is limited to three areas, there is a vast body of critical scholarship on biometrics and data privacy that has documented and analyzed the asymmetrical structures of digital capitalism as they fold into surveillance and governance. For a critical perspective on datafication and discrimination in biometric practices, see Ajana 2013; Leurs and Shepherd 2017; Madianou 2019; Rao 2013.
115 Budka 2019.
116 Duarte 2017.

4. KNOWLEDGE/CITATION

1 Macharia 2016.
2 Achille Mbembe, "Future Knowledge," Abiola Lecture, African Studies Association meeting, https://www.youtube.com/watch?v=Qa5NUW7aQAI retrieved on March 4, 2021.
3 Shringarpure 2020.
4 Christian 1987.
5 Foucault 2004.
6 Sandoval 2000, 44.
7 Ginsburg 2002, 44. For discussions on Indigenous media since the 1990s, see Ginsburg 1991, 2018.

8 Jobson 2020.

9 Pandian 2018. See also Boyer 2017; LaFlamme and Boyer 2018.

10 Nakassis 2012, 625.

11 Adair and Nakamura 2017.

12 Papacharissi 2013.

13 Gershon 2017.

14 Seaver 2017.

15 Zia 2018.

16 Alex Hern, "Twitter Apologizes for 'Racist' Image Cropping Algorithm," *Guardian*, September 21, 2020, www.theguardian.com.

17 Berardi 2009.

18 Terranova 2000.

19 Mignolo 2011.

20 Adair and Nakamura 2017.

21 Here is a link to the website: https://africasacountry.com/. We engaged with the site intensely from April 2021 to early January 2022.

22 "The Response by African States cannot be Generalized," *L.I.S.A.*, July 12, 2020, https://lisa.gerda-henkel-stiftung.de.

23 Ibid.

24 Mewburn and Thomson 2013.

25 Here we treat the *Footnotes* blog as an object of study, first accessed April 15, 2021. https://footnotesblog.

26 From the Cite Black Women website, https://www.citeblackwomencollective.org/.

27 Here we treat the Cite Black Women collective website as an object of study, first accessed April 20, 2021. https://www.citeblackwomencollective.org/.

28 Here we treat the Surviving Society podcast as an object of study, first accessed April 20, 2021, https://survivingsocietypodcast.com/.

29 Kelly Gillespie, Facebook post, https://www.facebook.com/kelly.gillespie.12, retrieved on May 5, 2021. See also Adair and Nakamura 2017 for a discussion of online syllabi as a form of political organizing.

30 Here we treat the Isuma.tv website as an object of study, first accessed April 15, 2021, http://www.isuma.tv/.

31 Here we treat the Dalit Camera as an object of study, first accessed April 20, 2021, https://www.dalitcamera.com/about.

32 For more on Delhi struggles for enfranchisement in the postcolonial state, see Yengde 2019. See also Ambedkar 2016.

33 Marcus 2000.

34 Stewart 2016.

35 Hearn 2010.

36 Papacharissi 2012.

37 Singh 2015.

38 Costa 2018.

39 Bhakti Shringarpure, "Notes on Fake Decolonization," *Africa Is a Country*, December 18, 2020, https://africasacountry.com/.

40 Search #HauTalk for an iterative, collective discussion about *Hau: Journal of Ethnographic Theory* as an indicator of the deep problems in the discipline.

41 Pia 2020.

42 For a broader sense of the unfolding of events, see Colleen Flaherty, "A Journal Implodes," *Inside Higher Ed*, June 15, 2018, www.insidehighered.com.

43 Nakassis 2016.

44 Tufekci 2017.

45 Lausan, "Non-Sovereign Revolutions: Thinking across Puerto Rico and Hong Kong," April 3, 2020, https://lausan.hk. See also Yarimar Bonilla, "Puerto Rican Politics Will Never Be the Same," August 2, 2019, https://jacobinmag.com.

46 Benjamin 1968, 2019.

47 Mirzeoff 2011.

48 Nishtha Jaiswal and Spoorthi Bammidi, "Data Societies 2020: Privacy Concerns amid Interplay of Capitalist Forces," *Economic and Political Weekly*, March 25, 2020, www.epw.in.

49 Foucault (1995) famously discussed how visibility is a trap in modes of modern governance as it subjects those who are made visible to forms of discipline and control.

50 Samuel Leighton-Dore, "Instagram Artist Depicts Queer Arabian Life: 'I Want to Break the Stigma,'" *Pride*, May 10, 2018, https://www.sbs.com.au.

51 Puar 2007. In *Queer Assemblages*, Puar draws our attention to the ways in which liberal discourse in Europe and North America rearticulates Islam as oppressive through the celebration of gay rights. This produces what she calls homonationalism, a kind of celebratory exceptionalism of liberal Western democracy. Puar shows how Muslim queer artists reject these ideas of a repressive/repressed Muslim by producing assemblages of creative work that are disruptive of liberal discourse. The examples we provide show how the digital works to circulate "amateur" disruptions of the same ilk.

52 String, "How Sikhism Will Be Extinct by 2050?," https://www.youtube.com/watch?v=45fPf4HERac&feature=youtu.be, accessed August 3, 2021

53 Ibid.

54 Udupa 2016b.

55 Mehta 2019.

56 Gabriel: As indicative of this, one of my cousins circulated a YouTube video in my family WhatsApp group documenting a talk that a Hindutva scholar, Rajiv Malhotra, gave at the University of Chicago. In the discussion after the talk, Malhotra was questioned about his chauvinistic politics and proceeded to push back by calling out the secular university as unable to engage with Hindu scholarship on the same terms as it would other forms of scholarship. See https://www.youtube.com/watch?v=G2ke7Higm-Y&feature=youtu.be, retrieved August 3, 2021.

57 In late 2020, Cambridge University's governing body decided to amend its free speech charter to remove "'welfare' considerations that sought to protect vulnerable groups from hostility and hate; and they banned forms of protest that include the 'non-platforming' of speakers who propagate racial hostility, xenophobia or anti-transgender sentiments." This move was championed as a victory for free speech and is indicative of the ways in which the use of free speech has been used to bolster right-wing politics on campus. See Priyamvada Gopal and Gavan Titley, "The Free Speech Row at Cambridge Will Restrict, Not Expand, Expression," *Guardian*, December 18, 2020, www.theguardian.com.

58 Ndlovu-Gatsheni 2018.

5. HOME/FIELD

Epigraph: Visweswaran 1994, 113.

1   See Simpson 2016.
2   Jackson 2014.
3   Simpson 2016.
4   Jackson 2014.
5   Simpson 2016.
6   Günel, Varma, and Watanabe 2020.
7   Gupta and Ferguson 1997.
8   Ibid.
9   Ibid., 32.
10 Ibid., 13.
11 Gupta and Ferguson 1997.
12 Appadurai 1996; see Escobar 1994.
13 Bao 2006, xiv.
14 Narayan 1993.
15 Mazzarella 2004, 346.
16 Gupta and Ferguson 1997, 12.
17 Sanjek 1990.
18 In applied research settings, where changes to policy and practice are the goal of the research and directly impact stakeholders, this formulation is complicated, of course. Stakeholders have a direct relationship to the research endeavor and its outcomes and do not necessarily utilize the countersurveillance of the digital in the ways we describe.
19 Dattatreyan 2020.
20 Gupta and Ferguson 1997, 6.
21 https://www.indiafacts.org.in, first accessed December 15, 2020. Some of the features of the website mentioned in this article were available in the earlier version, www.indiafacts.co.in, accessed February 17, 2014.
22 Simpson 2016.
23 Mukherjee 2020.
24 Malkki 1997.

25 The project is funded by the European Research Council Proof of Concept Grant 2020, Grant Agreement Number 957442.

26 A point on content analysis method that we also mention in the "Extreme" chapter.

27 See Buyse 2014; Gagliardone et al. 2015; and Siapera, Moreo, and Zhou 2018. Online Hate Index developed by Berkeley Institute for Data Science, www.adl.org

28 Perspective, "Using Machine Learning to Reduce Toxicity Online," accessed November 9, 2019, www.perspectiveapi.com.

29 See, for instance, Maarten Sap, Dallas Card, Saadia Gabriel, Yejin Choi, and Noah A. Smith, "The Risk of Racial Bias in Hate Speech Detection." In *Proceedings of the 57th Annual Meeting of the Association for Computational Linguistics*, 1668–78, Florence, Italy; Thomas Davidson, Dana Warmsley, Michael Macy, and Ingmar Weber, "Automated Hate Speech Detection and the Problem of Offensive Language," arxiv, March 11, 2017, ArXiv:1703.04009v1.

30 A point discussed in the "Extreme" chapter.

31 Freelon and Wells 2020.

32 Chakravartty et al. 2018, 254. The same article cites Catherine Lutz, who observed that even within disciplines such as anthropology that have a wide representation of female scholars, there is a "tendency for women social scientists to be cited far less frequently than are men." Also see Lutz 1990; Noble 2018.

33 Harrison 1991, 1, citing Magubane and Faris 1985. In the 1980s, the discipline underwent an introspection into its public responsibility in a changed politico-economic global order and modes of knowledge creation. Consumption, modernity, violence, gender, and other new themes were brought into the field of anthropology, leading to intense questioning of the traditional preoccupation with "primitive societies," a category that came into critical scrutiny because of its problematic teleology. See Clifford and Marcus 1986; Dirks, Eley, and Ortner 1994. See Harrison 1991 for the programmatic call to reexamine anthropological inquiry "as a historically specific set of discourses which the West deploys in order to make sense of, define, and figure out and render intelligible how a world ordered by [Western] capitalism works" (citing Magubane and Faris 1985, 93).

34 More details about the curated coding and labeling process are available in the policy brief, Udupa et al. 2021.

35 Ibid.

36 Collins, Durington, and Gill 2017.

37 Stoller 1992.

38 Dattatreyan and Marrero-Guillamón 2018.

39 Here we are referring to critiques of photovoice as a participatory modality in anthropology and development studies projects, as well as to a broader critique of participatory research often undertaken under the auspices of hegemonic interests. For a critique of photovoice, see Shankar 2016. For a critique of participatory methods, see Cooke and Kothari 2001.

40 Chen and Minh-Ha 1994.

41 For reference, see the work featured on CAMRA's website, https://www.cam-rapenn.org/, first accessed April 2, 2020.

42 Greenhouse 1985.

43 George Marcus develops the concepts para-site and para-ethnography to demonstrate how actors reflexively create their own sites of knowledge production that are complicit with and critical of the status quo. See Marcus 2000.

44 Sandoval 2000, 4.

CODA

1 Caduff, "Anthropology's Ethics." See also Lempert, "No Ordinary Ethics."

2 Das 2012.

3 Fraser 2017.

4 *Hindustan Times*, "Kangana Ranaut Reacts to Twitter Ban, Says It Proves White People Feel Entitled to 'Enslave' Brown People," May 4, 2021. www.hindustan-times.com.

5 Beller 2003, 6.

6 Beller 2003.

7 Shringarpure 2021.

8 Dattatreyan 2020b.

BIBLIOGRAPHY

Abidin, Crystal. 2020. "From 'Networked Publics' to 'Refracted Publics': A Companion Framework for Researching 'Below the Radar' Studies." *Social Media + Society* 7, no. 1 (January). https://doi.org/10.1177/2056305120984458.

Adair, Cassius, and Lisa Nakamura. 2017. "The Digital Afterlives of *This Bridge Called My Back*: Woman of Color Feminism, Digital Labor, and Networked Pedagogy." *American Literature* 89 (2): 255–78.

Agha, Asif. 2007. "Recombinant Selves in Mass Mediated Space Time." *Language and Communication* 27:320–35.

Aguilera-Carnerero, Carmen, and Abdul Halik Azeez. 2016. "Islamonausea, Not Islamophobia: The Many Faces of Cyber Hate Speech." *Journal of Arab & Muslim Media Research* 9 (1): 21–40.

Ahmed, Abdul Khayum. 2019a. *The Rise of Fallism: #RhodesMustFall and the Movement to Decolonize the University*. PhD diss., Columbia University. https://academiccommons.columbia.edu/doi/10.7916/d8-n7n3-e372.

———. 2019b. "#RhodesMustFall: How a Decolonial Student Movement in the Global South Inspired Epistemic Disobedience at the University of Oxford." *African Studies Review* 63, no. 2 (September): 1–23.

Ahmed, Hilal. 2019. *Siyasi Muslims*. New Delhi: Penguin.

Ahmed, Sara. 2004. *The Cultural Politics of Emotion*. Edinburgh: Edinburgh University Press.

———. 2021. *Complaint!* Durham, NC: Duke University Press.

Ajana, Btihaj. 2013. *Governing through Biometrics: The Biopolitics of Identity*. Basingstoke: Palgrave.

Ali, Syed Mustafa. 2016. "A Brief Introduction to Decolonial Computing." *XRDS: Crossroads, the ACM Magazine for Students* 22 (4): 16–21.

Allen, Jafari, and Ryan Jobson. 2016. "The Decolonizing Generation: (Race and) Theory in Anthropology since the 1980s." *Current Anthropology* 57 (2): 129–48.

Ambedkar, B. R. 2016 *Annihilation of Caste*. London: Verso.

Amrute, Sareeta. 2016. *Encoding Race, Encoding Class: Indian IT Workers in Berlin*. Durham, NC: Duke University Press.

———. 2020. "Bored Techies Being Casually Racist: Race as Algorithm." *Science, Technology, & Human Values* 45 (5): 903–33.

Appadurai, Arjun. 1996. *Modernity at Large: Cultural Dimensions of Globalization*. Minneapolis: University of Minnesota Press.

Aradau, Claudia, and Tobias Blanke. 2017. "Governing Others: Anomaly and the Algorithmic Subject of Security." *European Journal of International Security* 3, no. 1 (November): 1–21.

Arazna, Marzena. 2015. "Conflicts in the 21st Century Based on Multidimensional Warfare: 'Hybrid Warfare', Disinformation and Manipulation." *Security and Defence Quarterly* 8 (3): 103–29.

Article 19. 2021. "Emotional Entanglement: China's Emotion Recognition Market and Its Implications for Human Rights." Article 19, January. www.article19.org.

Asad, Talal. 1973. *Anthropology and the Colonial Encounter*. London: Ithaca Press.

———. 2003. *Formations of the Secular: Christianity, Islam, Modernity*. Palo Alto, CA: Stanford University Press.

Austin, John Langshaw. 1975. *How to Do Things with Words*. Oxford: Oxford University Press.

Bakhtin, Mikhail. 1981. *The Dialogic Imagination: Four Essays*. Austin: University of Texas Press.

Banerjee, Prasid. 2020. "Inside the Secretive World of India's Social Media Content Moderators." *Live Mint*, March 18. www.livemint.com.

Bangstad, Sindre. 2014. *Anders Breivik and the Rise of Islamophobia*. London: Zed.

Bangstad, Sindre, Enge Bjørn Berstelsen, and Heiko Henkel. 2019. "The Politics of Affect: Perspectives on the Rise of the Far-Right and Right-Wing Populism in the West." *Focaal—Journal of Global and Historical Anthropology* 83:98–113.

Bao, Xiang. 2006. *Global Body Shopping: An Indian Labor System in the Information Technology Industry*. Princeton, NJ: Princeton University Press.

Barney, Darin, Gabriella Coleman, Christine Ross, Jonathan Sterne, and Tamar Tembeck. 2016. *The Participatory Condition in the Digital Age*. Minneapolis: University of Minnesota Press.

Bar-On, Tamir. 2013. *Rethinking the French New Right: Alternatives to Modernity*. New York: Routledge.

Barrett, Paul M. 2020. "Who Moderates the Social Media Giants? A Call to End Outsourcing." NYU Stern Center for Business and Human Rights. https://bhr.stern.nyu.edus.

Bartlett, Jamie, Jonathan Birdwell, and Mark Littler. 2011. "The New Face of Digital Populism." *Demos*. https://www.demos.co.uk.

Bayer, Judit, and Petra Bard. 2020. "Hate Speech and Hate Crime in the EU and the Evaluation of Online Content Regulation Approaches." Brussels: European Parliament. https://www.europarl.europa.eu.

Beller, Jonathan. 2003. "Numismatics of the Sensual, Calculus of the Image: The Pyrotechnics of Control." *Image & Narrative*, no. 6 (February).

———. 2017. "The Fourth Determination." *E-Flux Journal*, October. www.e-flux.com.

Benjamin, Ruha. 2019. *Race after Technology: Abolitionist Tools for the New Jim Code*. Cambridge, UK: Polity Press.

Benjamin, Walter. (1968) 2019. *Illuminations: Essays and Reflections*. New York: First Mariner.

Benkler, Yochai, Robert Faris, and Hal Roberts. 2018. *Network Propaganda: Manipulation, Disinformation and Radicalization in American Politics.* Oxford: Oxford University Press.

Bennett, Lance W., and Alexandra Segerberg. 2012. "The Logic of Connective Action: Digital Media and the Personalization of Contentious Politics." *Information, Communication and Society* 15, no. 5 (April 10): 739–68.

Berardi, Bifo. 2009. *The Soul at Work: From Alienation to Autonomy.* Cambridge, MA: MIT Press.

Berry, David. 2014. *Critical Theory and the Digital.* New York: Bloomsbury.

Betancourt, Billy Ray. 2016. *A Poltergeist Manifesto. Feral Feminism*, no. 6 (Fall): 22–32. https://feralfeminisms.com.

Bhambra, Gurminder K., Dalia Gebrial, and Kerem Nişancıoğlu. 2018. *Decolonising the University.* London: Pluto Press.

Biddle, Jennifer. 2016. *Remote Avant-Garde.* Durham, NC: Duke University Press.

Blaya, Catherine. 2019. "Cyberhate: A Review and Content Analysis of Intervention Strategies." *Aggression and Violent Behavior* 45:163–72. https://doi.org/10.1016/j.avb.2018.05.006.

Boggs, Abigail, Eli Meyerhoff, Nick Mitchell, and Zach Schwartz-Weinstein. 2019. "Abolitionist University Studies: An Invitation." *Abolitionist Journal* (August). https://abolition.university.

Bollmer, Grant. 2018. *Theorizing Digital Cultures.* New York: Sage.

Bonilla, Yarimar. 2017. "Unsettling Sovereignty." *Cultural Anthropology* 32 (3): 330–39. https://doi.org/10.14506/ca32.3.02

Bonilla, Yarimar, and Jonathan Rosa. 2015. "#Ferguson: Digital Protest, Hashtag Ethnography, and the Racial Politics of Social Media in the United States." *American Ethnologist* 42 (1): 4–17.

Boromisza-Habashi, David. 2013. *Speaking Hatefully: Culture, Communication, and Political Action in Hungary.* University Park: Pennsylvania State University.

boyd, danah. 2010. "Social Network Sites as Networked Publics: Affordances, Dynamics, and Implications." In *Networked Self: Identity, Community, and Culture on Social Network Sites*, edited by Zizi Papacharissi, 39–58. New York: Routledge.

Boyer, Dominic. 2017. "Revolutionary Infrastructure." In *Infrastructures and Social Complexity: A Companion*, edited by Penny Harvey, Casper Bruun Jensen, and Atsuro Morita, 174–86. New York: Routledge.

Brown, Alexander. 2018. "What Is So Special about Online (as Compared to Offline) Speech?" *Ethnicities* 18 (3): 297–326.

Brown, Wendy. 2018. "Neoliberalism's Frankenstein: Authoritarian Freedom in Twenty-First Century 'Democracies.'" *Critical Times* 1, no. 1 (April): 60–79.

Browne, Simone. 2015. *Dark Matters: On the Surveillance of Blackness.* Durham, NC: Duke University Press.

Brubaker, Rogers. 2017. "Why Populism?" *Theory and Society*, no. 46 (October): 357–85.

Bruns, Axel, and Jean Burgess. 2011. "The Use of Twitter Hashtags in the Formation of Ad Hoc Publics." Paper presented at the European Consortium for Political Research conference, Reykjavik, August 25–27.

Bucher, Taina. 2018. *If . . . Then: Algorithmic Power and Politics*. New York: Oxford University Press.

Budka, Philipp. 2019. "Indigenous Media Technologies in 'the Digital Age': Cultural Articulation, Digital Practices, and Sociopolitical Concepts." In *Ethnic Media in the Digital Age*, edited by Sherry S. Yu and Matthew D. Matsaganis, 162–72. New York: Routledge. https://doi.org/10.4324/9781351045315.

Butler, Judith. 1997. *Excitable Speech: A Politics of the Performative*. New York: Routledge.

Buyse, Antoine. 2014. "Words of Violence: 'Fear Speech,' or How Violent Conflict Escalation Relates to the Freedom of Expression." *Human Rights Quarterly* 36 (4): 779–97.

Caduff, Carlo. 2011. "Anthropology's Ethics: Moral Positionalism, Cultural Relativism, and Critical Analysis." *Anthropological Theory* 11 (4): 465–80.

Caplan, Robyn. 2018. "Content or Context Moderation?: Artisanal, Community-Reliant, and Industrial Approaches." *Data & Society* (November 14). https://datasociety.net.

Carlson, Bronwyn, and Ryan Frazer. 2018. *Cyberbullying and Indigenous Australians: Review of the Literature*. Sydney: Macquarie University Press.

Casilli, Antonio A. 2017. "Digital Labor Studies Go Global: Toward a Digital Decolonial Turn." *International Journal of Communication* 11:3934–54.

Castells, Manuel. 2000. *The Rise of the Network Society*. Oxford: Blackwell.

———. 2012. *Networks of Outrage and Hope: Social Movements in the Internet Age*. Cambridge, UK: Polity Press.

Chakrabarty, Dipesh. 2000. *Provincializing Europe: Postcolonial Thought and Historical Difference*. Princeton, NJ: Princeton University Press.

Chakravartty, Paula, Rachel Kuo, Victoria Grubbs, and Charlton McIlwain. 2018. "#CommunicationSoWhite." *Journal of Communication* 68 (2): 254–66.

Chatterjee, Partha. 1993. *The Nation and Its Fragments: Colonial and Postcolonial Histories*. Princeton, NJ: Princeton University Press.

Chaudhuri, Pooja. 2020. "Old, Unrelated Video Shared as Muslims Licking Utensils to Spread Coronavirus Infection." *Altnews*, March 30. www.altnews.in.

Chaudhuri, Pooja, and Pratik Sinha. 2020. "Video of Sufi Ritual Falsely Viral as Mass Sneezing in Nizamuddin Mosque to Spread Coronavirus Infection." *Altnews*, April 1. www.altnews.in.

Chen, Adrian. 2014. "The Laborers Who Keep Dick Pics and Beheadings out of Your Facebook Feed." *Wired*, October 23. www.wired.com.

Chen, Nancy, and Trinh Minh-Ha. 1994. "Speaking Nearby." In *Visualizing Theory. Selected Essays from VAR 1990–1994*, edited by Lucien Castaing-Taylor, 433–51. London: Routledge.

Chow, Rey. 2012. *Entanglements, or Transmedial Thinking about Capture*. Durham, NC: Duke University Press.

Christian, Barbara. 1987. "The Race for Theory." *Cultural Critique*, no. 6 (Spring): 51–63.

Chun, Wendy Hui Kyong. 2009. "Introduction: Race and/as Technology; or, How to Do Things to Race." *Camera Obscura* 24, no. 1: 7–35.

Clifford, James. 1997. *Routes: Travel and Translation in the Late Twentieth Century.* Cambridge, MA: Harvard University Press.

Clifford, James, and George E. Marcus. 1986. *Writing Culture: The Poetics and Politics of Ethnography.* Berkeley: University of California Press.

Cody, Francis. 2018. "Millennial Ferment: The Networking of Tamil Media Politics." *Television & New Media* 21, no. 4: 392–406.

Bonilla, Yarimar, and Jonathan Rosa. 2015. "#Ferguson: Digital Protest, Hashtag Ethnography, and the Racial Politics of Social Media in the United States." *American Ethnologist* 42 (1) 4–17.

Coleman, Gabriella. 2014. *Hacker, Hoaxer, Whistleblower, Spy: The Many Faces of Anonymous.* London: Verso.

Collins, Sam, Matthew Durington, and Harjant Gill. 2017. "Multimodality: An Invitation." *American Anthropologist* 119, no. 1 (January): 142–46.

Cooke, William, and Usha Kothari. 2001. *Participation: The New Tyranny?* London: Zed.

Coser, L. Rose. 1961. "Insulation from Observability and Types of Social Conformity." *American Sociological Review* 26 (1): 28–39.

Costa, C. 2018. "Digital Scholars: A Feeling for the Academic Game." In *Feeling Academic in the Neoliberal University: Feminist Flights, Fights, and Failures*, edited by Y. Taylor and K. Lahad, 345–68. New York: Palgrave McMillan.

Couldry, Nick 2006. *Listening beyond the Echoes: Media, Ethics and Agency in an Uncertain World.* Boulder, CO: Paradigm.

Couldry, Nick, and Ulises A. Mejias. 2019. "Data Colonialism: Rethinking Big Data's Relation to the Contemporary Subject." *Television & New Media* 20 (4): 336–49.

Coulthard, Glen. 2014. *Red Skin, White Masks: Rejecting the Colonial Politics of Recognition.* Minneapolis: University of Minnesota Press.

Crawford, Kate. 2009. "Following You: Disciplines of Listening in Social Media." *Continuum: Journal of Media & Cultural Studies* 23 (4): 525–35.

Curtis, Bruce, and Cate Curtis. 2011. *Social Research: A Practical Introduction.* London: Sage.

Dagnaud, Monique. 2011. "Le lol (laughing out loud) sur le net un état d'esprit politique propre aux jeunes générations." In *La politique au fil de l'âge*, edited by Anne Muxel, 181–95. Paris: Presses de Sciences Po.

Das, Veena. 1998. "Specificities: Official Narratives, Rumour, and the Social Production of Hate." *Social Identities* 4 (1): 109–30. http://10.0.4.56/13504639851915.

———. 2012. "Ordinary Ethics. The Perils and Pleasures of Everyday Life." In *Ordinary Ethics: A Companion to Moral Anthropology,* edited by Fassin Didier, 133–49. Oxford: Wiley-Blackwell.

Dattatreyan, E. Gabriel. 2020a. "Circulating Ethnographic Films in the Digital Age." In *The Routledge International Handbook of Ethnographic Film and Video,* edited by Phillip Vannini, 293–301. Abingdon: Routledge.

———. 2020b. *The Globally Familiar: Digital Hip Hop, Masculinity, and Urban Space in Delhi, India*. Durham, NC: Duke University Press.

Dattatreyan, E. Gabriel, and Isaac Marrero-Guillamón. 2018. "Introduction: Multimodal Anthropology and the Politics of Invention." *American Anthropologist* 121 (1): 220–28.

Dattatreyan, E. Gabriel, and Akanksha Mehta. 2020. "Problem and Solution: Occupation and Collective Complaint." *Radical Philosophy* 2, no. 8 (Autumn). https://www.radicalphilosophy.com.

de Carvalho, José Jorge, and Juliana Flórez-Flórez. 2014. "The Meeting of Knowledges: A Project for the Decolonization of Universities in Latin America." *Postcolonial Studies* 17 (2): 122–39.

de Seta, Gabriele. 2021. "The Politics of Muhei: Ethnic Humor and Islamophobia on Chinese Social Media." In *Digital Hate: The Global Conjuncture of Extreme Speech*, edited by Sahana Udupa, Iginio Gagliardone, and Peter Hervik, 162–74. Bloomington: Indiana University Press.

De Sola Pol, Ithiel. 1983. *Technologies of Freedom*. Cambridge, MA: Harvard University Press.

de Sousa Santos, Boaventura. 2010. "From the Postmodern to the Postcolonial—and beyond Both." In *Decolonizing European Sociology: Transdisciplinary Approaches*, edited by Encarcacion Gutierrez Rodriguez, Manuela Boatca, and Sergio Costa, 225–42. Farnham: Ashgate.

Deloria, Vine. 1988. *Custer Died for Your Sins: An Indian Manifesto*. Norman: University of Oklahoma Press.

Dennis, Dannah. 2017. "Mediating Claims to Buddha's Birthplace and Nepali National Identity." In *Media as Politics in South Asia*, edited by Sahana Udupa and Stephen McDowell, 176–89. New York: Routledge.

Dhavan, Rajiv. 1987. *Only the Good News: On the Law of the Press in India*. New Delhi: Manohar.

Dhillon, Jaskiran. 2019. "Notes on Becoming an Accomplice in Joanne Barker's Guest Edited Special Issue, Indigeneity, Feminism, Activism." *American Indian Culture and Research Journal* 43, no. 3 (2019).

Dirks, Nicholas B., Geoff Eley, and Sherry B. Ortner. 1994. "Introduction to Culture/Power/History." In *Culture/Power/History: A Reader in Contemporary Social Theory*, edited by Nicholas B. Dirks, Geoff Eley, and Sherry B. Ortner, 3–46. Princeton, NJ: Princeton University Press.

Doctorow, Cory. 2020. "How to Destroy Surveillance Capitalism." *One Zero* (August 26). https://onezero.medium.com.

Doueihi, Milad. 2011. *Digital Cultures*. Cambridge, MA: Harvard University Press.

Duarte, Marisa Elena. 2017. *Network Sovereignty: Building the Internet across Indian Country*. Seattle: University of Washington Press.

Dube, Saurabh. 1998. *Untouchable Pasts: Religion, Identity and Power among a Central Indian Community, 1780–1950*. Albany: State University of New York Press.

Durrani, Mariam. 2015. "Digital Counterpublics: Black Twitter in the Aftermath of Ferguson." *Anthropology News* (blog), Society for Linguistic Anthropology. http://linguisticanthropology.org.

Edenberger, Christopher. 2019. "Landser." *Bundeszentrale für Politische Bildung.* https://www.bpb.de.

Escobar, Arturo. 1994. *Encountering Development: The Making and Unmaking of the Third World.* Princeton, NJ: Princeton University Press.

Fanon, Frantz. (1952) 1986. *Black Skin, White Masks.* Translated by Charles Lam Markmann. London: Pluto.

Féral, Josetta, and Teresa Lyons. 1982. "Performance and Theatricality: The Subject Demystified." *Modern Drama* 25 (1): 170–81.

Ferguson, Roderick A. 2017. *We Demand: The University and Student Protests.* Berkeley: University of California Press.

Ferreira da Silva, Denis. 2007. *Toward a Global Idea of Race.* Minneapolis: University of Minnesota Press.

Finn, Ed. 2017. *What Algorithms Want: Imagination in the Age of Computing.* Cambridge, MA: MIT Press.

Firdausi, Aabid. 2020. "The Social (Relations) Dilemma." *Developing Economics: A Critical Perspective on Development Economics.* https://developingeconomics.org.

Flores, Nelson, and Jonathan Rosa. 2015. "Undoing Appropriateness: Raciolinguistic Ideologies and Language Diversity in Education." *Harvard Educational Review* 85 (2): 149.

Forlano, Laura. 2018. "Invisible Algorithms, Invisible Politics." *Public Books* (February 2). www.publicbooks.org.

Forti, Venessa, Cornelis Peter Baldé, Ruediger Kuehr, and Garam Bel. 2020. *The Global E-waste Monitor: Quantities, Flows and the Circular Economy Potential.* United Nations University (UNU)/United Nations Institute for Training and Research (UNITAR)—cohosted by SCYCLE Programme, International Telecommunication Union (ITU) and International Solid Waste Association (ISWA), Bonn/Geneva/Rotterdam.

Foucault, Michel. 1995. *Discipline and Punish: The Birth of the Prison.* New York: Vintage.

———. 2004. *Society Must Be Defended: Lectures at the Collège de France 1975–76.* London: Penguin.

Fraser, Andrew. 2017. "We Go Inside the Guptabot Fake News Network." *Tech Central*, September 4. https://techcentral.co.za.

Fraser, Nancy. 1990. "Rethinking the Public Sphere: A Contribution to the Critique of Actually Existing Democracy." *Social Text*, no. 25/26, 56–80.

Freelon, Deen, and Chris Wells. 2020. "Disinformation as Political Communication." *Political Communication* 37 (2): 145–56.

Freeman, Carla. 2000. *High Tech and High Heels in the Global Economy: Women, Work, and Pink-Collar Identities in the Caribbean.* Durham, NC: Duke University Press.

Frenkel, Sheera, and Davey Alba. 2021. "In India, Facebook Grapples with an Amplified Version of Its Problems." *New York Times*, October 23. www.nytimes.com

Frére, Marie-Soleil. 2007. *The Media and Conflicts in Central Africa*. Boulder, CO: Lynne Rienner.

Fuchs, Christian. 2011. "New Media, Web 2.0 and Surveillance." *Sociology Compass* 5 (2): 134–47.

———. 2014. *Digital Labor and Karl Marx*. New York: Routledge.

Gagliardone, Iginio. 2019. *China, Africa and the Future of the Internet*. London: Zed Books.

Gagliardone, Iginio, Danit Gal, Thiago Alvs, and Gabriela Martinez. 2015. *Countering Online Hate Speech*. Paris: UNESCO.

Gajjala, Radhika. 2004. *Cyber Selves: Feminist Ethnographies of South Asian Women*. Walnut Creek, CA: Altamira.

Gamedze, Thulile. 2020. "Destruction Styles: Black Aesthetics of Rupture and Capture." *Radical Philosophy* 2, no. 8 (Autumn). www.radicalphilosophy.com.

Ganesh, Bharat. 2018. "The Ungovernability of Digital Hate Culture." *Journal of International Affairs* 71 (2): 30–49.

Gebrial, Dalia. 2018. "Rhodes Must Fall: Oxford and Movements for Change." In *Decolonising the University*, edited by Gurminder K. Bhambra, Dalia Gebrial, and Kerem Nişancıoğlu, 19–36. London: Pluto.

Genova, N. De. 2010. "Migration and Race in Europe: The Trans-Atlantic Metastases of a Post-colonial Cancer." *European Journal of Social Theory* 13 (3): 405–19.

Gere, Charlie. 2002. *Digital Culture*. London: Reaktion.

Gershon, Illana. 2017. "Language and the Newness of Media." *Annual Review of Anthropology* 46:15–31.

Getachew, Adom. 2019. *Worldmaking after Empire: The Rise and Fall of Self-Determination*. Princeton, NJ: Princeton University Press.

Gillespie, Kelly, and Leigh-Ann Naidoo. 2019. "#MustFall: The South African Student Movement and the Politics of Time." *South Atlantic Quarterly* 118 (1): 191.

Gillespie, Tarleton. 2014. "The Relevance of Algorithms." In *Media Technologies: Essays on Communication, Materiality, and Society*, edited by Tarleton Gillespie, Pablo J. Boczkowski, and Kirsten A. Foot, 167–94. Cambridge, MA: MIT Press.

Gillmor, Dan. 2004. *We the Media: Grassroots Journalism by the People, for the People*. Sebastopol, CA: O'Reilly.

Ginsburg, Faye. 1991. "Indigenous Media: Faustian Contract or Global Village." *Cultural Anthropology* 6 (1): 92–112.

———. 2002. "Screen Memories: Resignifying the Traditional in Indigenous Media." In *Media Worlds: Anthropology on New Terrain*, edited by Faye D. Ginsburg, Lila Abu-Lughod, and Brian Larkin, 39–57. Berkeley: University of California Press.

———. 2018. "The Road Forward." *Cultural Anthropology* 33, no. 2. https://doi.org/10.14506/ca33.2.06.

Gopal, Priyamvada. 2021. "On Decolonisation and the University." *Textual Practice* 35 (6): 873–99.

Gramsci, Antonio. 2007. *Prison Notebooks.* Vol. 3. Translated by J. A. Buttigieg. New York: Columbia University Press.

Greenhouse, Carol J. 1985. "Anthropology at Home: Whose Home?" *Human Organization* 44 (3): 261–64.

Günel, Gökçe, Saiba Varma, and Chika Watanabe. 2020. "A Manifesto for Patchwork Ethnography." *Fieldsights* (blog), Society for Cultural Anthropology, June 9. https://culanth.org.

Gupta, Akhil, and James Ferguson. 1997. "Discipline and Practice: 'The Field' as Site, Method and Location in Anthropology." In *Anthropological Locations: Boundaries and Grounds of a Field Science,* edited by Akhil Gupta and James Ferguson, 1–46. Berkeley: University of California Press.

Halder, Buddhadeb. 2020. "How the BJP Tried to Manipulate Public Opinion in Favour of the CAA." *Wire,* December 17. https://thewire.in.

Hall, Stuart. 1975. Introduction to *Paper Voices: The Popular Press and Social Change, 1935–1965,* edited by Stuart Hall and A. C. H. Smith, 11–24. London: Chatto and Windus.

Hallin, Daniel C., and Paolo Mancini. 2012. *Comparing Media Systems: Three Models of Media and Politics.* New York: Cambridge University Press.

Halverson, John. 1976. "Animal Categories and Terms of Abuse." *Man* 11 (4): 505–16.

Han, Byung-Chul. 2017. *In the Swarm: Digital Prospects.* Cambridge, MA: MIT Press.

Haraway, Donna. 1988. "Situated Knowledges: The Science Question in Feminism and the Privilege of Partial Perspective." *Feminist Studies* 14, no. 3 (Autumn): 575–99.

Hardaker, Claire. 2010. "Trolling in Asynchronous Computer-Mediated Communication: From User Discussions to Academic Definitions." *Journal of Politeness Research* 6 (2): 215–42. http://clok.uclan.ac.uk/4980/.

Harrison, Faye V. 1991. "Anthropology as an Agent of Transformation: Introductory Comments and Queries." In *Decolonizing Anthropology: Moving Further toward an Anthropology for Liberation,* edited by Faye V. Harrison, 1–15. Arlington, VA: Association of Black Anthropologists.

———. 1992. Introduction to *Decolonizing Anthropology: Moving Further toward an Anthropology of Liberation,* edited by Faye V. Harrison, vi. Arlington, VA: Association for Black Anthropologists.

Harvey, David. 1990. *The Condition of Postmodernity: An Enquiry into the Origins of Cultural Change.* Cambridge, MA: Wiley Blackwell.

Haynes, Nell. 2019. "Writing on the Walls: Discourses on Bolivian Immigrants in Chilean Meme Humor." *International Journal of Communication* 13:3122–42.

Headrick, Daniel R. 1988. *The Tentacles of Progress: Technology Transfer in the Age of Imperialism, 1880–1940.* New York: Oxford University Press.

Hearn, Alison. 2010. "Structuring Feeling: Web 2.0, Online Ranking and Rating, and the Digital 'Reputation' Economy." *Ephemera: Theory & Politics in Organization* 10 (3/4): 421–38.

Hegde, Radha S. 2011. *Circuits of Visibility: Gender and Transnational Media Cultures.* New York: New York University Press.

Hervik, Peter. 2011. *The Annoying Difference: The Emergence of Danish Neonationalism, Neoracism and Populism in the Post-1989 World*. New York: Berghahn.

———. 2019. "Ritualized Opposition in Danish Online Practices of Extremist Langauge and Thought." *International Journal of Communication* 13:3104–21.

———. 2021. "Racialization, Racism and Anti-racism in Danish Social Media Platforms." In *Digital Hate: The Global Conjuncture of Extreme Speech*, edited by Sahana Udupa, Iginio Gagliardone, and Peter Hervik, 131–45. Bloomington: Indiana University Press.

Hilderbrand, Lucas. 2009. "'Digital' Is Not a Noun." *Flow Journal*, July 23. www.flow-journal.org.

Hindman, Mathew. 2009. *The Myth of Digital Democracy*. Oxford: Oxford University Press.

Hu, Tung-Hui. 2015. *A Prehistory of the Cloud*. Cambridge, MA: MIT Press.

Hundle, Aneeth K. 2019. "Decolonizing Diversity: The Transnational Politics of Minority Racial Difference." *Public Culture* 31 (2): 289–322.

Intille, Stephan S., Emmanuel Munguia Tapia, John Rondoni, Jennifer Beaudin, Chuck Kukla, Sitij Agarwal, Ling Bao, and Kent Larson. 2003. "Tools for Studying Behavior and Technology in Natural Settings." In *UbiComp 2003: Ubiquitous Computing*, edited by Anind K. Dey, Albercht Schmidt, and Joseph F. McCarthy, 157–74. Berlin: Springer-Verlag.

Iqani, Mehita, and Sarah Chiumbu, eds. 2020. *Media Studies: Critical African and Decolonial Approaches*. Cape Town: Oxford University Press Southern Africa.

Irvine, Judith T. 1993. "Insult and Responsibility: Verbal Abuse in a Wolof Village." In *Responsibility and Evidence in Oral Discourse*, edited by Jane H. Hill and Judith T. Irvine, 105–34. Cambridge, UK: Cambridge University Press.

Jackson, John L., Jr. 2014. *Thin Description: Ethnography and the African Hebrew Israelites of Jerusalem*. Cambridge, MA: Harvard University Press.

Jaffrelot, Christophe. 1996. *The Hindu Nationalist Movement in India*. New York: Columbia University Press.

Jain, Ritika. 2020. "How India's Government Set Off a Spiral of Islamophobia." *Article 14*, April 20. www.article-14.com.

Jayal, Niraja Gopal. 2019. "Reconfiguring Citizenship in Contemporary India." *South Asia: Journal of South Asian Studies* 42 (1): 33–50.

Jee, Charlotte. 2020. "Facebook Needs 30,000 of Its Own Content Moderator, Says a New Report." *MIT Technology Review*, June 8. www.technologyreview.com.

Jobson, Ryan Cecil. 2020. "The Case for Letting Anthropology Burn: Sociocultural Anthropology in 2019." *American Anthropologist* 122 (2): 259–71.

Juris, Jeffrey. 2012. "Reflections on #Occupy Everywhere: Social Media, Public Space, and Emerging Logics of Aggregation." *American Ethnologist* 39 (2): 259–79.

Kaiser, Jonas. 2021. "Localized Hatred: The Importance of Physical Spaces within the German Far-Right Online Counterpublic on Facebook." In *Digital Hate: The Global Conjuncture of Extreme Speech*, edited by Sahana Udupa, Iginio Gagliardone, and Peter Hervik, 211–26. Bloomington: Indiana University Press.

Kavada, Anastasia. 2015. "Creating the Collective: Social Media, the Occupy Movement and Its Constitution as a Collective." *Information, Communication and Society* 18 (8): 872–86.

Khanna, Neetu. 2020. *The Visceral Logics of Decolonization*. Durham, NC: Duke University Press.

King, Tiffany Lebotho. 2019. *The Black Shoals: Offshore formations of Black and Native Studies*. Durham, NC: Duke University Press.

Koetsier, John. 2020. "Report: Facebook Makes 300,000 Content Moderation Mistakes Every Day." *Forbes*, June 9. www.forbes.com.

Kramer, Benjamin. 2017. "Populist Online Practices. The Function of the Internet in Right-Wing Populism." *Information, Communication and Society* 20 (9): 1293–1309.

Kuklick, Henrika. 1991. *The Savage Within: The Social History of British Anthropology 1885–1945*. New York: Cambridge University Press.

Kumar, Deepak. 1988. *Science and the Raj*. Oxford: Oxford University Press.

Kumar, Sangeet. 2021. *The Digital Frontier: Infrastructures of Control on the Global Web*. Bloomington: Indiana University Press.

Kundnani, Arun. 2020. "What Is Racial Capitalism?" Text of a talk presented by Arun Kundnani at the Havens Wright Center for Social Justice, University of Wisconsin-Madison, October 15, 2020. https://www.kundnani.org.

LaFlamme, Marcel, and Dominic Boyer. 2018. "Toward Adversary Anthropologies, Or, How to Build Your Own Revolutionary Infrastructure." *Cultural Anthropology* 33 (4): 526–35.

Lamont Hill, Marc. 2018. "Thank You Black Twitter: State Violence, Digital Counterpublics, and Pedagogies of Resistance." *Urban Education* 53 (2): 286–302.

Langton, Rae. 2018. "The Authority of Hate Speech." In *Oxford Studies in Philosophy of Law*, vol. 3, edited by John Gardner, Leslie Green, and Brian Leiter. Oxford: Oxford University Press.

Leach, Edmund. 1964. "Anthropological Aspects of Language: Animal Categories and Verbal Abuse." In *New Directions in the Study of Language*, edited by E. H. Lenneberg, 23–63. Cambridge, MA: MIT Press.

Lee, Ronan. 2019. "Extreme Speech in Myanmar: The Role of State Media in the Rohingya Forced Migration Crisis." *International Journal of Communication* 13:3203–24.

Lefort, Claude, and David Macey, trans. 1991. *Democracy and Political Theory*. Cambridge, UK: Polity Press.

Lempert, Michael. 2013. "No Ordinary Ethics." *Anthropological Theory* 13 (4): 370–93.

Leurs, Koen, and Tamara Shepherd. 2017. "Datafication and Discrimination." In *The Datafied Society*, edited by Tobias Mirko Schäfer and Karin van Es, 211–32. Amsterdam: Amsterdam University Press.

Lewis, David. 1979. "Scorekeeping in a Language Game." *Journal of Philosophical Logic* 1 (8): 339–59.

Lewis, Diane. 1973. "Anthropology and Colonialism." *Current Anthropology* 14:581–91.

Libirion, Max. 2021. *Pollution Is Colonialism*. Durham, NC: Duke University Press.

Liu, Roseann, and Savannah Shange. 2018. "Toward Thick Solidarity: Theorizing Empathy in Social Justice Movements." *Radical History Review* 131:189–98.

Lukose, Ritty. 2018. "Decolonizing Feminism in the #MeToo Era." *Cambridge Journal of Anthropology* 36 (2): 34–52.

Lutz, Catherine. 1990. "The Erasure of Women's Writing in Sociocultural Anthropology." *American Ethnologist* 17 (4): 611–27.

Macharia, Keguro. 2016. "On Being Area Studied." *GLQ* 22, no. 2 (April): 183–90.

Madianou, Mirca. 2019. "Technocolonialism: Digital Innovation and Data Practices in the Humanitarian Response to Refugee Crises." *Social Media + Society* 5 (3): 1–13. https://doi.org/10.1177/2056305119863146.

Mahendran, Dilan David. 2011. "Race and Computation: An Existential Phenomenological Inquiry Concerning Man, Mind and the Body." PhD diss., University of California Berkeley.

Malkki, Liisa H. 1997. "News and Culture: Transitory Phenomena and the Fieldwork Tradition." In *Anthropological Locations: Boundaries and Grounds of a Field Science*, edited by Akhil Gupta and James Ferguson, 86–101. Berkeley: University of California Press.

Maluleke, Gavaza, and Eileen Moyer. 2020. "'We Have to Ask for Permission to Become': Young Women's Voices, Violence, and Mediated Space in South Africa." *Signs: Journal of Women in Culture and Society* 45 (4): 871–902.

Mamdani, Mahmood. 2020. *Neither Settler nor Native: The Making and Unmaking of Permanent Minorities*. Cambridge, MA: Harvard University Press.

Mani, Lata. 1998. *Contentious Traditions: The Debate on Sati in Colonial India*. Berkeley: University of California Press.

Mankekar, Purnima. 2015. *Unsettling India: Affect, Temporality, Transnationality*. Durham, NC: Duke University Press.

Marcus, George. 2000. *Para-sites: A Casebook against Cynical Reason*. Chicago: University of Chicago Press.

———. 2008. "The End(s) of Ethnography: Social/Cultural Anthropology's Signature Form of Producing Knowledge in Transition." *Cultural Anthropology* 23 (1): 1–14.

Margetts, Helen, Peter John, Scott Hale, and Taha Yasseri. 2016. *Political Turbulence: How Social Media Shape Collective Action*. Princeton, NJ: Princeton University Press.

Marwick, Alice E., and danah boyd. 2011. "The Drama! Teen Conflict, Gossip, and Bullying in Networked Publics." In *A Decade in Internet Time: Symposium on the Dynamics of the Internet and Society* (September 12, 2011). Available at SSRN: https://ssrn.com/abstract=1926349.

Mathew, Leya, and Ritty Lukose. 2020. "Pedagogies of Aspiration: Anthropological Perspectives on Education in Liberalising India." *South Asia Journal of South Asian Studies* 43 (4): 1–14.

Maxwell, Richard. 2015. *The Routledge Companion of Labor and Media*. Oxford: Routledge.

Maxwell, Richard, and Toby Miller. 2012. *Greening the Media.* New York: Oxford University Press.

Mazzarella, William. 2004. "Culture, Globalization, Mediation." *Annual Review of Anthropology* 33:345–67.

———. 2020. "Populism as Political Theology." *Academia.* https://www.academia.edu.

Mbembe, Achille. 2015. "Decolonizing Knowledge and the Question of the Archive." https://africaisacountry.atavist.com.

———. 2016. "Decolonising the University: New Directions." *Arts & Humanities in Higher Education* 15 (1): 29–45.

McGranahan, Carole. 2017. "An Anthropology of Lying: Trump and the Political Sociality of Moral Outrage." *American Ethnologist* 44 (2): 243–48.

McIlwain, Charlton D. 2020. *Black Software: The Internet and Racial Justice, from the AfroNet to Black Lives Matter.* Oxford: Oxford University Press.

McKittrick, Katherine. 2006. *Demonic Grounds: Black Women and Cartographies of Struggle.* Minneapolis: University of Minnesota Press.

———. 2021. "Dear April: The Aesthetics of Black Miscellanea." *Antipode* 54, no. 1 (September 26): 3–18. https://doi.org/10.1111/anti.12773

Mehta, Akanksha. 2019. "Pedagogy and Violence: Mapping the Everyday Politics of Hindutva." *Hindutva Watch*, January 5. https://hindutvawatch.org.

Mejias, Ulises, and Nikolai Vokuev. 2017. "Disinformation and the Media: The Case of Russia and Ukraine." *Media, Culture & Society* 29 (7): 1027–42.

Menon, Nivedita. 2020. "The Virus, the Muslim and the Migrant." *Kafila*, April 22. https://kafilaonline.org.

Mewburn, Inger, and Pat Thomson. 2013. "Why Do Academics Blog? An Analysis of Audiences, Purposes and Challenges." *Studies in Higher Education* 38 (8): 1105–19.

Meyerhoff, Eli. 2019. *Beyond Education: Radical Studying for Another World.* Minneapolis: University of Minnesota Press.

Mignolo, Walter D. 2007a. "Introduction: Coloniality of Power and Decolonial Thinking." *Cultural Studies* 21 (2–3): 155–67.

———. 2007b. "Delinking: The Rhetoric of Modernity, the Logic of Coloniality and the Grammar of De-coloniality." *Cultural Studies* 21 (2–3): 449–514.

———. 2011. "The Global South and World Dis/Order." *Journal of Anthropological Research* 67 (2): 165–88.

———. 2015. *On Pluriversality.* waltermignolo.com.

Mignolo, Walter D., and Catherine E. Walsh. 2018. *On Decoloniality: Concepts, Analytics, Praxis.* Durham, NC: Duke University Press.

Milan, Stefania, and Emiliano Trere. 2019. "Big Data from the South(s): Beyond Data Universalism." *Television & New Media* 20 (4): 319–35.

Mills, Charles W. 2015. "Decolonizing Western Political Philosophy." *New Political Science* 37 (1): 1–24.

Mirzeoff, Nick. 2011. *The Right to Look: A Counter-History of Visuality.* Durham, NC: Duke University Press.

Moffitt, Benjamin. 2016. *The Global Rise of Populism: Performance, Political Style and Representation*. Stanford, CA: Stanford University Press.

Moosavi, Leon. 2020. "The Decolonial Bandwagon and the Dangers of Intellectual Decolonisation." *International Review of Sociology* 30 (2): 332–54.

Morozov, Evgeny. 2019. "Capitalism's New Clothes." *Baffler*, February 4. https://thebaffler.com.

Mossie, Zewdie, and Jenq Haur Wang. 2020. "Vulnerable Community Identification Using Hate Speech Detection on Social Media." *Information Processing and Management* 57 (3): 102087. https://doi.org/10.1016/j.ipm.2019.102087.

Moten, Fred, and Stefano Harney. 2004. "The University and the Undercommons: Seven Theses." *Social Text* 22 (2): 101.

Mukherjee, Rahul. 2020. *Radiant Infrastructures: Media, Environment, and Cultures of Uncertainty*. Durham, NC: Duke University Press.

Mumford, Lewis. (1963) 2010. *Technics and Civilization*. Chicago: University of Chicago Press.

Murray, Douglas. 2017. *The Strange Death of Europe*. London: Bloomsbury.

Nagle, Angela. 2017. *Kill All Normies: Online Culture Wars from 4Chan and Tumblr to Trump and the Alt-Right*. Alresford: Zero.

Nakassis, Constantine. 2012. "Brand, Citationality, Performativity." *American Anthropologist* 114 (4): 624–38.

———. 2016. *Doing Style: Youth and Mass Mediation in South India*. Chicago: University of Chicago Press.

Narayan, Kiran. 1993. "How Native Is a Native Anthropologist?" *American Anthropologist* 95 (3): 671–86.

Ndlovu-Gatsheni, Sabelo. 2018. *Epistemic Freedom in Africa—Deprovincialization and Decolonization*. New York: Routledge.

Negroponte, Nicolas. 1995. *Being Digital*. New York: Knopf.

Newsinger, John. 2016. "Why Rhodes Must Fall." *Race & Class* 58 (2): 70–77.

Newton, Casey. 2019. "The Trauma Floor: The Secret Lives of Facebook Moderators in America," *Verge*, February 25. https://www.theverge.com.

Neyazi, Tabarez Neyazi. 2019. "Digital Propaganda, Political Bots and Polarized Politics in India." *Asian Journal of Communication* 30 (1): 39–57.

Noble, Safiya Umoja. 2018. *Algorithms of Oppression: How Search Engines Reinforce Racism*. New York: New York University Press.

Noble, Safiya Umoja, and Brendesha M. Tynes. 2016. *The Intersectional Internet: Race, Sex, Class and Culture Online*. New York: Peter Lang.

Odell, Jenny. 2020. *How to Do Nothing. Resisting the Attention Economy*. New York: Melville House.

Oldenburg, Silke. 2020. "Going Off-the-Record? On the Relationship between Media and Identity Formation in Post-genocide Rwanda." In *Theorizing Media and Conflict*, edited by Philipp Budka and Birgit Bräuchler, 277–94. New York: Berghahn.

Ong, Jonathan Corpus, and Jason V. Cabanes. 2018. "Architects of Networked Disinformation: Behind the Scenes of Troll Accounts and Fake News Production in
the Philippines." University of Massachusets Scholar Works. https://scholarworks.
umass.edu.

Orisakwe, Orish Ebere, Chiara Frazzoli, Cajetan Elochukwu Ilo, and Benjamin Oritse-
muelebi. 2019. "Public Health Burden of E-waste in Africa." *Journal of Health and
Pollution* 9 (22): 1–12.

Pandian, Anand. 2018. "Open Access, Open Minds." *Fieldsights* (blog), Society for
Cultural Anthropology. June 15. https://culanth.org.

Papacharissi, Zizi. 2012. "Without You, I'm Nothing: Performances of the Self on Twitter." *International Journal of Communication* 16:18.

———. 2013. "On Networked Publics and Private Spheres in Social Media." In *The Social Media Handbook*, edited by Jeremy Hunsinger and Theresa Senft, 144–58. New
York: Routledge.

———. 2014. *Affective Publics: Sentiment, Technology, and Politics.* Oxford: Oxford
University Press.

———. 2015. "Affective Publics and Structures of Storytelling: Sentiment, Events, and
Mediality." *Information, Communication & Society* 19 (3): 307–24.

Partridge, Damani J., and Matthew Chin. 2019. "Interrogating the Histories and Futures of Diversity." *Public Culture* 31 (2): 197–214.

Penfold-Mounce, Ruth. 2010. *Celebrity Culture and Crime: The Joy of Transgression.*
London: Springer.

Perrigo, Billy. 2019. "Facebook Says Its Removing More Hate than Ever Before: But
There's a Catch." *Time*, November 27. https://time.com/.

Phillips, Whitney. 2018. "The Oxygen of Amplification: Better Practices for Reporting
on Extremists, Antagonists, and Manipulators." *Data & Society*, May 22. https://
datasociety.net.

Pia, Andrea, et al. 2020. "Labour of Love: An Open Access Manifesto for Freedom,
Integrity, and Creativity in the Humanities and Interpretive Social Sciences." *Com-
monplace.* https://commonplace.knowledgefutures.org.

Pillay, Suren. 2015. "Decolonizing the University." *Africa Is a Country.* https://africasa-
country.com.

Pinney, Christopher. 1990. "Colonial Anthropology in the 'Laboratory of Mankind.'"
In *The Raj, India and the British 1600–1947*, edited by C. A. Bayley, 252–63. London:
National Portrait Gallery.

Pohjonen, Matti, and Sahana Udupa. 2017. "Extreme Speech Online: An Anthropological Critique of Hate Speech Debates." *International Journal of Communication*
11:1173–91.

Ponzanesi, Sandra. 2020. "Digital Cosmopolitanism: Notes from the Underground."
Global Perspectives 1 (1): 12548. https://doi.org/10.1525/gp.2020.12548.

Postill, John. 2018. "Populism and Social Media: A Global Perspective." *Media, Culture
& Society* 40 (5): 754–65.

Puar, Jasbir. 2007. *Queer Assemblages: Homonationalism in Queer Times*. Durham, NC: Duke University Press.

Punsmann, Burcu Gültekin. 2018. "Three Months in Hell." *Süddeutsche Zeitung Magazin*, January 6. https://sz-magazin.sueddeutsche.de.

Puschmann, Cornelius, Julian Ausserhofer, and Josef Slerka. 2018. "Converging on a Populist Core? Comparing Issues on the Facebook Pages of Pegida Movement and the Alternative for Germany." Paper presented at the international workshop on Global Digital Media Cultures and Extreme Speech, Munich, February.

Quijano, Anibal. 2007. "Coloniality and Modernity/Rationality." *Cultural Studies* 21 (2): 168–78.

Rajagopal, Arvind. 2001. *Politics after Television: Hindu Nationalism and the Reshaping of the Indian Public*. Cambridge, UK: Cambridge University Press.

Rao, Rahul. 2020. "Neoliberal Antiracism and the British University." *Radical Philosophy*. https://www.radicalphilosophy.com.

Rao, Ursula. 2013. "Biometric Marginality: UID and the Shaping of Homeless Identities in the City." *Economic and Political Weekly* 48 (13): 71–77.

Rao, Ursula, and Vijayanka Nair. 2019. "Aadhaar: Governing with Biometrics." *South Asia: Journal of South Asian Studies* 42 (3): 469–81.

Richardson, Allissa V. 2017. "Bearing Witness while Black." *Digital Journalism* 5 (6): 673–98.

Richey, Mason. 2017. "Contemporary Russian Revisionism: Understanding the Kremlin's Hybrid Warfare and Strategic and Tactical Deployment of Disinformation." *Asia Europe Journal* 16 (1): 101–13.

Rietzschel, Antonie. 2018. "Nazi Hipsters in Crisis." *Süddeutsche Zeitung*, April 28. sueddeutsche.de.

Roberts, Sarah T. 2019. *Behind the Screen: Content Moderation in the Shadows of Social Media*. New Haven, CT: Yale University Press.

Rogers, Katie, and Nicholas Fandos. 2019. "Trump Tells Congresswomen to Go Back to the Countries They Came From" *New York Times*, July 14. www.nytimes.com.

Rongbin, Han. 2015. "Manufacturing Consent in Cyberspace: China's 'Fifty-Cent Army.'" *Journal of Current Chinese Affairs* 44 (2): 105–34.

Rosa, Johnathan, and Yarimar Bonilla. 2017. "Deprovincializing Trump, Decolonizing Diversity, and Unsettling Anthropology." *American Ethnologist* 44 (2): 201–8.

Rosales, Jose. 2016. "Of Surrealism and Marxism." *Blind Field*, December 1, https://blindfieldjournal.com.

Ross, Andrew. 2013. "In Search of the Lost Paycheck." In *Digital Labor: The Internet as Playground and Factory*, edited by Trebor Scholz, 14–32. New York: Routledge.

Russell, Catherine. 1999. *Experimental Ethnography: The Work of Film in the Age of Video*. Durham, NC: Duke University Press.

Sabbatini, Whitten. 2019. "New Book Explores 'Concept of the Ordinary'—100 Words at a Time." *UChicago News*. https://news.uchicago.edu.

Saberwal, Satish. 2006. Introduction to *Assertive Religious Identities: India and Europe*, edited by Satish Saberwal and Mushirul Hasan, 9–27. New Delhi: Manohar.

Saint Laurent, Constance de. 2018. "In Defence of Machine Learning: Debunking the Myths of Artificial Intelligence." *Europe's Journal of Psychology* 14 (4): 734–47.

Salzborn, Samuel. 2018. "Heidegger für Halbgebildete—Identitäre Heimatideologie zwischen Fiktion und Propagandaa." Institut für Demokratie und Zivilgesselschaft. Idz-jena.de. doi:10.19222/201803/13.

Sandoval, Chela. 2000. *Methodology of the Oppressed*. Minneapolis: University of Minnesota Press.

Sanjek, Roger. 1990. "The Secret Life of Fieldnotes." In *Fieldnotes: The Makings of Anthropology*, edited by Roger Sanjek, 39–44. Ithaca, NY: Cornell University Press.

Sap, Maarten, Dallas Card, Saadia Gabriel, Yejin Choi, and Noah A. Smith. 2019. "The Risk of Racial Bias in Hate Speech Detection." In *Proceedings of the 57th Annual Meeting of the Association for Computational Linguistics, ACL Anthology*. https://aclanthology.org.

Schaflechner, Juergen. 2021. "Blasphemy Accusations as Extreme Speech Acts in Pakistan." In *Digital Hate: The Global Conjuncture of Extreme Speech*, edited by Sahana Udupa, Iginio Gagliardone, and Peter Hervik, [[Pages]]. Bloomington: Indiana University Press.

Schroeder, Ralph. 2018. *Social Theory after the Internet: Media, Technology and Globalization*. London: UCL Press.

Schullenberger, Geoff. 2016. "The Scapegoating Machine." *New Inquiry*, November 30. https://thenewinquiry.com.

Seaver, Nick. 2017. "Algorithms as Culture: Some Tactics for the Ethnography of Algorithmic Systems." *Big Data & Society* 4, no. 2. https://doi.org/10.1177/2053951717738104.

Segura, Maria Soledad, and Silvio Waisbord. 2019. "Between Data Capitalism and Data Citizenship." *Television & New Media* 20 (4): 412–19.

Shange, Savannah. 2019. *Progressive Dystopia: Abolition, anti-Blackness, and Schooling in San Francisco*. Durham, NC: Duke University Press.

Shankar, Arjun. 2016. "Auteurship and Image-Making: A (Gentle) Critique of Photovoice Method." *AnthroSource* 32 (2) (November): 157–66.

———. n.d. "'Brown Saviors' and Their Others: Diasporic Connection and the Racialized Hierarchies of India's Help Economy." *Current Anthropology*.

Shilliam, Robbie. 2018. *Race and the Undeserving Poor: From Abolition to Brexit*. London: Agenda.

Shirky, Clay 2011. *Here Comes Everybody: The Power of Organizing without Organizations*. New York: Penguin.

Shoshan, Nitzan. 2016. *The Management of Hate: Nation, Affect, and the Governance of Right-Wing Extremism in Germany*. Princeton, NJ: Princeton University Press.

Shringarpure, Bhakti. 2019. *Cold War Assemblages: Decolonization to Digital*. London: Routledge.

———. 2020. "Notes on Fake Decolonization." *Africa Is a Country*. https://africasacountry.com.

————. 2021. "A Demanding Relationship with History: A Conversation with Priyamvada Gopal." *Los Angeles Review of Books*, August 30. https://lareviewofbooks.org.

Siapera, Eugenia, Elena Moreo, and Jiang Zhou. 2018. "Hate Track: Tracking and Monitoring Racist Speech Online." Dublin: Dublin City University.

Simpson, Ed. 2016. "Is Anthropology Legal? Earthquakes, Blitzkrieg, and Ethical Futures." *Focaal. Journal of Global and Historical Anthropology*, no. 74, 113–28.

Singh, Karan Deep, and Raj, Suhasini. 2021. "India Says It Will Prioritize Hindus and Sikhs in Issuing Emergency 'Visas' to Afghans." *New York Times*, September 15. www.nytimes.com.

Singh, Sava Saheli. 2015. "Hashtagging #HigherEd." In *Hashtag Publics: The Power and Politics of Discursive Networks*, edited by N. Rambukkana, 267–77. New York: Peter Lang.

Stalder, Felix. 2018. *The Digital Condition*. Cambridge, UK: Polity Press.

Stewart, Bonnie. 2016. "Collapsed Publics: Orality, Literacy, and Vulnerability in Academic Twitter." *Journal of Applied Social Theory* 1 (1): 61.

Stocking, George W. 1988. *Functionalism Historicized: Essays on British Social Anthropology*. Madison: University of Wisconsin Press.

Stoller, Paul. 1992. *The Cinematic Griot: The Ethnography of Jean Rouch*. Chicago: University of Chicago Press.

Subramaniam, Ajantha. 2019. *The Caste of Merit: Engineering Education in India*. Cambridge, MA: Harvard University Press.

Suhr, Christian, and Rane Willerslev, eds. 2013. *Transcultural Montage*. New York: Berghahn.

Terranova, Tiziana. 2000. "Free Labor: Producing Culture for the Digital Economy." *Social Text 2* 18 (2): 33–58.

Thirangama, Sharika, Tobias Kelly, and Carlos Forment. 2018. "Introduction: Whose Civility?" *Anthropological Theory* 18 (2–3): 153–74.

Treitler, Vila Bashi. 2013. *The Ethnic Project: Transforming Racial Fiction into Ethnic Factions*. Palo Alto, CA: Stanford University Press.

Treré, Emiliano, and Alejandro Barranquero Carretero. 2018. "Tracing the Roots of Technopolitics: Towards a North-South Dialogue." In *Networks, Movements and Technopolitics in Latin America*, edited by Francisco Sierra Caballero and Tommaso Gravante, 43–63. Cham: Springer.

Tuck, Eve, and Wayne K. Yang. 2012. "Decolonization Is Not a Metaphor." *Decolonization: Indigeneity, Education & Society* 1 (1): 1–40.

Tufekci, Zeynep. 2017. *Twitter and Tear Gas: The Power and Fragility of Networked Protest*. New Haven, CT: Yale University Press.

Tuohy, Wendy. 2020. "It Makes You Want to Throw Your Phone in the Bin: The Film Turning Teens off Social Media." *Age*, September 27. https://www.theage.com.au.

Tynes, Brendescha, Joshua Schuschke, and Safiya Umoja Noble. 2016. "Digital Intersectional Theory and the #BlackLivesMatter Movement." In *The Intersectional Internet*, edited by Safiya Umoja Noble and Brendesha M. Tynes, 21–40. New York: Peter Lang.

Udupa, Sahana. 2016a. "Faith Online: Transnational Religious Politics in India and Europe." European Research Council starting grant project. https://cordis.europa.eu/project/id/714285/it.

———. 2016b. "Archiving as History-Making: Religious Politics of Social Media in India." *Communication, Culture and Critique* 9 (2): 212–30.

———. 2017. "Gaali Cultures: The Politics of Abusive Exchange on Social Media." *New Media and Society* 20 (4): 1506–22.

———. 2019. "Nationalism in the Digital Age: Fun as a Metapractice of Extreme Speech." *International Journal of Communication* 13:3143–63.

———. 2020. "Decoloniality and Extreme Speech." Paper presented at the 65th e-seminar, Media Anthropology Network, European Association of Social Anthropologists, June 17–30, 2020. www.easaonline.org/downloads/networks/media/65p.pdf.

Udupa, Sahana, Iginio Gagliardone, and Peter Hervik. 2021. *Digital Hate: The Global Conjuncture of Extreme Speech*. Bloomington: Indiana University Press.

Udupa, Sahana, Elonnai Hickok, Antonis Maronikolakis, Hinrich Schuetze, Laura Csuka, Axel Wisiorek, and Leah Nann. 2021. "AI, Extreme Speech and the Challenges of Online Content Moderation." AI4Dignity Project, https://doi.org/10.5282/ubm/epub.76087.

Udupa, Sahana, and Max Kramer. Forthcoming. "Multiple Interfaces: Social Media, Religious Politics and National (Un)belonging." *American Ethnologist*.

Udupa, Sahana, and Matti Pohjonen. 2019. "Extreme Speech and Global Digital Cultures." *International Journal of Communication* 13:3049–67.

Udupa, Sahana, Shriram Venkatraman, and Aasim Khan. 2019. "Millennial India: Global Digital Politics in Context." *Television & New Media* 21 (4): 343–59.

Upadhya, Carol. 2009. "Imagining India: Software and the Ideology of Liberalization." *South African Review of Sociology* 40 (1): 76–93.

———. 2016. *Reeingineering India: Work, Capital and Class in an Offshore Economy*. New Delhi: Oxford University Press.

van der Veer, Peter. 1994. *Religious Nationalism: Hindus and Muslims in India*. Berkeley: University of California Press.

———. 2001. *Imperial Encounters: Religion and Modernity in India and Britain*. Princeton, NJ: Princeton University Press.

Vannini, Phillip. 2015. *Non-representational Methodologies: Re-envisioning Research*. London: Routledge.

Varnelis, Kazys, ed. 2008. *Networked Publics*. Cambridge, MA: MIT Press.

Visweswaran, Kamala. 1994. *Fictions of Feminist Ethnography*. Minneapolis: University of Minnesota Press.

Vizenor, Gerald. 1999. *Manifest Manners: Narratives on Postindian Survivance*. Lincoln: University of Nebraska Press.

Walsh, Catherine E., and Walter D. Mignolo. 2018. Introduction to *On Decoloniality: Concepts, Analytics, Praxis*, edited by Walter D. Mignolo and Catherine E. Walsh, 1–12. Durham, NC: Duke University Press.

Warner, Michael. 2002. *Publics and Counterpublics*. New York: Zone Books.

Weheliye, Alexander G. 2014. *Habeas Viscus: Racializing Assemblages, Biopolitics, and Black Feminist Theories of the Human*. Durham, NC: Duke University Press.

Wekker, Gloria. 2016. *White Innocence: Paradoxes of Colonialism and Race*. Durham, NC: Duke University Press.

Weller, Katrin, Axel Bruns, Jean Burgess, Merja Mahrt, and Cornelius Puschmann. 2013. *Twitter and Society*. New York: Peter Lang.

Whttaker, Zack. 2020. "Facebook to Pay $52 Million to Contenr Moderators Suffering from PTSD." *Tech Crunch*, May 12. techcrunch.com.

Wynter, Sylvia. 2003. "Unsettling the Coloniality of Being/Power/Truth/Freedom: Towards the Human, after Man, Its Overrepresentation-An Argument." *New Centennial Review* 3 (3): 257–337.

Yengde, Suraj. 2019. *Caste Matters*. New York: Penguin.

Yu, Henry. 2001. *Thinking Orientals*. New York: Oxford University Press.

Zia, Ather. 2019. "Block List: How Facebook Helps Silence Kashmiris." *Caravan*, December 1. https://caravanmagazine.in.

Zuboff, Shoshana. 1988. *In the Age of Smart Machine: The Future of Work and Power*. New York: Basic Books.

———. 2019. *The Age of Surveillance Capitalism: The Fight for a Human Future at the New Frontier of Power*. New York: Public Affairs.

Zúquete, José Pedro. 2018. *The Identitarians: The Movement against Globalism and Islam in Europe*. Notre Dame, IN: Notre Dame University Press.

INDEX

Abiola Lecture on Future Knowledges, 126
academic mediation, digital technologies
   effect on, 14
academic migration, immigrant migration
   compared to, 20, 58
academics: gatekeeping of marginalized,
   126–28; migration of, 20, 58; right-
   wing attacks on, 51–54, 156–57, 164, 165,
   202n74; on social media, 162; surveillance of, 183
#AcademicTwitter, 143–44, 146
activism, digital, social media in, 7
Adair, Cassius, 130, 135
AfD. *See* Alternativ für Deutschland
affects, social media channeling, 41, 42–43,
   44–45
affirmative action, at US universities, 49
Africa Is a Country (AIAC), 135–36, 145
Ahmed, Sara, 42, 68–69, 88, 92–93
AI. *See* artificial intelligence
AI4Dignity, 168, 171–73, 174–75, 177
AIAC. *See* Africa Is a Country
algorithmic systems: bias in, 173; as culture, 132–33, 134–35; racism in, 24, 97,
   105–8, 133; radicalization by, 90, 96; on
   social media, 15–16, 184; for surveillance, 123–24
Algorithms of Oppression (Noble), 106
Ali, Syed Mustafa, 106, 115
alliance building, decolonial sensibility
   in, 19
Alternativ für Deutschland (AfD), 80, 83,
   84–85
Ambedkar, B. R., 141

American Anthropological Association,
   147–48
American Anthropologist, 147–48
American Association of Geographers,
   199n26
Amristar Massacre, 152
Amrute, Sareeta, 108, 115–16
animal names, in online vitriol, 74,
   204n60
annotation, of extreme speech, 171–72
anthropology: colonial relations in,
   197n43; crisis of legitimacy in, 129,
   213n33; data capture in, 100–102;
   decoloniality in, 173–74; digitalization
   effect on, 25–26; ethnographic, 102–3,
   159, 168, 171–75, 177, 185–87; fieldwork
   in, 160–62; *Hau* journal of, 145–46;
   montage in, 197n47; multidisciplinary
   research in, 160; multimodal production in, 175, 176–77; para-ethnography
   in, 142–43; rationality in, 62–63; as science of the colonizer, 97; spatial tropes
   in, 163–64; status quo in, 137–38
anthropology, media, 13–14, 21–22
#AnthroTwitter, 146
anti-immigrant policies: of AfD, 84–85;
   extreme speech of, 88; of GI, 87
anti-racist struggles, at universities, 10
anxiety: of digital consumption, 155; in
   networked exposure, 157–58, 181–82; of
   researchers, 164
Anzaldúa, Gloria, 135
apartheid, #RhodesMustFall as response
   to, 27–28

China, state surveillance in, 124
Christian, Barbara, 127
Cicarello-Maher, George, 202n74
citation: of Hindu nationalists, 153; in knowledge production, 130; on Twitter, 144, 148–49
@citeblackwomen, 25
#CiteBlackWomen, 138–39
The Citizenship (Amendment) Act (2019) (India) (CAA), 1, 119–21
Cleaners (documentary film), 111
Clouthard, Glen, 48
collaboration: of CAMRA, 177–78, 179; Indigenous peoples and media anthropologist, 14; in knowledge production, 175–76, 191–92; in multimodal production, 176–77; for online content moderation, 168, 174–75; technical disciplines and social science, 168, 171–73, 174–75, 181; universities and online knowledge production, 140
collective disruption, in knowledge production, 145
colonial capture, social physics compared to, 104
colonialism, 29–30; COVID-19 pandemic exacerbating, 183; effect on Indigenous peoples, 183–84
colonialism, data, 24, 99, 102–3
coloniality: in data capture, 99–102, 103–4, 105, 106–7, 108–9, 118–19; in Deptford, 34–35; digitalization relation to, 2, 11, 14–15, 184–85; in extreme speech, 94; hashtags to index, 36–37; in hierarchical structures, 11–12, 19, 93–94, 115–16; in market relations, 89; in online spaces, 3–4, 23–24, 57–58, 145; in open access publishing, 146; performance contrition relation to, 50–51; protests against, 27–28, 39; in religion, 123–24; of universities, 30–31, 36, 42, 46, 47–48
colonial power, technologies of surveillance protecting, 35–36

colonial relations, in anthropology, 14–15, 100–102, 105, 160–61, 177, 197n43
Colston, Edward, statue of, 1
commons, digital, logics of, 6–7
communication, digital, 7, 187; effect on journalism, 56–57, 205n80
complaint, hashtags as archive of, 42
connection, decolonial sensibility for, 18–19
consciousness, collective, emotions effect on, 65–66
consumption, digital, anxiety of, 155
content moderation: by AI, 174; bias in, 168, 170–71, 172; BPO of, 109–15; of CAA protests, 120–21; of extreme speech, 116–17; of misinformation, 118; NYU Stern Centre for Business and Human Rights report on, 110, 112–13; online propaganda comingled with, 122
contrition, performance, coloniality relation to, 50–51
Couldry, Nick, 100
Counter Abuse Technology project, Google, 170
counter-hegemonic knowledge projects, in research, 128–29
counterpublics, 30, 45–46; of #DalitLivesMatter, 40–41; on social media, 39–40, 44
COVID-19 pandemic, 121, 183
critical digital method, montage as, 17, 22–23, 160
cultural production, digital, montage in, 17
culture, 89, 91; algorithmic systems as, 132–33, 134–35; COVID-19 pandemic effect on, 183; digitalization of, 162; effect on extreme speech, 59–61; German culture, 85–87
curriculation, Black Lives Matter uprisings effect on, 139–40
cyberbullying, of Indigenous peoples, 93

English Defence League, 79
epistemology, of European Renaissance, 63
Equality Labs, 118, 200n46
ethics, 189–91; in anthropological ethnography, 185–87; in multimodal production, 192
ethnography, anthropological, 102–3, 159; of AI4Dignity, 168, 171–75, 177; ethics in, 185–87
ethnopluralism, 87, 88
European Association of Social Anthropologists, Media Anthropology Network of, 21–22
European Enlightenment, 24, 96, 99–100, 115
European Renaissance, epistemology of, 63
e-waste, in Global South, 115
exclusionary politics, decolonization in, 188
expropriation, of digital labor, 190
extraction, data, 3, 118–19, 130; political economy of, 12
extreme speech, 79–80, 82, 190; annotation of, 171–72; anti-immigrant, 88; capitalism relation to, 90; categorization of, 171–72, 174; coloniality in, 94; content moderation of, 116–17, 168, 170–71; culture effect on, 59–61; data capture in, 108–9; decoloniality in, 64; hegemonic power relation to, 61–62, 133; humor in, 169; as performance, 60–61, 90–91; right-wing, 57–58; in #Troll_event, 75; of white supremacists, 93

Facebook, 87, 118, 133; content moderation of, 109–11, 116–17, 120–21
"The Facebook Papers," 118
Fallist movements, in South Africa, 33
Fanon, Frantz, 69
far-right, 55; in Germany, 82
#FeesMustFall, 28

feminists, in India, 43
Ferguson, James, 159, 160, 162
Ferguson, Roderick, 27, 32
Ferreira da Silva, Denis, 62, 67
field, 163–64; home as, 178; home compared to, 159, 160; territorial borders relation to, 166
fieldwork, 14, 160–63; decolonization of, 175; on Twitter, 70
financial stability, of academic adjacent writing projects, 136–37
Finn, Ed, 105
Firdausi, Aabid, 96
Floyd, George, murder of, 1, 49
Footnotes, on status quo in anthropology, 137–38
Forment, Carlos, on hierarchical structures, 11–12
Foucault, Michel, 128
France: Bloc Identitaire in, 87; la Ligue du LOL in, 91
Franco-Bavaria, Recht in, 83
Fraser, Nancy, 39
Frazer, James G., 101
Frazer, Ryan, 93
free speech, 92; at universities, 31, 51–54, 156, 212n57
French revolution, digital revolution compared to, 55–56, 62
Friedrich, Caspar David, 86
fun: to escape speech regulation, 92; in extreme speech, 91, 133

gaali cultures, extreme speech as, 61
Gamedze, Thulile, 41
Ganesh, Bharat, 80
GARA. See Goldsmiths Anti-Racist Action
gatekeeping, academic, of marginalized scholars, 126–28
Gebrial, Dalia, 51
Génération Identitaire (GI), right-wing nationalism of, 87–88

home, 163, 177; as field, 178; field compared to, 159, 160; territorial borders relation to, 166
human behavior, 99, 102–3, 105
humor, in extreme speech, 169
Hundle, Aneeth Kaur, 9, 48–49

#Iam, 42
Identitäre Bewegung, 92
immigrant migration, 67, 93; academic migration compared to, 20, 58; surveillance of, 107–8
imperialism, European, ethnopluralism relation to, 88
India, 43, 61, 79, 97, 119–21, 133; caste in, 20, 40, 200n52; content moderation outsourced to, 113–14; Dalit Camera in, 25, 141–43; Delhi, 179–80; elections in, 80, *81*, 168–69; general elections in, *81*; hate speech in, 63–64, 118; Hindu nationalists in, 10–11, 24, 77–78, *78*, 90, 91, 122, 152–54, 156, 158, 163, 165, 188, 211n56; missed-call campaigns in, 208n100; nationalism in, 1, 10, 186; religious majoritarian politics in, 123–24
Indiafacts.com (Indiafacts.org.in), 165
Indigenous peoples, 14, 23, 47, 93, 146, 183–84; media production of, 128, 140–41; sovereignty of, 10, 33–34, 125; *survivance* relation to, 196n35
informants, researchers tracked by, 158
information infrastructure, of Google, 106
Instagram, 36, 42, 83, 84–85, 110–11, 151
integrity, electoral, digital communication effect on, 7
internet, 5–6, 56, 89, 95–96, 99, 131; academic adjacent writing projects on, 136–37
Internet of Things, 115
Islamophobia, 121–22, 151
Israel, 53, 158
Isuma.tv, 140–41, 142

Jackson, John Lester, Jr., 158
Jacobs, Sean, 135–36
jargon, digitally native, in #Troll_event, 75–76
Jasmine Revolution, Tunisia, 150
Jigsaw, Perspective API of, 170
journalism, 56–57, 62, 205n80
Junge Alternative München, AfD, 83, 84–85
Juris, Jeffrey, 35
juxtaposition, in montage, 15–16

Kelly, Tobias, on hierarchical structures, 11–12
Kill All Normies (Nagle), 78
Kincaid, Jamaica, 19, 190–91
King, Tiffany Lebotho, 33–34
Kitchen Table: Women of Color Press, 135
knowledge production, 140–42, 145–46, 147–48, 181; of AIAC, 135–36; collaboration in, 175–76, 191–92; counterhegemonic, 128–29; data monetization in, 130–31; decolonization of, 138–39; gatekeeping in, 127–28; of Hindu nationalists, 153–54; on social media, 134–35, 143–44, 150
Krishnamurthy, Jiddu, 86–87
Kuklick, Henrika, 101–2
Kumar, Sangeet, 89–90
Kundnani, Arun, 116

labor, digital, 116, 134; academic adjacent writing projects as, 136–37; disinformation as, 111–12; expropriation of, 190
la Ligue du LOL (Laughing Out Loud League), 91
Lamont Hill, Mark, 40
Latin America, campus protests in, 28
Laughing Out Loud League (la Ligue du LOL), 91
Leach, Edmund, 74
Leurs, Koen, 107
Lewis, David, 80

ABOUT THE AUTHORS

Combining ethnography, policy, and community collaboration, SAHANA UDUPA has researched digital politics, extreme speech, artificial intelligence, and urban cultures, centering the question of mediation as a socio-technological, performative, and experiential space to articulate political practice. Supported by the European Research Council, the United Nations Department of Peace Operations, and other organizations, she has founded the For Digital Dignity program to translate research findings into possibilities in the real world. She is the author of *Making News in Global India: Media, Publics, Politics* and coeditor of *Digital Hate: The Global Conjuncture of Extreme Speech* and *Media as Politics in South Asia*.

For almost a decade ETHIRAJ GABRIEL DATTATREYAN has utilized collaborative, multimodal, and speculative approaches to research how digital media consumption, production, and circulation shape understandings of migration, gender, race, and urban space. His first monograph, *The Globally Familiar: Digital Hip Hop, Masculinity and Urban Space in Delhi* narrates how Delhi's young working class and migrant men adopt hip-hop's globally circulating aesthetics—accessed through inexpensive smartphones and cheap internet connectivity that radically changed India's media landscape in the early aughts—to productively refashion themselves and their city.